34028051734979

D1160109

Watching TV: the American family, glued to the set, in 1957.

Karal Ann Marling

As Seen on TV

The Visual Culture
of Everyday Life
in the 1950s

Harvard University Press · Cambridge, Massachusetts · London, England

Copyright © 1994 by the President and Fellows
    of Harvard College
All rights reserved
Printed in the United States of America

Seventh printing, 2002

First Harvard University Press paperback edition, 1996

Library of Congress Cataloging-in-Publication Data
Marling, Karal Ann.
    As seen on TV : the visual culture of everyday life in
    the 1950s / Karal Ann Marling.
        p.   cm.
Includes bibliographical references (p.   ) and index.
ISBN 0-674-04882-2 (cloth)
ISBN 0-674-04883-0 (pbk.)
1. United States—Social life and customs—1945–1970.
2. Television broadcasting—Social aspects—United States.
3. Popular culture—United States—History—20th century.
I. Title.   II. Title: As seen on television.
E169.02.M3534   1994
973.92—dc20   94-2814

Designed by Gwen Frankfeldt

Contents

As Seen on TV

The MIT-designed Monsanto House of the Future at Disneyland, 1957: real life inside a giant TV set.

Prologue

*G*iant (1956) is one of the great, big-screen epics of the 1950s. It's got everything. A radiant Liz Taylor. Rock Hudson in his first major role. James Dean, teen idol, wearing blue denim jeans, in his last. Dean died in a car crash during post-production work on the film. "There were only two people in the fifties," remembers the actor Martin Sheen. "Elvis Presley, who changed the music, and James Dean, who changed our lives."[1]

Giant is long, too. *Gone with the Wind*, to which Louella Parsons, for one, compared George Stevens's dynastic saga of oil, prejudice, and married life in the American West, is only thirty-seven minutes longer. And the scope is equally vast: cultivated Maryland belle Leslie Lynnton (Taylor) is wooed by raw Texas rancher Bick Benedict (Hudson) in the flapper era, but by the end of the story, as the couple sit together minding their grandchildren, the 1950s have arrived with a vengeance. The big house on Benedict's spread—a gloomy, three-story Victorian horror that Warner Brothers shipped from Hollywood to Marfa, Texas, in pieces on five railroad flatcars—has become a white-and-gold, ranch-house-moderne fantasy of sectional sofas and recumbent cocktail tables, with a picture window, a swimming pool, a patio, and a built-in barbecue out back.

In the form of Cadillacs, oil wells, private planes, mink stoles, twin beds, and dresses from Neiman-Marcus, civilization has clearly tamed the frontier. A film critic of the 50s thought the key image in the picture was that of the glossy Elizabeth Taylor in a Cadillac convertible. She stood for the awesome power that flowed from generations of wealth and a half-million acres of real estate.[2] But others thought *Giant* was about new money, about diamond rings on fingers still puckered from the washtub.

Edna Ferber, who wrote the novel upon which Warner Brothers loosely based *Giant*, was fascinated by the Texas *nouveaux riches*. She did her research in Texas in 1948 and 1949, when the place was awash in new oil money; for Ferber, the Lone Star State became a metaphor for the postwar United States and its material prosperity. Her description of the company town where the Chicano ranch hands and their wives shop attests to an abundance that transcends old class barriers, even as Ferber mocks the products on display. "Plate glass windows reflected, glitter for glitter, the dazzling aluminum and white enamel objects within," she writes of the show windows. "Vast refrigerators, protean washing machines, the most acquisitive of vacuum cleaners. . . . Plastic things, paper things, rayon things. Gadgets."[3]

The filmscript is another matter, though. Written around a TV set during the Army-McCarthy hearings, it attacks contemporary social issues implicit in but hardly central to the novel. The Mexican workers on the Benedict ranch, for example, stand for all people of color, and for the civil rights movement in the year of the Montgomery bus boycott: the movie ends with a vision of future racial integration, two Benedict heirs, one white and the other brown, sharing a single playpen (in case the point is not abundantly clear, the children are juxtaposed with a white lamb and a Black Angus calf). The American family will solve the largest national problems at the level of father and mother and children, ranch house and Cadillac. Jett Rink (Dean), the villain of the piece, is an orphan, an outsider who pines for the amenities of house and home but winds up the unhappy owner of a fancy, empty hotel.

Despite changes in emphasis, however, the rich, textural qualities of Ferber's original persist, mainly in the details—in the set decoration by Boris Levin, and the flouncy pastel dresses by Moss Mabry. And the burnished look of the film, especially in the chic interiors, undercuts the ostensible social message. In the end, *Giant* is a house-centered family melodrama, a domestic Western which, despite the big screen, has the feel of an evening of television, interrupted by commercials for new cars and plush wall-to-wall carpeting. In the nullity of the flat, brown Texas landscape, the house assumes visual as well as symbolic importance; it is the changes in its appointments from scene to scene that create the illusion of time passing. The epic dimensions of the story, in other words, depend almost completely upon the labors of designers and dressmakers. History is pure style. A 1952 reviewer of the book accused Ferber of churning out a pot-boiler with "money-snob appeal for the masses."[4] The movie is a celebration of *House Beautiful* interiors over exteriors, Liz Taylor's domain over Rock Hudson's, perhaps, the bright, modern home and all the artful paraphernalia that fills it over issues, 9-to-5 careers, and an inconvenient, dark, and dingy past.

In his pioneering study of Hollywood films of the 1950s, Peter Biskind argues that the pictorial emphasis on the house puts the consciousness of Taylor's Leslie at the very center of *Giant*. She is the "Queen of Hearth," and *Mother* (not Father) knows best on the Benedict ranch. It is the cinematic housewife, he says, who shapes and finally controls the man's environment and his values.[5] But secure in their artfully contrived setting, Leslie and Bick don't seem very different by the time the 50s come to Texas: they are full domestic partners, both of them equally at ease with the postwar gadgets, the low-slung living room suites, with tail fins and togetherness.

Despite the classical man-and-wife bickering and their ultimate renunciation of the two-ton, forty-foot mobile home that literally propels the plot, Desi and Lucy (as newlyweds Nicky and Tacy Collins) seem delighted with all of the above, too, in *The Long, Long Trailer* of 1954. If *Giant* and movies like it tried to outdo TV in spectacle, sumptuousness, scale, and stereo sound, *The Long, Long Trailer* represents a concession to the popularity of *I Love Lucy* and small-screen, middle-class, family sitcoms. MGM made the movie in June and July of 1953, when the Arnazes' weekly comedy series was on hiatus and at a time when the studio's own contract players were still forbidden to appear on television. The idea was to wean addicts away from the black-and-white tube (which offered *free* entertainment, of course) with familiar characters enhanced by the magic of Hollywood. In the case of Desi and Lucy, the moguls toyed with the idea of 3-D but settled for Anscocolor: for the first time, ads proclaimed, America would see its favorite dizzy redhead in her true colors.[6] And as in the Texas of *Giant*, the Western landscape through which the honeymooners drag their home on wheels pales in comparison to the trailer's colorful interior, replete with built-in sectionals and appliances, and the camera's pastel views of luxurious roadside trailer courts which are really instant, overnight suburbs, with swimming pools. If the Benedicts are upwardly mobile, beyond the wildest dreams of the audience, the Collins family is simply mobile. But in both cases, the viewer's eye is seduced by creature comforts, all shiny and new.

So is Tacy-Lucy, in her fashionable, wide-skirt dress and clutch coat (by Helen Rose), as she drags her intended off to the annual trailer show to inspect a lime-green and turquoise model as lavishly decked out as herself. She likes the stove with the glass picture window in the door of the oven "so you don't have to open it to look in." And when the papers are signed and the trailer loaded up with wedding presents—matching sets of pastel towels and kitchen gadgets—she lays plans for home improvements, in the form of a deep freeze and a TV set. The latter, she argues, is the telling detail that will make a rolling house into a true home, where a husband can enjoy a relaxing evening in the bosom of his family.

Nicky-Desi is the one who must cope with his bride's several domestic enthusiasms. He pilots the spiffy new Mercury convertible with the automatic top that pulls the trailer. He puts on his jeans and jacks up the rear end when a rainstorm threatens to upend the sunken living room. He waxes enthusiastic over her stabs at gourmet cooking. Only when Tacy's latest hobby—collecting rocks from tourist sites along the route—threatens to send convertible, trailer, glass-front range, and the couple's vast wardrobe plummeting into a gorge in the Rockies does Nicky make a half-hearted effort to rebel against the dollhouse domesticity that has led him to the brink of disaster. But there's something a little disingenuous about his protests. In 1953 Desilu Enterprises, the growing Arnaz TV empire, was licensing *I Love*

Lucy dolls, aprons, bedroom furniture, and outfits for men and women, including a line of "Desi Denims" for vacation and leisure wear. *I Love Lucy* kitchen flooring, with a "thrilling plastic glow," was being advertised in the pages of *McCall's*. The same glow of color and style—the seductive blue glow of a TV set—lights up *The Long, Long Trailer*.[7]

There isn't much difference, however, between the comedy exploiting the newly made celebrities of the small screen and the epic, illuminated by some of Hollywood's last and brightest superstars. Gender roles, homemaking, the myth of the West, dressing for a part: the same themes resonate through both films, just beneath the texts articulated by their divergent plots. *Giant* and *The Long, Long Trailer* are both set in densely material worlds, crowded with remarkably similar artifacts, too. Whatever the story—farce or ponderous message—the effect is a visual, visceral dazzle, an absorbing sense of pleasure in the act of perusal. Costumes. Things. Things to look at. New things. The latest things. High style. The glass door lets Lucy peep into her oven: she loves it because it lets her see inside. And seeing is absolutely central to the meaning of the 1950s. The only thing wrong with movies was that they weren't TV, offering a free look at the contents of other people's lives, and houses, on demand. This book is about dressing up (How do I look?), taking up a hobby (How does this look?), taking a vacation (Look at that!); it's about Cadillacs and rebel teens and cake-mix cakes and how they were adorned and why; about shiny new kitchens with pass-throughs from which the TV set could always be glimpsed and the suburbs they were created for; about parking lots and paintings and plastic crocodiles; and expositions, exhibitions, and TV shows, tailored to the visual sensibility. It's all about what people looked at in the 1950s, and what there was to see.

And who. Stars: Mamie Eisenhower, Elvis Presley, Betty Crocker, Richard Nixon, Grandma Moses, Ed Sullivan, Walt Disney, and Nikita Khrushchev, who wanted more than anything else to see Disneyland during his American tour of 1959. Ike wanted to take him to Levittown to show the Soviet leader how mass production could give everyone a new home just as efficiently as Detroit cranked out new cars. In the end, both excursions were scrubbed.[8] But had Khrushchev made it to Disneyland (to "Tomorrowland," therein) he would have seen a house—the Monsanto House of the Future—that resembled a giant TV set, or rather, four of them, protruding from a single stalk like some monstrous electronic flower.

The house was made of plastic panels, cast in sensuous, pliable curves. It was crammed with microwave ovens and pictophones and the latest in domestic gadgetry: it had an "Atoms for Living Kitchen," a vinyl floor with embedded flakes of synthetic pearl, and closed-circuit TV in every room, for looking at one's own stuff. It had regular TV sets, too, for watching *I Love Lucy* or the Wednesday night favorite, *Disneyland* (and other people's no-wax floors) in homey comfort.[9] For the House of the Future wasn't *that* different, except in its video-syncratic shape, from the standard picture-window model in Levit-towns everywhere. And the picture in the picture window was like the picture on the TV set or the view into Lucy's oven. They all provided framed views of what was going on inside. Look! Look at that! So the person sitting in the living room window watching the set was a kind of minor-league star as well as a spectator. Look at me! Look at my house and my new color TV! Life in the 1950s imitated art—as seen on TV.

Ike's 1953 inauguration was one of the first big TV events of the decade. The cameras caught every detail of Mrs. Eisenhower's costume: the mink coat, the silly hat worn over bangs, the suit with the nipped-in waist and flared hipline, the charm bracelet, and high heels that pinched.

Mamie Eisenhower's New Look

*I*n December of 1946, according to legend, Christian Dior retreated to the chateau of a friend in Fontainebleau. Fifteen days later he emerged with the sketches for his première collection, his so-called Corolle Line. "We were leaving a period of war, of uniforms, of soldier-women with shoulders like boxers," he later mused. "I turned them into flowers, with soft shoulders, blooming bosoms, waists slim as vine stems, and skirts opening up like blossoms." The world press saw Dior's designs for the first time in Paris on February 12, 1947—and came away enchanted. After seven long years of wartime make-do, rationing, and stringent rules governing the amount of fabric permissible in a given garment, after seven years of skimpy, asexual suits and silence from the great French couturiers, fashion and femininity were back at last. Dior's suits were sensuous, positively luxurious—gloriously full in the skirt, and topped off with great, extravagant cartwheel hats. Nipped at the waist, rounded at the hips and bustline, sloping gracefully through the shoulder, they defined the body's every womanly, *viva la différence* contour. The silhouette was so different, so utterly novel that *Life* magazine christened it "The New Look."[1]

The New Look. It was a phrase like "The Middle Ages" or "The Four Freedoms." It signified an entity, an institution to be reckoned with, permanent, significant. And Dior's line was all those things—

1947

Dior's New Look of 1947, according to *Harper's Bazaar*. This was the style that set the tone for the "look" of the 1950s in the United States.

and more. Suddenly, peplums and petticoats were everywhere. Hemlines plunged. Women used to piecing together an outfit from a hand-me-down dress, an old jacket, and a newish hat learned to covet ensembles in which shoes, bags, and even perfume were carefully coordinated by a designer to achieve an artful totality. An American woman returning from China after a year abroad first encountered the long skirts and unpadded shoulders in Calcutta and thought they "looked like something out of a masquerade party," but by the time she reached New York she "felt conspicuous" in her out-of-date clothes.[2]

Everybody was wearing or copying the New Look, it seemed, and the renascent fashion business had become a matter of churning out Paris knockoffs as quickly as possible. "If there could be a composite, mythical woman dressed by a mythical, composite couturier," *Vogue* opined, "she would probably wear her skirt about fourteen inches from the floor" and it would be modeled on a flower. By 1952 or so, variants had appeared. Jacques Fath went in for pencil-slim skirts topped off by exuberant, flower-like jackets, for example, and Dior himself eventually renounced the big hat in favor of sleek little heads that did not distract attention from the sculptural qualities of his models. For make no mistake about it: the New Look was a form of living sculpture, created by ingenious corsetry, inspired design, and an intricate dressmaking technique that amounted to a kind of body engineering.[3]

The molded, hourglass shape was achieved through a variety of means: padding hidden in the lining of jackets to accentuate the swelling of the hips; boning, stays, or other constricting devices built into waistlines; and an internal framework composed of layers of tulle, organza, silk pongee, and a new "miracle fabric"—nylon. A well-wrought Dior, it was said, could stand up by itself in a corner, after the wearer had gone to bed. It could be argued, of course, that the woman inside was irrelevant to the dress, that she was the victim of fashion, enslaved and oppressed by her own dinner gown. Edmund Bergler, an American psychoanalyst of the 1950s, dismissed the fashion industry as a "gigantic unconscious hoax" perpetrated on women by homosexual men who wanted to make them look ridiculous.[4] The New Look was just one more sign of the rampant sexual malaise of the times.

Christian Dior saw things differently. The women tottering precariously about on the high heels that completed the Corolle costume were rediscovering the grace of the dance, he insisted, while his ankle-grazing hemlines had "restored all its former mystery to the leg." Husbands weren't so sure, though. Who was this Frenchman, this Dior character, to cover up the female leg? The leg which, thanks to Betty Grable's famous G.I. pinup, had become as American as baseball and Mom's apple pie! The New Look "shows everything you want to hide and hides everything you want to show," their wives complained. On aesthetic grounds alone, a Little Below the Knee Club founded in Dallas (where pickets were thrown up around an award ceremony honoring the great Dior) attracted a nationwide membership. "The Alamo fell but our hemlines will not!" cried the fashion holdouts.[5]

Others, including a League of Broke Husbands organized in Georgia, objected to the whole concept of style, obsolescence, and change. In England, as shortages persisted and Princess Elizabeth chose calf-length skirts for her trousseau, New Look wardrobes became the subject of serious political debate on grounds of waste, unwholesome "over sexiness," and ideology. The costume historian James Laver, writing in British *Vogue* in 1944, had described a "fashion of collaborators" then being worn in Occupied Paris. The Germans went down to defeat but this *Küche und Kinder* style—frilly, wasp-waisted, romantic, and reactionary—seemed to have won the war for the hearts and minds of the well-dressed victors. In *The Second Sex*, published in Paris in 1949, at the high water mark of Dior's influence, Simone de Beauvoir toyed with the notion of fashionable "elegance as bondage."[6]

The New Look has never really stopped being controversial. Fashion experts still squabble over Dior's authorship of the style. Weren't Scarlett O'Hara's laced corsets and crinolines in the 1939 movie *Gone With the Wind* as "new look" as anything turned out by the House of Dior? Hadn't the so-called American Look designers, like Claire McCardell, introduced natural shoulders, fuller skirts, and cinch belts back in 1946? Others, less concerned with issues of primacy and more interested in meaning, recoil from what the designer and fashion photographer Cecil Beaton called the "wanton fantasy" of the New Look—an artificial, manufactured woman whose anatomical differences were exaggerated to conform to the sexual dimorphism of the 40s and 50s. Was a woman who stuffed herself into a girdle and high

My parents on a second honeymoon in Washington, D.C., circa 1948. My mother and her mother made the New Look outfit: long, full skirt; fitted peplum jacket; wild hat.

heels a woman at all, by the hard-body, in-your-face standards of the 1990s? Wasn't she some form of sexual chattel? A piece of pretty, consumer-culture, top-of-the-TV-set bric-a-brac?[7]

She was, without question, artful, and the harbinger of what one design specialist dubs "a radical shift in aesthetic" which would, by the middle of the 1950s, transform everything from bric-a-brac and automobiles to cakes, plastic cups and saucers, high-style furniture, and off-the-rack department store outfits.[8] The postwar aesthetic asserted the importance of deliberate artfulness, of close attention to matters of color, line, and form. The Diors of the world readily achieved celebrity status in such an atmosphere, but so did Harley Earl (chief stylist for General Motors), Russel Wright (creator of American Modern dinnerware), Charles Eames (designer of spindly-legged, full-bodied chairs made of new high-tech materials), and Jackson Pollock (Abstract Expressionist painter). One strain of 50s design was organic—a synonym for curvilinear, volumetric, vaguely bosomy shapes. The New Look was organic to a fault but so were the lazy, sexy sag of a Wright cream pitcher and the tumescence on the back fender of the Cadillac (1948–ca. 1953) that would shortly become a full-fledged tail fin. A second strain was two-dimensional, textural, and richly patterned, like a vintage Pollock. It was colorful, obtrusive, and lavish. A little too much, perhaps. Like yards of figured *peau de soie* with dyed-to-match gloves and shoes.

The design critic Thomas Hine uses the term "populuxe"—that is, glitz and glitter for the masses—to describe the consumer products of the postwar era, including the retail versions of the New Look. He's right about the obsession with the outsides of things. The kitchen-matching finish ("New Colorama Styling!") of the Frigidaire electric range for 1954, for instance, probably weighed as heavily in customer buying decisions as any technical features described in the small print. But the new stove also came with a "Visi-door," allowing the housewife to look inside without opening the oven.[9] Cooking as television. The very construction of the artifact makes it clear that looking and viewing were central acts of consciousness. In the most fundamental of ways, the New Look is about looking, too—about distinctive forms, eye-catching patterns and textures, and attractive

Most modern design in the early 1950s resembled a woman wearing a New Look dress. Even lamps had waistlines, hips, busts, and slender legs.

colors; about looking at people and their clothes and being looked at in turn; about thinking about looking. Looking: not the judgmental "gaze" of contemporary feminist theory, but something more like a scrupulous, pleasurable regard for both shape and surface.[10] In this respect, there is something post-literate about the 50s. And the association of a diagnostic habit of vision with sensual enjoyment makes the New Look all the harder to talk about. Or rather, it is all too easy to dismiss as trivial and superficial the lives of those who looked for their own reflections in the era's glittering surfaces.

Applied to the female body, the principles of the New Look exuded a palpable optimism. If its basic shape could be changed, so could the human condition or, at the very least, the life of the lady in the son-of-Dior suit. Things were always perfectible, just as form—one's own included—was invariably improved by the complex play of pattern against contour and volume. So the old rules of finality no longer pertained. In the design ethos of the New Look, everything was always brand, spanking new.

To understand the New Look in this way suggests that people and artifacts engage in a complex sensual dialectic. Women may or may not have been the pawns of manufacturers engaged in a conspiracy to keep them homebound (and busily breeding more consumers) by a sort of invalidism of fashion: heels too high for walking, dresses too confining for real freedom of movement.[11] But they did experience actual physical changes—a corporeal transformation—within their own persons when they put on New Look clothes. They felt a constant pressure at the waistline, a flutter of drapery around the legs, the friction of flesh and close-fitting fabric across the breasts. With the torso both contained and sensitized by the cut of the garment, the movement of the leg became, by sheer contrast, a significant gesture.

"A garment that squeezes the testicles makes a man think differently," observes Umberto Eco in his famous essay on wearing jeans. By pinching and poking him in unfamiliar ways, his clothing drove Eco to an "epidermic self-awareness" of a charged relationship between self, garment, and society—or precisely the aesthetic of the New Look. He sees nothing of value in that relationship, however, concluding instead on a note of pity for women, perpetually enslaved by fashion and forced to "live for the exterior." But the autoerotic aspects of the Dior ensemble are clear enough to women who wore New Look styles. "High heels and corsets provide intense kinesthetic stimulation for women," writes Beatrice Faust, "appealing to the sense of touch by extending more than skin deep. These frivolous accessories are not just visual stimuli for men; they are also tactile stimuli for women." The frivolous externals of fashion may themselves trigger deeply internalized consequences.[12]

Because externals are the usual bases of advertising, the notion that style and appearances may actually matter is distressing to many critics of American mass culture weaned on Vance Packard's 1957 exposé of Madison Avenue.[13] Frederic Jameson traces the beginnings of the postmodern malaise to the point just after World War II when the empty blandishments of advertising accelerated the already "rapid rhythm of fashion and styling changes." By virtue of its intimate proximity with the body, however, fashion also functions as an extension of personality, a medium through which autobiographical statements (true *or* false ones) are made manifest. "Clothes are a sort of theatre where the leading player—the self—is torn between function and decoration, protection and assertion, concealment and display," posits the British design critic Stephen Bayley. In fitting rooms all across America, women twirling before mirrors in their first New Look skirts understood the dynamic perfectly. Pretty clothes not only enhanced the self; the theater of fashion also allowed the wearer to explore multiple identities and potential starring roles. In her satiric memoir of suburban life in the 1950s, Margaret Halsey described a shopping excursion to the city that changed a dutiful housewife into a sex goddess the moment she tried on "a silk print which, worn with very high heels and my hair in a French roll, makes me look properly carnal . . ., as if I had my mind on lower things." Ironically, the mass-produced New Look uniform of the 50s invited the shopper to try on a new persona, primal and highly individualized—a self usually hidden from the public gaze by skirts and hats and little silk prints.[14]

Clothing manufacturers and marketers were sensitive to the intrinsic theatricality of fashion and its dual capacity to influence the perceptions of both audience and actress. The first in a long and famous series of theater-of-the-absurd lingerie ads, released in October of 1949, pictured a woman mysteriously out and about at the local supermarket clad only in a New Look skirt (with coordinating purse and beads) and a brassiere. "I dreamed I went shopping in my Maidenform bra," the copy announced. The highly successful Maidenform campaign drew on suburbanized Surrealism and bowdlerized Freud to glamorize the underpinnings demanded by the new style: the model's "dream" discloses suppressed yearnings of a distinctly genteel sort—to shop, to be an artist, a lady editor, a fashion designer, a *grande dame* bound for the opera with a neckful of jewels and a mink stole. Nevertheless, her state of demi-nudity establishes the missing costume as the link between a private, interior life of repressed desires and the public world of action, from which unclothed persons are firmly barred. By the absence of garments, Maidenform ads speak to the intricacies and pleasures of fashion and its importance as a signifier of meaning. And in the heyday of the

I dreamed
I went
shopping
in my
maidenform bra

Asleep...but it all seemed so real! Leafing through
lettuce, browsing over broccoli...all eyes gave my figure
a big "aye." And all because of my Maidenform
brassiere. No figure can ever get out of line with Maidenform at the controls. Uncanny the fit, wonderful
the comfort! Maybe you've dreamed of a bra like this!

A.M. You want to look your best...accentuated, lifted...
it's Maidenform's Allo-ette* for you! **P.M.** You're wearing as
I-dare-you neckline...choose Dec-la-tay * Or for the
no-straps-at-all look...Maidenette Strapless.*

Shown: Maidenform's Allo-ette in white rayon satin.
Just one from a vast collection of styles and fabrics.
There is a *Maiden Form* for Every Type of Figure

Maidenform's famous "dream" series of
the 1950s began with this ad: the New
Look surrealized.

New Look the refrain of the nocturnal dreamer with nothing to wear became a national watchword. The press was properly delighted one day early in her husband's first term, therefore, when Mamie Eisenhower—an unrepentant clotheshorse—dropped in backstage at a Washington fashion show. Quipped a flustered model, caught in her underwear by the First Lady: "Gosh, I never dreamt I'd meet Mrs. Eisenhower in my Maidenform bra!"[15]

As her choice of a White House wardrobe demonstrated, Mrs. Eisenhower was a passionate but prudent devotee of the New Look throughout the 1950s, preferring the less extreme American adaptations of Dior's original concept. She was an early convert, too, quick to equate the "New" with a youthfulness of attitude she cultivated and freely discussed. Being young meant trying the latest thing. And whether that novelty was the packaged cake mix with which she stocked the family pantry at 1600 Pennsylvania Avenue, the "1950s modern" furniture with which she redecorated the presidential retreat at Camp David, or the new TV soap operas she adored (*As the World Turns* was her hands-down favorite), Mamie Eisenhower was determined to give it a whirl.[16]

In 1948, years before the General decided to run for public office, the *Brownsville Herald* interviewed "Ike's wife" about her taste in clothes. The reporter found her looking much younger than her 51 years and partial to unmatronly fashions. "Hats don't interest her particularly," the writer noted, "but she loves shoes. She likes the longer dresses of the 'new look' but hopes they don't get too close to the ankles." She liked fitted bodices, sweetheart necklines, and flirty skirts that swished when she walked—an ultra-feminine version of Dior filtered through Hollywood—and wore them for the next decade, when a grandmother of more sedate disposition might have settled into Mother Hubbards.[17] In the popular imagination, though, ankle-length dresses were still for old ladies, whatever the fashion magazines said about the Parisian chic and sophistication of a hemline less than a foot above the pavement. Mamie wanted to be stylish, forever young, wholesomely, girlishly sexy, and well turned out on all occasions. Since she was constantly in the public eye and known for her delight in her well-stocked closets, Mrs. Eisenhower became

Mrs. Eisenhower, wearing a Sally Victor hat, backstage at a fashion benefit for the National Symphony, March 1953. The fashion show became a popular form of entertainment for both "official" wives and women of the middle class in general; like watching TV serials with friends over lunch, it was intimate and aesthetic. Here, the scrumptious gowns are by Pierre Balmain.

both an exemplar of the new fashion sensibility of her day and an example of the precise terms in which the New Look appealed to postwar America.

In 1950 President Truman sent Ike to Europe to head NATO. Mamie joined him in 1951, emerging as a newsworthy figure in her own right for the first time, partly because of fashion. French journalists were intrigued by the likes and dislikes of a lady from exotic Iowa, while women's pages back home wondered how one of their number would fare in the dazzling world of *haute couture*. The powerful mystique of the dress salon was explored in a spate of fashion movies beginning with the 1952 *Lovely to Look At*, starring Kathryn Grayson as part-owner of a struggling Paris design establishment. What these films have in common—from *Funny Face* (1956) with its ethereal Givenchy gowns to the 3-D raunchiness of *The French Line* (1953)—is an aura of exclusivity and wealth (French fashion is for the rich), a sense of womanly competence, and an emphasis on headgear. In the Hollywood version of the fashion business, the salon is a place in which men are tolerated for the sake of romantic duets or financial expertise. But it is a woman's place, ultimately governed by her preferences and skills. The hat is a badge of membership in the sisterhood of the empowered: fashion commentators and editors, poker-faced mannequins, salesgirls, brisk *premières*, designers, and knowing customers all wear outrageous confections atop their carefully coiffed heads.

It should come as no surprise, then, that Mamie Eisenhower discovered hats in Paris. Thereafter, she wore a hat to complete a costume, to signify a public appearance or a special occasion, to announce her kinship with other hatted ladies who ran the charity functions she attended. The hat was a luxury item as well, too small and delicate to shield the head from the elements, but visually obtrusive and subject to radical seasonal change, a prime example of what Packard meant by a "status symbol." Yet, in America's vibrant new consumer culture, luxuries once reserved for the rich were within reach of everybody. When asked about a stunning new hat she wore to a state affair in Paris, Mamie replied: "I got it by mail order from home. It cost me $9.95!" Much to the chagrin of the French press, she then launched into a gleeful account of rummaging through the racks

Despite the prominence of names like Dior and Balmain, the dress salon was one of the few places where the professional competence of women was unquestioned in the popular culture of the 1950s. This is Lily Daché's New York salon during the launch of the 1954 winter collection.

The hat was the ultimate mark of feminine empowerment. A woman in a hat meant business.

at department stores for high fashion bargains. Mamie, it seems, had no interest in one-of-a-kind New Look clothes when the same thing could be had for a song in Macy's or Bloomingdale's. She attended the Paris shows regularly but never bought a thing. "Can you see my paying seven hundred dollars for a dress?" she asked a visiting columnist from the States.[18]

Once ensconced in the White House, Mamie's rummaging days were over. She drew mobs whenever her gleaming black Chrysler pulled up to a store, and sale-rack frugality was politically inexpedient besides. "We had a hard time convincing her that she couldn't wear two-year-old dresses," said Mollie Parnis, her favorite American designer. "I told her, 'It's like driving [an old] Cadillac around Washington. You just can't *do* it. It would be bad for our industry.'" During the 1952 campaign, however, there were no such constraints on her fashion instincts. She wore her mail-order hats (and a couple of numbers bought in Paris). And she made excellent copy by being most emphatic about her personal fashion dos and don'ts.[19]

Photographed for a biography in *Collier's* wearing a sleeveless, halter-top sundress with a billowing skirt that "made her look more like a girl than a mature woman," Mrs. Eisenhower made it clear that she had chosen her wild cotton print deliberately: "I hate old-lady clothes. And I shall never wear them." As much as a friendly smile and an ease of manner, her insistence on young lines and cuts—after all, teenagers were wearing big felt skirts decorated with poodle dogs in 1951 and 1952—may have encouraged the public to call her "Mamie." At any rate, during the Eisenhowers' whistle-stop tour of the nation, her sense of style soon became familiar to anybody who followed the campaign in the media. *Life* insisted that her photogenic political wardrobe had been specially ordered in Paris. But *Newsweek* scooped its rivals by tracing six of the outfits to the Seventh Avenue salesrooms of Mollie Parnis in New York City. Mamie liked Parnis's clothes, she explained, because they had bouffant skirts and that "little extra flair."[20]

Letters to the designer from the campaign trail date the beginning of their long relationship to the early summer of 1952 and Mamie's purchase of a navy blue silk shantung Parnis dress at Bonwit Teller. The dress had acquired a prominent spot somewhere around Chicago, possibly as the result of water leaking from a bouquet of flowers presented by the party faithful. Mamie complained—and promptly ordered five more dresses and a faille suit which caught up with the entourage in Minnesota on an October day too cold for any of the new finery. In late November, with the election won, Parnis and Eisenhower were engrossed in fittings for a Washington wardrobe. In December Parnis found herself on the official guest list for the forthcoming inauguration ceremonies. At Christmas, she sent her client a bright red taffeta dress for a gift. "What a perfectly beautiful . . . dress," wrote Mamie gratefully, "and in a style that is so becoming to me, too!"[21]

A typical Mamie Eisenhower outfit, in navy blue—what the 1950s called the "Mamie Look." Mollie Parnis became her favorite designer and Sally Victor her favorite milliner.

The style Mamie found most becoming was a one-piece dress (sometimes a suit) with a full skirt and a thirteen-inch hemline, usually made up in a fabric with a reflective or slightly iridescent surface—like silk taffeta. The dress itself was a fancy, ornamental variation on the shirtwaist, the relaxed, suburban edition of the New Look seen everywhere from shopping centers to junior high schools in the Americana ginghams introduced in the spring of 1950. It was a "lady look": neat, coherent, feminine, and yet, without the more extreme forms of corsetry and built-in structure, one which permitted a freedom of movement in keeping with car pools, servantless homes, and the other conventions of modern housewifery. Mollie Parnis did not admit to any interest in "designing for the average housewife," but the Parnis dress did stake out a middle ground between Paris and Levittown. Her firm, wrote one fashion historian, "produced flattering dresses . . . for the well-to-do woman over thirty, emphasizing becomingness in beautiful fabrics [and] a conservative interpretation of current trends."[22]

Unlike high fashion clothes, the Parnis shirtwaist made a woman look well turned out but *normal,* a term the designer also used to describe her most famous client in the mid-1950s. "That is the nicest thing about her," Parnis gushed. "She's so normal! [And] Mrs. Eisenhower brings a new viewpoint on clothes to the White House. She's proving that a grandmother needn't be an old lady. She's making maturity glamorous." In later years Parnis could be cruel in her criticisms, claiming that she had been forced to accessorize Mamie's outfits lest the First Lady commit some awful error of taste: "You know, she really didn't have much fashion sense."[23] Other members of the design profession also sniffed at Mamie's relish for dyed-to-match shoes and colored stockings, mink coats, charm bracelets, and bangs. In the end, however, what she called "looking high class"—adorning a basic style with marks of familial success and individuality—came to be known as "the Mamie look." Subordinating dress to ensemble and ensemble to personality, it was not a look calculated to advertise a designer's product: the ultimate Mamie-ness of a given outfit all but overshadowed the contribution of a Mollie Parnis or a Nettie Rosenstein. And when she decided that she looked "high class," even the contrary opinions of the experts fazed her not at all. Dior raised hems in the spring of 1953 but Mamie didn't. *Life* magazine made fun of her hairstyle but she ignored suggestions for a change so studiously that bangs became a key element of "the Mamie look."[24]

In 1951 the fringe of hair across her high forehead was already being called "the famous bangs" in published profiles of the General's lady. The bangs were noteworthy because the "modified Lillian Gish" style seemed old fashioned for a woman bent on staying young. In Mamie's case, however, they were not some hangover from the silent era but the last decorative vestige of an elaborate sculptural coiffure,

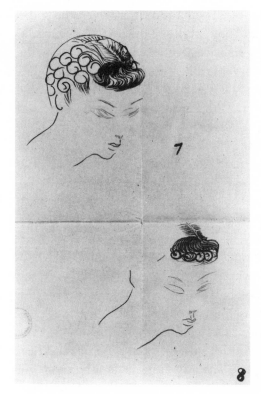

The cutting and setting diagram for Mrs. Eisenhower's celebrated bangs, by Elizabeth Arden, 1953.

typical of the mid-1940s, that she began to wear after Ike returned from his wartime service in Europe. The historian Carl Sferrazza Anthony thinks they amounted to "a private symbol" for Mamie, a reminder of the end of the Eisenhowers' long marital estrangement. The public was fascinated by her perky forelock: while fashion trends seemed calculated to turn women into so many mass-produced robots in pseudo-Diors, Mamie Eisenhower's hairdo called attention to itself by its sheer oddity. Hollywood columnist Hedda Hopper facetiously asked whether, if she became First Lady, Mamie would expect all the women in America to wear bangs. A week after the election, *Life* demanded that she trim the bangs and get a poodle cut instead, and provided retouched pictures to prove that with that one simple change she could be "the best looking first lady we have ever had."[25]

The poodle cut was a bold attempt to do for heads what the New

Look had already done for figures. The hairdo from which the softer Italian cut and the various short "boy" styles of the decade eventually descended, the poodle seems to have begun on Broadway, in the musical *South Pacific*, with Mary Martin's washable cap of ringlets (1949). But it was not until the style was taken up by the TV star Faye Emerson that the term entered the American vocabulary. *Life* showed Emerson and three other rising television personalities wearing the head-hugging crown of curls (the result of a Toni home permanent or sleeping on upwards of 125 curlers every night) in January of 1952; by February, Emerson's distinctive clip had filtered down to the picture digests sold at supermarket checkout counters.[26] In keeping with its origins in television and postwar do-it-yourself beauty technology, the poodle cut was gorgeously new, exciting—and young. As hairdressers were quick to point out, it was an unforgiving style, too, because the hair was curled away from the face, exposing every sag and wrinkle. It was a young look best suited to the young complexion of an authentic gamin, whereas the customers who filled Washington's beauty salons on the eve of the inauguration, demanding "The Mamie," wanted instead the youthful illusion the wife of the President-elect so buoyantly projected. The adventurous among them got a haircut. The timid settled for false bangs priced from $10 to $17.50.[27]

The "Mamie look" of the early 50s had an additive quality: bangs appended to the hairline, gauntlet gloves pulled up over dress sleeves, ditzy hats atop an elaborate hairdo (Elizabeth Arden even provided a diagram to insure complete uniformity in cut and set), and a mink tossed over everything. The effect was busy and acquisitive, somehow, as if each layer—brooch on bodice under coat; hat plus hair plus lipstick and earrings—were too important in its own right to subside quietly into some fashion ensemble. It was possessive, obtrusive, infinitely pleased with things that shimmered and glistened, or swished, or dangled. The noisy, hopelessly jejune charm bracelet was Mamie-ism in its purest form. Most photos of Mrs. Eisenhower campaigning with her husband show her posing so as to call attention to a lucky "Ike" charm or a huge four-leaf-clover medallion. She owned several similar bracelets, including one with twenty-one charms representing important milestones in her husband's career, made by a

Two versions of the "Full Mamie": (top) receiving an award from the Women's Medical College of Pennsylvania in the White House Rose Garden, 1953; (bottom) with her husband in Denver, summer 1953.

One of Mamie's biographical charm bracelets. Note the miniature White House at left.

Fifth Avenue jeweler who specialized in expensive versions of a fad more popular among teenagers, coeds, and debutantes. But the presentation of a biographical bracelet was also a highlight of *This Is Your Life*, a popular new Wednesday night television show devoted to humanizing celebrities by revealing incidents from their private lives. With the charm bracelet, life literally became a fashion statement. It was a sign of accomplishment, a proof that the good life of fame and stardom and obtrusive jewelry had been well earned.[28]

The formal components of 1950s fashion appear in other artifacts of the decade which also expressed and enhanced the pleasures of ownership by means of accretion. The 1952-model kitchen stoves didn't work better for having pushbuttons and colored trim applied to the surface; cars didn't idle more smoothly thanks to a two-tone paint job or several pounds of chrome "gorp" on the front bumper; improved reception in a radio or television set was not a function of the woven and textured finishes and the metallic highlights adorning the cabinet. Yet these superfluous details were the visual luxuries, "the little extra flair," Mamie also looked for in her clothes. They made life sparkle and glitter. They made it fun to get dressed in the morning, to cook, to drive. The extras were the bright lights, the music, the glamour, the excitement, the pizzazz, the gleaming charms.

Fur was the ultimate 1950s extra. By the time of the 1952 elections, the ranch mink coat had also acquired partisan connotations. A year earlier, a congressional committee investigating corruption in the Truman administration had turned up evidence of bribery in the form of a $9,540 pastel mink hanging in the closet of a White House stenographer. The televised "Checkers" speech, in which Eisenhower's running mate, Richard Nixon, attempted to clear himself of charges that he had tapped a secret slush fund, exploited that symbol of decadent luxury shamelessly. His wife, Pat, didn't own a mink coat, the candidate boasted: "But she does have a respectable Republican cloth coat, and I always tell her that she would look good in anything." There matters rested until Mamie waded in on the side of fashion. On December 1, wearing what seemed to be a full-length mink, she turned up to accompany the departing First Lady on the traditional tour of the executive mansion. As the women posed for pictures at the door (Bess Truman in a modest Persian lamb topper), reporters eyed the glossy Republican fur and needled Mrs. Eisenhower about it, trying to get a newsworthy quote. What was her coat made of, anyway? "Mink, of course," shot back Mrs. Eisenhower with a broad smile and a winning tinkle of her charm bracelet.[29]

Her fur labeled Mamie a winner, a success. Democrat, Republican: those were dim abstractions. Fur was real and so was Mamie's transparent joy in finding herself under the White House portico equipped with all the sartorial trappings of the American Dream: a pearl choker; a drop-dead mink pulled back to reveal a Mollie Parnis shirtwaist with pleats, a ruffle, and covered buttons; matching Cuban-heel pumps; a big, shiny alligator purse; and a little velvet hat. Texture, color, complexity, contrast: dressed to kill, she was a walking compendium of the aesthetic principles that governed the marketplace. And for that reason, she managed to look very much like the woman next door. The velvet hat was by Sally Victor, who told the *New York Times* that Mamie exemplified "good American taste."[30]

Sally Victor began her career in the 1930s as a protégée of Dorothy Shaver, the influential Lord and Taylor vice president who promoted American fashion in the Fifth Avenue windows of the store. The American quality Victor prized in fashion was a kind of purposeful playfulness best expressed in millinery. Specifically, she thought of hats in psychological terms, as disguises, indices of character, mirrors of mood, or means of trying on new aspects of a complex personality. "A woman becomes what her hat means to the world and to herself," the milliner wrote. Fighting the postwar drift toward a more casual, hatless lifestyle—despite the pictures in fashion magazines, younger women and teens owned far fewer hats than their elders—Victor stayed at the top of her profession in the 1950s by conceding the avant-garde end of the trade to Mr. John and to her arch-rival, Lilly Daché. The "Sally V" subsidiary, which accounted for half of her business, produced hats for the mass market, priced within the reach of most bareheaded suburbanites. They sold briskly because Victor emphasized the concept of prettiness: "All you have to do" to sell hats, she counseled, "is show a woman that she looks prettier with a hat on than off."[31]

Pretty was not chic, of course. Whereas chic required external verification, pretty was an entirely more comfortable concept, grounded in how a woman felt about herself. "Good fashion is an individual matter," Victor asserted. "It is whatever makes you look better. I do not believe in any style that does not make the wearer prettier." Prettiness was ageless, besides. Pretty girls were like melodies; children called their mothers "pretty"; women used the term to describe one another, or a new hat. Meeting Pat Nixon for the first time at the Republican convention in Chicago, Mamie Eisenhower turned to her and blurted out, "Why, you're the prettiest thing!" "The little flowered one is just as pretty as it can be and terribly sweet," she told Sally Victor after her 1953 Easter bonnet arrived at the White House.[32] And if Mrs. Eisenhower worried that another woman was feeling unpretty and ill at ease, her folk remedy was always a new hat. She ordered four Sally V's—"Young hats—she's so pretty!"—as a gift for Elizabeth of England when the Queen paid a state visit in 1957 dressed in matronly British woolens, and another in 1959 for the dowdy Nina Khrushchev, who didn't dare wear such a blatant emblem of capitalist excess in public.[33]

Mamie's most celebrated hat, the "airwave" model, was the one she wore to her husband's 1953 swearing-in and to the massive inaugural parade that followed. It was a Sally Victor, of course (the designer had

The "airwave" hat by Sally Victor, for the outdoor ceremonies at Ike's first inaugural, was designed to set off Mamie's Hattie Carnegie suit.

earned her place on the official guest list by creating special campaign berets, with cockades to hold milady's "I Like Ike" buttons). Shaped like a shallow, inverted bowl or an iced cupcake, the hat was made of soft gray felt, contoured into four scalloped layers and slashed to show flashes of a bright green lining.[34] Because the festivities were covered at length on television, Mamie's costume came in for unprecedented scrutiny. Her gray Hattie Carnegie dressmaker suit was hidden under her mink, and her charm bracelet peeped out of her sleeve only when she waved, but the cheerful little hat was hard to miss, especially in "human interest" shots of the First Lady slipping off a shoe and bending over to massage an aching arch as the parade dragged on toward nightfall.

Macy's sold knockoffs by the gross. Of the seven hundred letters per week directed to Mrs. Eisenhower by the general public following the inauguration, many asked for that hat, or one just like it. Mamie's letter to Sally Victor—one of the first pieces of post-inaugural business to be attended to—proved the latter's point about psychology and headgear. "All your hats were beautiful and styled so becomingly," she wrote, "but I think the one that attracted the most comment and admiration was the soft grey hat with the lovely green lining peeking through. An attractive, flattering hat always helps me feel my best and look my most confident, so you can see your selections were so important in boosting my morale."[35]

The other components of her Washington wardrobe paled into insignificance, however, beside the all-important inaugural ballgown. Stories circulated about the special plywood crate built to convey the

Mrs. Eisenhower in her pink Nettie Rosenstein ball gown. Glitter was added, as per her instructions, in the form of 2,000 hand-sewn pink rhinestones. The artificial jewels were by Trifari.

dress to Washington, about the three hours it took to dispose the built-in petticoats properly, as the President ("By golly, Mamie, you're beautiful!") paced the floor in a fit of impatience. Magazines ran inch-by-inch descriptions of the gown. Mamie dolls and figurines were garbed in Renoir pink *peau de soie* dresses with matching above-the-elbow gloves, shoes, and evening bags.[36] Like the gray suit, the dress and all its accessories were ordered through Neiman-Marcus of Dallas. Lawrence Marcus selected the designers and commissioned

Dolls and figurines reflected the popularity of Mamie's New Look.

the clothes, but in the case of her gown, Mrs. Eisenhower personally specified a wide skirt, chose the color, and insisted that Nettie Rosenstein supply additional glitter in the form of 2,000 hand-sewn rhinestones in four sizes and several shades of pink.[37] Concentrated in the gathers just below the dropped waistline, where the gown was at its fullest, the stones drew attention to the lavish use of material and to feminine curves already exaggerated by stiff taffeta underskirts. It was a New Look extravaganza, embellished and enriched American style.

In stylistic terms the ballgown anticipated most of the ingredients of vintage Mamie-ism. All the designers who made clothes for Mrs. Eisenhower during her White House years—Parnis, Carnegie, Elizabeth Arden's fashion division—would use some variation on the bouffant skirt with added fullness at the sides, most often placing bunches of unpressed pleats like panniers over each hipbone or achieving the same effect with peplum jackets. Gathered into narrow twists of silk at the shoulder, the gown exposed what *Life* called her "pretty neck and shoulders": the shoulder would be soft, unseamed, and natural in her daytime outfits, too. And her street clothes would be decorated, the basic structure already enhanced with unusual or nonfunctional buttons, cording, false pockets, and plackets before she began to add jewelry and accessories on her own initiative. The inaugural extras—*faux* pearls and brilliants by Trifari, an evening bag encrusted with pink stones and beads—matched the gown but were in no way subordinated to it: the things Mrs. Eisenhower carried or pinned to her everyday dresses would remain equally distinct, as if to call attention to the fact that they were hers and that she alone had decided to wear them. This was an American style, a newer, showier, happier, shop-'til-you-drop New Look. It was everything that *haute couture* was not: pretty, busy, flouncy, clothes-proud, quirkily personal, oblivious of age, all decked out, studied but still a little slapdash. Garnished like a colorful Jell-O salad. After details of the ballgown hit the papers, the New York Dress Institute named Mamie to its list of the world's twelve best-dressed women.[38]

She made the lists every year. Best-dressed (along with the Duchess of Windsor, Mrs. William Paley, and other high priestesses of fashion orthodoxy). Best-hatted. Best-shod. Her shopping trips, and every item purchased, were considered newsworthy.[39] So was the story of Mamie and a lobbyist's wife arriving at a diplomatic reception in virtually the same Mollie Parnis. As the offending party retreated into a distant room clutching her mink cape over the blue and green print—"Don't hide it," cried Mamie. "I think it's pretty!"—Parnis explained that many of Mrs. Eisenhower's "originals" were off-the-rack models with fuller skirts and special trim. Anybody could dress just like Mamie and manufacturers counted on her down-to-earth taste to revive the retail end of the business. "She is as likely to buy a dress she likes for $50 as she is to order an exclusive custom-made one," noted an economic observer. "What pleases the moguls of the nation's $11 billion fashion industry is that Mrs. Eisenhower can be counted on to wear either with an air."[40]

The best way to guarantee Mamie's presence at a charity event, the joke went, was to hold a fashion show. A typical list of engagements for a two-week period in the spring of 1953, for example, included style show benefits mounted by the Naval War College Officers' Wives Club, the Cherry Blossom Festival, and the National Symphony Orchestra.[41] A popular form of activity for women's organizations in the 1950s, the fashion show was a highly specialized dramatic form— a ritualized pantomime of shopping, and a play in which audience and performers were equally well costumed. Indeed, model and viewer were often one and the same person, as club officers did their

At a 1953 fashion show sponsored by the Navy Doctors Women's Club, Mamie eyes a pink wool suit topped off with a mink stole.

turns on the runway, reminding the rest of the spectators that fashion always had the dual aspect of looking and being looked at, performing and appraising.

An episode of *I Love Lucy* first telecast in February 1955 described the heroine's efforts to acquire a $100 "original" by appearing in a charity fashion show at the Hollywood salon of Don Loper. The funniest moment involves Lucy's unwitting parody of a model's mannered runway slouch: thanks to a terrible sunburn, Lucy can't help walking stiffly. But the program as a whole played off expensive originals against virtually identical clothes suited to the modest budgets of Lucy and Ethel, society women against aspiring suburbanites, and "normal" patterns of movement and decorum against the way a haughty beauty acts when she invites attention through her choice of dress—only to conclude that the forced comedic contrasts were skin deep after all. Fashion was a classless American universal.

I Love Lucy was one of the Eisenhowers' favorite TV shows. Two years earlier, despite charges that Lucille Ball was a "Red," Mamie had invited the cast to dine at the White House.[42] Perhaps it was in tribute to their hostess that the ballgown worn in the finale of Lucy's fashion burlesque was trimmed in sequins and *pink* mink. By 1955, because it was Mamie's favorite, "First Lady Pink" had become a bona fide color for hats, gloves, dresses, linoleum flooring, dishware, plastic buckets, nylon curtains, bathroom fixtures, and hardware-store paint chips. Also known as "Mamie Pink," it was the shade in which she redecorated her boudoir in the family quarters of the White House: from the pink-topped jars of Elizabeth Arden cosmetics to the pink tufted headboard of her queen-size bed, from her pink bedjackets to the fluffy pink rugs in the bathroom, her private world was a monotone confection. The First Lady's suite in the retirement home the Eisenhowers were building in Pennsylvania—"Mamie's Dream House"—was a study in pink tiles and soap dishes. So was her bedroom in "Mamie's Cabin," the presidential vacation hideaway overlooking the Augusta National Golf Club. She favored pink evening gowns and pink hats. She kept two brandy snifters full of pink rosebuds at her elbow.[43]

At first blush, pink seems a maidenly, even infantile color prefer-

The cast of *I Love Lucy* entertained the Eisenhowers on November 23, 1953, along with Eddie Fisher and Walter Cronkite.

ence, redolent of sentimentality, nurseries, and girlish innocence. The costume historians Jo Paoletti and Carol Kregloh point out, however, that pink and blue gender coding began to harden into dogma only after World War II, as fashion began the process of shaping adult clothing to exaggerate anatomical differences between men and women. Before the postwar baby boom, red and its pastel derivatives were as likely to signify a boy as a little girl. Widely publicized between 1951 and 1953, Mamie's fetish for pink may have helped to confirm the ultimate feminization of the color. But pink also bore into the 1950s a residue of zany, unpredatory sexiness associated with the designer Elsa Schiaparelli. In the 1930s, when major fashion changes were undermined by economic realities, Schiaparelli made news by espousing touches of color—"shocking" pink was her favorite—that could wake up a tired wardrobe in "shocking" and unexpected ways in the form of a ribbon, a fabric rosette, or a bright slash of lipstick. Color was a pick-me-up, the visual symbol for the shock of the new. In design circles, it was axiomatic that the whole postwar world had had enough of penury, khaki, and navy blue, and, in the words of the fashion retailer Stanley Marcus, "was hungry for a color explosion."[44]

Manufacturers of consumer durables were not the first to conclude that big-ticket items, like refrigerators and cabinet units, were potential fashion items, to be changed as frequently as hats. Nervous discussions of color in trade journals of the early 1950s show that corporate planners initially resisted the trend toward supplying items in a variety of shades only to be bowled over by the vehemence of popular demand for new hues, and a wide choice thereof. Pink and green and yellow appliances were what customers clamored to buy, along with "Coloramic" light bulbs from G.E. and boxes of Trix, the nation's first multicolored breakfast cereal. Color where color had never been before showed that a product was brand, spanking new— a new acquisition—and that the buyer was modern and forward looking, too. A sassy pink was the hottest color of the decade. Sexpot Jayne Mansfield once held a press conference in a pink swimming pool full of pink champagne to promote a career that caricatured the operative feminine stereotypes of the mid-50s. Male heartthrob Elvis Presley was addicted to the same candy shade, however. While Mamie was turning the White House pink, Elvis was wearing flashy pink pegged pants to Humes High School in Memphis. He showed up for his first singing dates in an outlandish pink suit, bought his parents a new pink Ford with his first big check, and slept in a mock-erotic pink bedroom in the suburban ranch house he gave them after he hit the big time. Teenage Presley fans craved lipsticks of "Heartbreak Hotel Pink."[45]

Pink was young, daring—and omnisexual. In 1955 respectable gray-flannel executives suddenly began finding pink shirts and ties under the family Christmas tree. The colorization of men's sports- and leisurewear was part of the general fascination with chromatic variety. Even so, the social critic Russell Lynes was unnerved by the spectacle of the American male standing over a backyard barbecue "dressed like a bird of paradise. For some reason food seems to taste better to him if he has on blue canvas shoes, brick-red or canary-yellow slacks, and a pastel blue sports shirt which hangs free, like a young matron's maternity smock, outside the pants." In casual duds, color probably stood for an after-hours revolt from the conformity and routine of the office, Lynes reasoned, but he was less certain of what to make of pink dress shirts. Were there buried motives at work here, as complicated as the psychology governing ladies' hats? Did the pink shirt represent some deep-seated need on the part of men to "glamorize and sexualize" their clothes, too? Was this a New Look for Him? A sign of creeping effeminacy brought on by too much "togetherness"? Or only a fad that had somehow managed to sweep up Mamie Eisenhower, Elvis Presley, Jayne Mansfield, and most of adolescent America, along with buyers of pink Cadillacs and steam irons, and hordes of Dads in new pink buttondowns? The sudden ubiquity of pink seemed to signify a culture in love with novelty, change, and visual stimulation. Rock 'n' roll singles justly celebrated the joys of acquiring "Pink Pedal Pushers" (1958), "Pink Shoe Laces" (1959), and a "White Sport Coat [with a Pink Carnation]" (1957).[46]

Or were there *two* pinks on either side of a growing generational divide? Mamie's pretty, ladylike shade versus the aggressively hot pink of the teenagers, the former a visual code for receptivity to new styles and products, the latter a mark of rebellion against social conventions, including the rigid sexual coding of blues and pinks? Between 1953, when Mamie brought pink to the White House, and 1955, when the rest of America went pink, too (that decisive moment is parodied in the Audrey Hepburn movie *Funny Face:* a Diana Vreeland-like fashion editor tells her readership to "Think Pink" and everything on screen from airplanes and trains to the offices of her magazine instantly turns a violent pink!), a genteel battle was being waged within the fashion industry between the form-fitting, womanly silhouette of the New Look and the short, ungirdled chemise known as The Sack. Fashion was about to desert its most faithful client—the woman whose age was a perennial thirty-five—to court the baby-boomer.

Unlike Dior's New Look, the sack had no readily discernible point of origin. In April 1955 Sportwhirl, an American manufacturer, made the cover of *Vogue* with a $13 cotton knit t-shirt dress, an unstructured, straight-up-and-down shift; over the next two years, more than 400,000 were sold. The 1957 fall season in Paris saw these same lines everywhere. Dior's last collection, his Free Look, was unfitted in the back; Balenciaga's "chemmy dress" was completely unfitted and tapered to a narrow hem; Givenchy also disavowed darts and waistlines.[47] Although the fashion writers finally agreed that credit for the definitive breakthrough belonged to Balenciaga, who had been experimenting with various loose shapes since 1951, the distinction was a dubious one since the sack or bag was one of the most hated styles in recent memory. Women who had fought for their figures with "saccharin and Slenderella" objected to hiding what the young could take for granted. Husbands who paid the bills found the middy style hideous. "The U.S. male has fallen to the most degraded position in history," a California reader complained in a letter to the editor of *Newsweek*. "He bellows his rage, but his womenfolk ignore him. The sack is an affront to man's esthetic sensibilities."[48]

Grownups—those who had accepted the gender marking of the New Look as the natural order of things—were most apt to be enraged by sacks. At times the anti-sack movement took on the overtones of an ideological crusade. Former Secretary of State Dean Acheson, speaking to students at the University of New Hampshire, noted that there are fashions in everything—even horrors. "By the couturier's alchemy," he concluded, "our most curvaceous charmers are turned into bags of Idaho's famous product." But Adlai Stevenson whimsically blamed the sack on Moscow: "Its purpose is to spread discontent, unrest, antagonisms, and hostilities." Comedian Bob Hope, in the Soviet Union to film a TV special, claimed that Russian women, unfashionable by American standards, had "been wearing sack dresses for years." In fact, under Nikita Khrushchev, Moscow's GUM department store had begun to carry adaptations of the new Western styles, including sack dresses with hems fourteen inches from the floor.[49]

In the United States, the hemlines were higher, creeping inexorably toward the knee and defining a new erogenous zone. And that was one major problem with the chemise in the eyes of potential buyers. Hosiery companies hoped the colored stockings often shown with the sack would perk up lagging sales, but mature women dreaded exposure of that much calf. Queen Elizabeth was said to be captivated by an American sack that buttoned down the front like an oversize sweater; Marilyn Monroe wore one to announce the start of production on her new movie, *Some Like It Hot*. Most women over thirty wouldn't be caught dead in one, regardless. "No sack for me," cried the sultry Italian actress Gina Lollobrigida. "Poor men, they are offered pregnant women or fake little girls. What would become of Gina if I showed myself thus?" The lack of a waistline evoked fecundity or the little-girl shapelessness of a doll's dress: in either case, the sack was a young, ready-to-wear style, for high school girls and teenage brides with money to spend. The sack, writes the fashion historian Barbara Schreier, "marked the end for the celebrated mature woman of the 1950s. In their efforts to emulate the new standard of beauty, i.e. a narrow, underdeveloped body, women seemed to shrink in size. . . . The eccentricities of youth became the new target of exploitation."[50]

Fashion writers still disagree about whether the sack—subject of a two-year "Battle of the Chemise" waged in the nation's department stores—was a success or a miserable failure, a telling middle-class revolt against the dictates of a design elite or just another flop. Early on, trade journals recognized that the poster-like silhouette, the pointy shoes, the inverted-bucket hats, and the skimpy shirts were extreme enough to be risky. Women, if they bought shifts at all, tended to buy one of them: most of the sales came in the junior and teen size ranges. *McCall's* and the *Ladies' Home Journal* took note of the chemise, but magazines for girls with allowances raved about sacks and showed them in their most intemperate forms, with billowing backs, hobble skirts, and huge plastic belts circling the widest point of the hip. The sack became the first significant fashion statement of the generation reared after World War II, the first style to serve as a uniform of an emerging youth culture. Phenomenal spring sales for 1958 had been restricted almost entirely to the young, the *New York Times* decided:

Comic books pitched at fashion-conscious teens lampooned the sack in 1958 but young readers bought such dresses for themselves regardless.

"They will try anything new. From the University of Missouri . . . it was reported . . . that the 'co-eds are taking to the trend full force, without the usual delay.' In the Prudential Building, Chicago, the chemise is now an office uniform for secretaries."[51]

The crucial test for the sack came in the spring of 1958, the traditional time for getting a new outfit. As the chorus of derision continued—"eggs on legs," "sad sacks," "bags"—women looked to Washington for fashion cues. She was adventurous, always fond of the latest thing. She loved wild hats. What would Mamie do about the sack? Furriers claimed the chemise was all wrong with mink. A soft, long-haired fox was required to enhance the straight lines of the new style.[52] Would Mamie scrap her trademark minks on the say-so of some Paris designer? The first hint came in a wire service photograph of a model wearing a green silk shantung sack reportedly chosen by Mrs. Eisenhower for Easter; a Suzy Perette of New York creation decorated with self bows below the bust and hip bone, it retailed in less expensive fabrics for $39.95. The dress was not a conventional sack but its apparent successor, a looser empire or trapeze style which at least offered the advantage of comfort. When the White House scurried to issue an official denial, however, the rumor mill had it that Ike himself vetoed the green silk number. The story gained credence in September. Attending a Navy benefit fashion show at which similar dresses were shown, Mrs. Eisenhower applauded when conventional New Look skirts appeared while she merely smiled as the empire gowns paraded by. "The sack is probably the only style that was completely wiped out because too many husbands said 'I just won't let my wife wear it'," the runway commentator remarked. "She's so right!" Mamie was overheard telling the woman seated next to her. "She's so right!"[53]

Mamie Eisenhower's New Look was finally eclipsed by something newer still, a vision of the ideal woman as a leggy girl in a proto-miniskirt. The continuous fashion shows mounted in the American pavilion at the 1958 Brussels World's Fair featured sacks and more sacks, barely long enough to graze a knee. Although the all-American fashion parade organized by *Vogue* showcased the sack and thus banished older styles to a quasi-official fashion limbo, the fact that

The sack at the U.S. Pavilion at the Brussels World's Fair of 1958; moderately priced fashions stood for American classlessness and freedom of choice.

dresses commanded a position of such prominence within the U.S. display was a tribute of sorts to Mamie's influence and to the pivotal position of fashion in an American culture of affluence. Even Edward Durell Stone's circular American pavilion, centered on the open-air atrium where the models appeared, owed as much to jewelry or dressmaking as it did to conventional architecture.[54] A vast, billowing, skirtlike tent of gossamer plastic, the pavilion achieved its effect through decorative devices—pierced screens, patterned metal grids, and meshwork in shiny metallic tones—that were hung from the underpinnings of the building like so many charms on a bracelet or rhinestones on a gown. A monument to the effect of the New Look aesthetic on all aspects of American design, the Stone pavilion resembled fashion in its seeming frivolity, too: it was an unapologetic pleasure dome, bedecked with lovely bits of glitter to feast the eye—architecture to be looked at in passing, like the dressed-to-the-nines models who twirled down the runway every few minutes.

To critics of the American self-presentation in Brussels, the pavilion and its contents seemed lightminded and ornamental rather than substantive. The Russians, right next door, were scoring major propaganda points with their Sputniks, heavy industrial machinery, and heavy-duty high culture (the Bolshoi, for example). The U.S. display, a collection of amusing gadgets, kitchen appliances—including a pink built-in oven—frozen food packages, Coke machines, bits of back-home streetscape, and fashions scattered willy-nilly across an indoor pond containing a series of "islands for living," was playful and incoherent by contrast. Hollywood movies were expected to be a big draw for the United States; *South Pacific* (Mamie loved musicals) and *High Noon* (Ike liked Westerns) topped the playbill. The design team, in fact, considered its overall exhibition plan highly cinematic or tele-matic in character: the audience was invited to draw its own conclusions from a barrage of visual stimuli, delivered in short filmic "takes." Packaged in this way, the United States was not a written text, arguing for a particular interpretation of the meaning of America, but a "look," a style, a lifestyle appealing on precisely the same grounds as those on which fashion captivated the senses. With the help of some show-biz, Seventh Avenue razzle-dazzle, the exhibition celebrated abundance, choice, "the positive cultural effects of material progress and a high standard of living."[55]

As such, it disgusted both intellectuals and patriots. Thomas B. Hess, in a blistering editorial in *Art News*, charged that the building would "hold up to visitors a mirror to reflect their own mental picture of a cultureless America, land of soft-headed high-living, of thoughtless epicures whose taste deals with chromium and carbonated drinks." Liberals called the America on display at Brussels (the first post-atomic world's fair) "a Pompeii among nations, a huge holiday resort whence all care has been banished." Conservatives deplored the absence of some comforting sign of American military might to cheer up European guests. Did the evident "concern over 'gracious living'," they wondered, engender real admiration for the free enterprise system from which the built-in ovens and off-the-rack fashions flowed?[56] Of all the specifics of the American spectacular in Brussels, the fashion show proved the easiest target. There was much grousing about the use of European mannequins (although Elizabeth Arden did their makeup). About the wisdom of showing sacks and other beyond-the-pale styles that the typical American woman would never wear ("Maybe they *do* wear those sack things in New York," offered an indignant tourist from Michigan). But many Yankees abroad in 1958, like the correspondent for *The Nation*, simply couldn't fathom "what message the fashion show is supposed to convey about America or Americans. If the designers wanted a circular building, and needed something in the middle which was in the nature of a circular exhibit, why a fashion show?" Why not a basketball game?[57]

Even *Vogue* dithered over the message issue. The earliest Brussels shows stressed the affordability of American high style, or the trickle-down system whereby the First Lady and the average shopper might easily wear the same outfit for Easter. Prices ranged from $15 for a mail-order sack to $7,500 for a genuine mink coat, with every possible permutation and variation in between. But the democracy of fashion was lost on some observers distracted by the sheer gaudiness of what Belgium's largest newspaper called "the last word in carnival clothes from New York."[58] Flower-print pumps, short skirts, and wandering waistlines outraged conservative taste in Brussels as much as these same sack-related details had already offended America's First Husband. The notion that New York—not Paris—was a prime source of fashion trends was something altogether novel, however. The Brussels fair defined America as an engine of change in the popular culture, where ludicrous new dresses were flaunted and enjoyed.

For the second in its series of fashion shows, *Vogue* toned down the radicalism and rebellion of the collection, as well as the costs. The thirty-five outfits, priced from $4 (for a "red cotton chemise splashed with a misty flower print") to $25, were still sacks, to be sure, but they were shown in real-life situations. In the real world, the sack was the costume of the working woman and the active student: the *Vogue* show domesticated the ideology of fashion change by minimizing the differences between housewives and coeds, secretaries and suburbanites, single girls and busy moms. Instead of slinking down the runway wearing vacant looks, the models pushed shopping carts and pretended to barbecue or run the vacuum cleaner, in total indifference to the preferences of invisible, sack-hating spouses.[59] Reflecting the theme of "more taste than money," the taste in question was the wearer's alone and the show openly equated American fashion with the ready-to-wear industry. These were clothes for women who vacuumed and shopped. If the unfitted shift with the shrinking skirt had not yet become the everyday norm in the suburbs of New York, Chicago, Los Angeles, and Washington, D.C., the 1958 Brussels fair helped to make it so.

The newest "New Look" dramatized the American woman as an eternal American girl, as Mamie's younger sister in spirit—pert, sleek, peppy, and born to shop. In a dozen years the wheel of imagery had turned from slow, voluptuous curves to abrupt angles, from continental elegance to American energy, from romantic retrospection to the uncharted potential of the girl-woman. What remained the same was the sense that how things looked counted for a great deal, the delight in the play of images that Mrs. Eisenhower and her generation of shoppers brought to the task of looking their best in the 1950s.

TV's Nelson family—
Ozzie, Harriet, David, and Ricky—
advertised the new paint-by-numbers
kits in 1953.

Hyphenated Culture: Painting by Numbers in the New Age of Leisure

*T*here had never been anything quite like it before in the history of civilization. The new American leisure, that is. "Never have so many people had so much time on their hands—with pay—as today in the United States," crowed a special *Business Week* report on postwar trends in American living. The forty-hour week was the norm. And that meant two-day weekends, a three-week annual vacation, daily lunch and coffee breaks, and early retirement on a pension. World War II had put an end to Saturday half-days. Union contracts made paid holidays standard throughout the workforce. The sociologists Reuel Denney and David Riesman, just beginning a major study of the leisure issue, noted that if Americans "were willing to accept the standard of living of 1870, most of us could presumably get by with a five-hour week."[1] But almost a third of the increased productivity made possible by mechanization and gains in efficiency went toward subsidizing free time.

For the first time, leisure was a mass phenomenon, too. Thorstein Veblen's old "leisure class" had expanded to include almost everybody. So many people had joined the ranks, said the *New Yorker*, that the term was obsolete. Leisure was classless nowadays, a textbook example of democracy in action. In 1954, with a major recession just ended and business and labor leaders well satisfied with the status quo, *Fortune* was already plumping for a four-day work week as a

New suburban homes, like Levittown's Cape Cods, were rudimentary affairs that left lots of room for home improvements.

boost to consumption. Pooh-poohing all the old objections to shorter hours—the Bible, after all, had allocated only one day of rest—the editors pointed out that leisure spending currently accounted for $30 billion annually, or "half again as much as the American consumer spends on clothing or shelter" and twice what the average family put into new cars and items for the home. Given idle hours, the consumer was rapidly filling them up with recreational shopping, travel, watching a new TV set or listening to a new hi-fi, with do-it-yourself projects, and with hobbies of all kinds. For makers of power tools, snack foods, and recliners, the emerging culture of leisure was highly profitable.[2]

It was also problematic. Ancient capitalist folklore held that the worker with time on his hands was a threat to the public order. Equating leisure with laziness, professional moralists looked for the average Joe or Jill to run riot with drink, dissipation, and wretched excess. Television entered the equation, too, confirming the worst fears of intellectuals who expected a steady diet of pro wrestling, sitcoms, and commercials to turn the masses into passive nitwits, ripe for exploitation. But many thinkers saw themselves as part of the problem, their critical sensibilities blunted by their own middle-class affluence and the blandishments of leisure. Betraying a deep-seated suspicion of consumption, and a preference for the act of production, they thought leisure demanded careful preparation and management. The historian David Potter, writing in 1954, enjoined the postwar American "to cultivate interests that are appropriate to an enlarged leisure." People ought to be *doing* something, something significant with all those extra hours.[3]

The evidence suggested that they were—or wanted to. National surveys taken in the 1930s, when the Depression curtailed spending on equipment and travel, disclosed a sedentary pattern of recreation: respondents were reading magazines and listening to the radio and visiting with friends. What they really wanted to do, however, was to

Oddly enough, the heaviest watchers of TV were also the folks most likely to have hobbies.

play tennis and golf, plant a garden, go swimming or skating. In the 1940s, wish became reality. Between 1947 and 1953, revenues for spectator sports and amusements showed a marked dip, despite increases in population and income and the insatiable demand for TV sets. The popular singer and CBS star Perry Como said that his favorite home pastime was "to create a still life consisting of TV set, bowl of fruit, paring knife, cigarette, and Como stretched out on the couch." But he was the indolent exception. Market research proved that it was the heaviest TV-watchers who were liable to be most interested in painting a still life or reupholstering the living room sofa. Power tools and other do-it-yourself accessories were a $12 billion industry by the end of the decade; $30 million more went for amateur art supplies. "There seems to be a major trend away from passive, crowd amusements toward active pursuits that people can carry on independently," concluded a highly regarded study of this "Changed America" with plenty of time on its hands.[4]

Although hobbies often were pursued independently, the notion of making or collecting or generally doing things on the weekends was fostered by large institutions. The Boeing Airplane Company was one of many postwar industries to sponsor employee hobby shows, for example: the 1952 exhibition, held in a hanger-size plant cafeteria, drew 27,652 visitors and included thirteen competitive categories, ranging from a working airplane and a tablecloth crocheted on the bus to work to elaborate model trains. Models and other hobby crafts became popular during the 1930s. Thanks to enforced leisure, hobby shops (along with miniature golf courses) were one of the few new businesses to flourish during the Depression. Making miniature trains and planes was a cheap, weatherproof form of recreation and a comfort for hands accustomed to holding the tools of full-scale industry.[5]

Toward the end of the war, the Navy opened its first hobby craft shop at the Alameda Naval Air Station in California in an effort to improve morale. Hobby outfits had already been included in forward base supplies for the Pacific Theater to promote the mental health of men stranded on remote beachheads.[6] Physical and occupational therapy programs for the wounded also cultivated manual dexterity through courses in pottery, fingerpainting, carving, leatherwork, cabi-

Power tools for do-it-yourselfers were one of the major growth industries of the 1950s.

netry, and various home and auto repairs. Specialists in recreation began to speak of hobbies as the fifth freedom—along with freedom of speech and worship and freedom from want and fear. They provided wholesome emotional release for workers "bored and cramped" by tedious routine. And, when hobbyists came together to examine one another's work, such occasions met "the important need of being accepted by, and belonging to, some group." In a book entitled *Emotional Reactions Created from the War,* the eminent psychiatrist William C. Menninger advised his readers to have some fun, take it easy, and "develop a hobby. . . . It is as important in the maintenance of good mental health as good food is to physical health."[7]

Franklin Roosevelt, America's wartime president and father of the Four Freedoms, was himself an avid hobbyist. He collected postage stamps. The enthusiast of the 1950s was more apt to be creative, however. Polls taken in the early 50s still ranked collections—stamps, dolls, coins, autographs—high on the Top Ten list, but activities that involved making things for oneself were on the rise. Defense workers and G.I.s had both learned new mechanical skills and the postwar labor shortage encouraged their use. First-time buyers saved money on tract houses by buying models with unfinished attics and basements. Painting and fixing a new home, remarked one overzealous do-it-yourselfer in 1954, "[is] a form of play!"[8]

There were almost as many good reasons for taking up a hobby as there were merchants eager to furnish the necessary supplies and attire for any given creative pastime. Hobbies offered spiritual compensation to those forced to spend their working lives being told precisely what to do. They promoted individuality in the face of terrible pressures for conformity, including the "prefabricated emotional cliches" of TV; they were the weekend revenge of the beleaguered organization man.[9] Conversely, they promoted family togetherness. Fathers and sons could share a backyard workshop. New interests might keep restless parents at home and nip juvenile delinquency in the bud.[10]

In contrast to the workplace, success or failure did not matter much in hobbyland, nor was the livelihood of the amateur boatbuilder at stake if he could not get his creation out of the basement. But small victories counted just the same. Do-it-yourselfism, in particular, was the last refuge for the exercise of control and competence in a world run by the bosses and the bureaucrats. It was a throwback, a rebuke to a buy-it-in-a-box world of TV dinners and ready-made everything. The home handyman was a neo-pioneer, following in the footsteps of his resourceful forebears. "The push-button mechanisms, both domestic and industrial, have repaid with extra leisure for what they've taken from the spirit," wrote a reviewer of the 1953 Do-It-Yourself Show at New York's 71st Regiment Armory. Hobbyists knew what it meant to make things, to come face to face with personal, tangible accomplishments. They alone retained a sense of mastery and potency, reclaiming in small ways what technology had appropriated in big ones.[11]

Husbands who tinkered with home improvements had nothing to

In the postwar years, Armstrong linoleum used this his 'n' hers work center—her kitchen, his shop—as a promotional device.

apologize for: unlike model-makers or Sunday painters, their after-hours labors were expected to produce practical, money-saving results. But do-it-yourselfers also garnered media respect as heavy-duty buyers of wallpaper, pipe, lumber, instruction manuals, hobby magazines, and expensive power tools. When whole new industries arose to cater to the weekend contractor, self-styled experts began to speculate on the deep-seated appeal of lathes and electric drills. It was a male issue, many thought. Movie idols who used to pose with buxom starlets to assert their masculinity were now apt to pose with decorative fences they had built themselves, as Glenn Ford did in a 1957 issue of *Better Homes and Gardens*. Ads pitched at the man's man showed rugged types surrounded by their hobby gear. In the largely ungendered spaces of the suburban, open-plan house, in the cloying atmosphere of domestic "togetherness," handiness seemed to be the last badge of unabashed manliness.[12] But men who bought pricey tools to save money on household projects often ended up building a nifty home workshop (11 million of them in 1954) to store the equipment—and not much else. Possessing the fetishistic tool was the object of the hobby. "Men love things that whirr," wrote the social critic Russell Lynes. Using them was almost an afterthought.[13]

Within the corporate structure, hobbies were generally approved of as effective aids to the development of junior executives. They were "broadening." Ways to become more interesting to prospective clients. Sources of self-confidence. Major overhauls of the house were another matter, however. The up-and-coming commuter was admonished not "to become a nut over some interest outside his business life." Competence was one thing. Professionalism was quite another. Dreams of making fabulous profits from painting fabric, tinting photos, or shaping old phonograph records into useful objects were left to starry-eyed retirees and housewives, the latter newly liberated for craft projects by the proliferation of home appliances. Increasingly, men's hobbycraft tended to the useless, the unprofitable, and the nostalgic.[14]

Model trains of an earlier era and model planes of World War II were the top products of home workshops in the 1950s. In the 1930s and 40s, tinkerers had built working models from scratch. In 1945, Monogram Models put together three rudimentary kits for the construction of ships from lengths of balsa wood. These were relatively hard to assemble and finish. Manufacturers joked that they were catering to "model spoilers, not model builders." Noting the frustration and the high failure rate, the president of a small toy firm in Venice, California, took a different tack. He made an exact, detailed replica of the ancient Maxwell automobile publicized by the comedian Jack Benny and then broke it down into pieces, ready to reassemble at home. There was a wide margin for error. Satisfaction was virtually guaranteed. The first Revell hobby kits, with parts made of injection-molded thermoplastics, hit the stores in 1951 and were an instant success. Suddenly, men everywhere seemed intent on recreating in miniature their days of glory in the service or some bygone, golden era of chuffing locomotives and Tin Lizzies, back before the advent of traffic jams and last-minute dashes to catch the morning's last commuter local to the city.[15]

Why were the Revell kits an overnight sensation? Lou Glaser, the inventor, believed they appealed to the child in the man: models were, after all, toys for grownups. Because they were easy to make but looked so complicated when finished, they also generated a disproportionate and addictive upsurge of pride in achievement. The biggest single seller in the line in 1954 was a plastic model of the battleship *Missouri* (for $1.98) that fairly bristled with tiny guns and turrets and anchors. Industry analysts suggested that hobbyists were people who craved realism, precision, and certainty in lives lived in the shadow of nuclear terror. Others thought there was some intrinsic appeal in plastic. "Plastics are definitely *it*," a trade association representative told the *New Yorker* in 1956. "Plastic models are the trend. Dollar-wise, more money is being spent on plastic models than on any other hobby. Second come metal trains."[16]

By the end of the 1950s there were hobby kits for almost everything: stained glass panels, decorative tiles and trivets and trays, Mickey Mouse Club regalia, tasteful figurines, "design-it-yourself" neckties. A do-it-yourself show at California's Pan-Pacific Auditorium featured a kit for making a mink coat.[17] Jon Gnagy, the Saturday-morning-TV artist, sold boxed "learn to draw" and "learn to paint" kits to his viewers for $4.95 apiece. But the paint-by-numbers set was the biggest hobby breakthrough of the decade and a fad so contagious that it amounted to a national mania. Over the 1953 Christmas holidays, if Americans weren't playing Scrabble, they were filling in the spaces on a printed canvasboard panel. Each space bore a number corresponding to one of twenty or so capsules of ready-mixed oil paint supplied with the kit. When all the spaces were filled in, why there it was. Voila! An instant masterpiece. Da Vinci's *Last Supper*. A dog. A New England seascape. "Every man a Rembrandt!" just like it said on the box. "Anyone can paint a picture, from 8 to 80!" Industry-watchers predicted sales of $200 million before the end of 1954. But the paint-by-numbers craze had caught the oracles flatfooted and nobody was too confident about the future. "We pray a little, keep our fingers crossed, and hope that when the herd finally turns to glass blowing, enough will stay behind to keep us in business," said a nervous paint kit magnate. "In the meantime, we're cleaning up."[18]

There are several strong claimants to the idea of painting by the numbers. Fill-in books for children had been around for years, too.[19] But the adult version originated in Detroit, in November of 1951, when a chemist and former merchandising researcher for General Motors acquired a small paint plant. According to one account, Max Klein was approached by two employees of the Picture Craft Company of Decatur, Illinois, which already produced a crude art set consisting of a rolled canvas and glass jars containing paint. Picture Craft had sold their sets primarily to the military through mail order and was seeking a broader national market for a line of "mystery" pictures, the subjects of which only became clear as the various colors were applied. Under the terms of the agreement worked out between the principals, Klein's company, Palmer Paint, was to manufacture similar kits in quantity for Picture Craft. The hitch came when the Illinois group could not come up with the capital. Klein and Palmer were stuck with the sets and launched a high-powered campaign to get rid of existing stock. Four-color ads were placed in Sunday supplements. Deep discounts were given to department stores that agreed to run their own ads for the "Craft Master" system. In less than two years, $10 million worth of paint-by-numbers sets were sold. Gimbel's in Philadelphia was forced to set up a special Craft Master department to handle the crush. Red-faced judges at a San Francisco art show were fooled by a Craft Master painting that took third prize.[20]

A more fanciful version of the story had Max Klein yearning to paint but failing miserably until a Palmer employee sketched scenes for him on canvas, complete with numbers.[21] Whether aesthetics or the prospect of financial ruin inspired the paint-by-numbers movement in the first place, however, the artists ultimately responsible for the sets went about their task in a thoroughly businesslike way. Dan Robbins, age 26, headed a staff of twenty-five painters who designed the master pictures "with an eye to public demand." Pets and landscapes were customer favorites. Despite a complicated pattern with

Now **YOU** can paint **ORIGINAL** **OIL PAINTINGS** *the first time you try!*

IT'S QUICK . . . IT'S EASY! WITH *Picture Craft*

DECORATE YOUR HOME . . .

Or Sell Your Paintings For Profit

With this fun-filled hobby you can paint genuine oils, beautiful beyond dreams, from the very start—*even though you've never held a brush!* No lessons, no training . . . not even any hard-to-follow instructions! PICTURE CRAFT's "Mystery" canvas guides your hand like a Master Painter, yet the painting is your own *original* work — signed with your name, expressing YOU!

GUARANTEED!

Men and women of all ages paint lovely, large pictures — suitable for framing on their first try. *We guarantee that YOU can do the same.* Full satisfaction or your money back! No special equipment needed — everything's in the PICTURE CRAFT package. Choose from 21 gorgeous, artist-designed subjects today . . . dogs, horses, birds, landscapes and circus scenes. If there isn't a PICTURE CRAFT dealer in your town, write to us at the address below.

2^{95} per set

including:

● "Mystery" Artist Canvas (16" x 12")
● Ready-Mixed Oil Colors
● Special Artist's Brush
● Complete Painting Instructions

SOLD BY STATIONERY, ART, HANDICRAFT, HOBBY and DEPARTMENT STORES OR WRITE TO

Picture Craft

790 N. WATER ST.   DECATUR, ILL.

An early ad for what would become the paint-by-numbers set featured a "mystery canvas:" fill in the spaces and be surprised!

hundreds of numbered areas, *Three Kittens* was an early hit, widely copied in rival shops that sprang up almost overnight. Stanley Silver of Master Artists Materials followed Robbins's lead with a kit called the *Twin Scotty*. "Where else can you get two genuine original oil paintings for only $1.79?" Silver asked. Meanwhile, back at Palmer, the design department was reading letters solicited from users, calling for seascapes, horses, ballet dancers, religious themes, and more adult "artistic" challenges. Thus the new "Masterpiece" line of larger pictures included nudes, a single abstraction, celebrity portraits, and do-it-yourself versions of the Old Masters, of which an $11.50 *Last Supper* became the all-time paint-by-numbers bestseller. The treatment of some of the upgraded subjects had a more contemporary "foreign flavor," too, according to Robbins, involving a poster-like application of bright primaries derived from French modernism.

The total lack of originality in this assembly-line Impressionism bothered Robbins at first. "I felt a little uneasy," he remembered. "But then we began getting letters from art supply stores telling how people who had done several of our paintings had gone on to original work. . . . Our sets started them in the painting hobby on their own." Yet most Craft Master artists were perfectly content to stay inside the lines and indifferent to mounting ridicule of their precooked, predigested "art." And their ranks grew by the week. The demographics of painting-by-numbers cut a broad swath through the new leisure class—"bankers, pilots, housewives, nurses, and cab drivers," according to a hasty corporate survey. Of that diverse group, homemakers were most apt to buy one kit after another and to write in demanding better ones. A testimonial from a Baltimore woman was typical: "My home is disgraceful and I sit there all day and paint. I am spending money which I ought to be saving. Please send me a list of any new subjects you have." Perhaps because women were so heavily represented among the connoisseurs of numbered canvases, the popular press did not always treat the pastime kindly. In a satirical look at the new leisure written for *Life*, Russell Lynes ranked "fillers-inners of numbered pictures" among the peasant class, at the bottom of his scale of good taste and refinement, or several notches below Sunday painters of the bourgeoisie who had dispensed with lines and capsules.[22]

A closeup of a finished picture shows a strong formal similarity to Impressionism and abstract art.

Was it art or just a hobby? Product or process? A store owner run off his feet by the Christmas rush for painting sets in 1953 thought he knew: "I can tell the difference between money and art. This is money." Boosters of amateur painting often cited sales figures for "number painting" as proof of a growing national art-mindedness. Since they explained Sunday dabbling as a form of mild rebellion against the standardizations and frustrations of an age of mass production, however, promoters of the fine arts gagged a little at including paint-by-numbers "addicts" in their movement. And professional artists were apoplectic at the prospect of being run out of business by do-it-yourselfers with their pre-mixed, pre-drawn "Snow-Covered Forest[s] with Elk." The art historian Alfred Werner, author of a recent book on Utrillo, cordially detested all daubers. In a diatribe against "paintitis" written for the *American Mercury* at the end of 1952, he reserved special scorn for the "self-indulgent philistines" who presumed to work from numbered paint pots. They debased the standards of artistic excellence, Werner thundered. They devalued the originality that was the essence of great art.[23]

The following Christmas, with paint-by-numbers sets under every tree, *American Artist*, house organ of the profession, opened its monthly amateur page to a spirited forum on the fad. The first letter came from a convert: "Why oh why didn't you . . . tell me before how much fun it is to use these wonderful 'paint-by-number' sets?" The correspondent had never been able to paint, but wanted to, and was so thrilled with the results that he or she had already completed five pictures, and was looking forward to the next one. The letter concluded with a plea that *American Artist* commend the sets to anyone who loved pictures and was stymied by a lack of innate artistic ability: "They will be proud to show their paintings to their friends!" The second writer believed paint-by-numbers sets portended the demise of the republic since "thousands of people . . . are willing to be regimented into brushing paint on a jig-saw miscellany of dictated shapes and all by rote." Painting-by-numbers was turning Americans into a race of morons. The final comment, from an art teacher, was that "there ought to be a law!" The better students thought they were being highly creative when they brushed "Color 9 into Areas 1 and 7" and the rest didn't care. Originality was dead.[24]

Michael O'Donoghue, a screenwriter who collects and exhibits number pictures, calls them "a great metaphor for life in rigid McCarthy America. You stayed in the lines." In the 1950s social rigidity was one possible explanation among many for their popularity. "Machines taking over from housewives, higher birth rates, dull jobs that produce a need for creative outlets, the desire to emulate the President and the British Prime Minister, and, of course, television," were all reasons for the boom in paint kits, declared the savants from *Business Week*. Winston Churchill, to be sure, was a cut above the average number painter: he didn't buy kits and in 1950 Hallmark bought the rights to eighteen original Churchill landscapes for use on its Christmas cards.[25] Ike was another story altogether. Although he began to paint using a real palette left behind by an artist called in to do Mrs. Eisenhower's portrait, he was not unduly interested in originality. He copied postcards, photos, and greeting card designs and treated the whole affair like a kind of indoor sport or exercise regimen. He set up his easel twice a week, come hell or high water, was unperturbed by conversation or the TV set, painted fast (the Eisenhower record was seven in ten days), and often wiped off the picture when it was done and started another one right on top. "They're no fun when they're finished," he told a friend. Nor was Ike above painting-by-numbers. In fact, at the height of the craze, the President gave sets to his White House staff for Christmas presents. And if an endorsement from the First Family was not enough, the television Nelsons—Ozzie, Harriet, David, and Ricky: "America's Favorite Family"—also began to advertise Picture Craft kits for holiday giving in 1953. "35 Beautiful Subjects! It's fun, relaxing, you need no experience—and it's GUARANTEED!"[26]

There was some feeling that completed sets were a form of fine art; after all, as Picture Craft proudly stated in its ads, all of the available templates had been drawn for use in kits "by real artists." But no

Ike painting a portrait of his grandchildren from a family photo. He often painted and watched TV at the same time.

artistic talent whatsoever was called for on the part of the "painter" who filled in the blanks. Talent seemed to demand a commitment on the part of those who possessed it, a seriousness at odds with having fun. Ike was the first to admit a distinction between serious art, which required talent, and tossing off pictures for pleasure, which did not. Although his cooking really was done by the numbers—aides reportedly cut and chopped and measured before Eisenhower ever entered the kitchen to assemble his famous lemon pies or his vegetable soup—he was quicker to take credit for his abilities as a chef than for any artistic gifts. And some proponents of numberless art for amateurs also assured novices that talent had nothing to do with painting pictures. "Whether you have talent or not," counseled a 1952 hobby manual, "you can find enjoyment in putting on canvas or paper what *you* see in the way *you* see it." It was easy! Painting was pure expression, a glorious release—except when the object was to execute a representational work. That took training, a knowledge of the rules of perspective, and a lot of talent. Or, perhaps, a paint-by-numbers set.[27]

Winston Churchill is the key figure in the "splash and wallop" school of self-expression. A doughty Cold Warrior much admired in the United States, Churchill was also beloved for his human quirks: the florid prose, the cigar, and most of all, the paint set. When Sir Winston visited the White House in 1954 for foreign policy talks, the press and the President both badgered him about his hobby. Had he brought his paints along? Would he like to borrow Ike's? The Prime Minister's association with art began in 1915, during a trying period in his public life. Thereafter, in times of crisis, he retired to the country and his easel. "Painting is a complete distraction," he wrote. "Whatever the worries of the hour or the threats of the future, once the picture has begun to flow along, there is no room for them in the mental screen." Churchill's reflections on his hobby reached American admirers in 1948, in a slender volume entitled *Painting as a Pastime*. Quoted widely whenever art, hobbycraft, or the private lives of celebrities were under discussion, the book exhorted inhibited amateurs to splash about in the turpentine and wallop the colors down in "large fierce strokes" for therapeutic reasons. An antidote to boredom, a comfort in times of loneliness, a relief for anxiety and tension, the canvas couldn't "hit back" either, he observed. It existed to be dominated. It "grinned in helplessness" before the flailings of the Sunday painter. It restored one's "psychic equilibrium."[28]

Inherent in this popular view of art were several ideas pertinent to the fine art debates of the 1950s. Churchill's insistence that art was cheap psychotherapy or a way of releasing pent-up feelings found some resonance in the "splash and wallop" technique of the Abstract Expressionists, whose turbulent emotional lives and alienation came to form the basis of their heroic public image. Although Winston Churchill never painted in blue jeans and a t-shirt, the procedures he recommended came close to the drip-and-dribble methods shown in photographs of Jackson Pollock that enjoyed wide circulation in the early 50s.[29] The Churchill approach also lent credence to Surrealist claims about the close relationship between art and the sub- or unconscious. While the Churchillian argument explained what was happening on the New York art scene in blunt, lay terms, and probably contributed to the media's sudden interest in the antics of America's professional artists, it subtly devalued legitimate painting, too. For

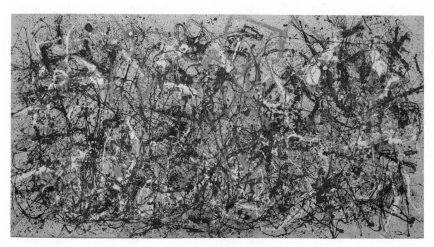

Jackson Pollock's *Autumn Rhythm* (1950) looked the way Churchill's "splash and wallop" theory of art sounded.

painting required no talent—merely a litany of frustrations to be exorcised on canvas. And because anybody could splash and wallop, the critical reverence for *real* artists who did so seemed disproportionate to their accomplishments. And the prices! Why pay thousands for somebody else's nightmares when a lovely *Twin Scotty* set retailed for $1.79?

Art as a violent, unpremeditated eruption of the psyche was an idea current in other quarters as well. In 1950 *Art News* inaugurated a nationwide contest for amateurs, crediting the newfound fashionableness of Sunday painting to Irving Stone's novelized biography of Vincent Van Gogh. Stone's *Lust for Life* first appeared in the 1930s but when the film rights were sold to Hollywood a new edition was issued in 1946 and became a surprise bestseller. The story of a tormented genius whose inner demons surface on canvas in the form of distorted images of reality was a perfect illustration of the Churchill thesis: a painting was a fever chart of temporary madness. Nor did the 1956 movie version, starring a rabid Kirk Douglas, do much to tip the scales in the direction of talent, training, hard work, and skill. As MGM portrayed it, art was instinctual, irrational, and highly entertaining.[30]

Jacob Getlar Smith, in an *American Artist* feature article of 1957, blamed Stone, Churchill, and Van Gogh for a new wave of ignorant, speed-is-of-the-essence, dilettante painting that denigrated the traditional values of the artist, including "humility, love of craft, [and] sincerity." One of the luminaries of a major 1957 touring exhibition called "From the Executive Easel"—a self-taught New York clothing manufacturer—confessed to *Newsweek* that "he was inspired by a biography of Vincent van Gogh and . . . borrowed from the violent style of that tortured master." Other weekend painters in the group (which included a surgeon, the president of I. Magnin, and the 78-year-old owner of a Brooklyn underwear factory who called himself "Grandpa Moses") had taken Ike or Winston Churchill as their exemplars. Indeed, while the executive paintings continued their two-year circuit of the nation, forty pictures by Churchill went on view at the Metropolitan Museum in New York early in 1958. They were mostly sunny landscapes or flower pieces, set down in a style that resembled Impressionism and paint-by-numbers sets in roughly equal measure.

Detail was all but eliminated; motifs were reduced to the flat, simple shapes of the color areas Churchill saw in the subjects observed. And even critics stung by the thought of Sir Winstons hanging in the Met praised his color sense and good, clear English eye for decoration. The problem, and what ultimately distinguished the professional from the amateur product, was the latter's complete absence of originality. Churchill and Eisenhower and their disciples painted for sport while their real creative energies found expression in war or politics or business. On a daily basis, the amateurs dominated those worlds. But in the world of the artist, they remained weekend guests, exploring what someone else had already imagined and defined.[31]

The fact that a high percentage of the amateurs whose work was hung in galleries and reproduced in magazines had thriving careers in other fields was one of the things that fascinated the public about the art craze of the 1950s. Some were cabbies and housewives and executives but some were very big stars. And they made art of all kinds popular—including the paint-by-numbers variety. A 1948 benefit auction of celebrity art held at New York's Associated American Artists (AAA), for example, featured masterpieces by actor Clifton Webb, boxer Joe Louis, and beauty adviser Helena Rubenstein. Since the 1930s AAA had aimed at getting original American art into the hands of ordinary citizens: the art historian Erika Doss has reconstructed the campaign to democratize the fine arts through selling inexpensive prints by big-name artists and involving member artists in advertising and commercial product design.[32] In a sense, AAA demystified art by treating it as a readily accessible consumer product, like a new appliance or a paint-by-numbers set. Showing the work of amateurs further suggested that art was something for—and by—everybody. When the "artist" was a well-known celebrity with whom the public was already familiar and even comfortable, the cultural product came to resemble the bottle of shampoo or the pack of cigarettes endorsed by a movie star. Or the paint-by-numbers pictures Ozzie Nelson and his smiling family sold on TV.

There was no shortage of genuine, beret-wearing artists in the movies of the 1950s. In *An American in Paris* (1951) Gene Kelly defined the character of the boy from back home in search of artistic fame and glory on the naughty Left Bank where paintings come to life in

Technicolor dance routines. But despite his picturesque studio and a portfolio of touristy Eiffel Tower views, Kelly plays a sort of amateur who is patently better at dancing and turning a buck than he is at painting. His star appeal shines through the flimsy tissue of art and makes him into a dabbler with a day job, like Ike. Nonetheless, the music, the dance, and a series of magical scenes staged within the fictive spaces of paintings by Toulouse-Lautrec and Van Gogh put *An American in Paris* at the forefront of Hollywood's drive to win audiences back from television with spectacle, color, and culture. Showing the stars in a new light—as persons of culture and consequence—was a part of the strategy, too, and as if by the magic of the movies, everybody in the film colony took up painting, *circa* 1951. Frank Sinatra did clowns. Henry Fonda liked still lifes: plums were his favorite subject. Claudette Colbert read Churchill's book, began to splash and wallop the next day, and specialized in portraits. Dinah Shore began to paint in a corner of her Beverly Hills living room in 1954 and was willing to try anything: flowers, scenery, still lifes, *and* the occasional portrait. Van Johnson and Linda Darnell were rumored to be "good enough to be professionals." Jose Ferrer took his pictures to a National Amateur Art festival held in New York in 1954, where TV comic Herb Shriner served as a genial model for a sketching contest.[33]

Then everybody got into the act. Washington wives hired a teacher and formed an art club in 1954; Senator Kefauver's spouse, who enjoyed painting her children, took several local prizes. A supermarket in Eau Claire, Wisconsin, hung student pictures of the town over the frozen food case and sold $218-worth. *Life* went to Attica, Kansas (pop. 622) to profile a thriving art group that raised money for lessons and drew eight hundred sidewalk critics to its annual summer show. For those who lacked the confidence of a Claudette Colbert, professional instruction was easy to come by. Nor was it necessary to go to art school. Jon Gnagy taught the fundamentals on TV in fifteen minutes a week. Radio personality John Anthony invented the "Talking Paints" system, which consisted of a six-minute recording that talked the aspirant through completion of an unnumbered canvas (the art supplies came with the record). The Sargent Progressive Painting Portfolio pledged to guide the pupil from a numbered painting to

In a New Jersey supermarket, amateur art competed with boxes of detergent.

"your own original picture" in three easy steps. Stodgy news journals and chirpy home-and-hearth periodicals alike promised foolproof results, if the reader followed the printed instructions, sent away for the patterns, bought the recommended items. These included pantographs, or instruments that reflected an image onto a sheet of paper

Sidewalk art sale in New York; pictures to match every sofa.

for tracing. "An Amazing Invention—Magic Art Reproducer," the pantograph meant the owner could "draw from the first day," even if he or she couldn't draw the proverbial straight line. NO LESSONS! NO TALENT![34]

The notion that a machine, a record, or a kit could turn a rank novice into a competent artist discloses a remarkable faith in instrumentality. In a 1954 essay about off-duty scientists who put together elaborate hi-fi sets, the sociologist Reuel Denney pointed out that their array of speakers and turntables allowed them "to identify at once with the gadgeteering do-it-yourself impulse and with imported elements of high culture." The pantograph bridged the same gap between culture and tinkering. Art was a semi-science, a matter of the right equipment and formulae. Or listening to the experts. In the 1930s thousands of Americans who might otherwise have been at work took painting lessons in WPA studios set up by relief agencies to provide federal jobs for starving artists.[35] The WPA experience, and the popularity of art instruction in veterans' hospitals and union halls, seemed to prove that the rudiments could be taught to almost anybody. In 1948, Famous Artists Schools of Westport, Connecticut, put that thesis to the test in the marketplace.

Famous Artists Schools founder Albert Dorne remembered that the idea came to him during a conversation with the illustrator Norman Rockwell about the unique "know-how" experts like themselves had to offer to people who truly needed clear, simple tutelage in art: veterans on the G.I. Bill, amateurs, and students who had graduated from art schools knowing how to paint Picassos but not how to earn a living. It was the aspiring illustrator that Famous Artists Schools targeted first with a three-year, do-it-at-home correspondence course consisting of twenty-four printed lessons and more than 5,000 instructional drawings and diagrams prepared by the twelve "famous artists" listed in the ads: the folksy Norman Rockwell, cover king of the *Saturday Evening Post;* Stevan Dohanos, his heir apparent; glamourgirl specialist Jon Whitcomb; Ben Stahl, the Degas of periodical fiction; and eight others, each of whom earned more than $50,000 per annum as an art professional. By 1954, however, with the amateur painting craze in full swing, Famous Artists Schools began to zero in on paint-by-numbers addicts with catchy ads stating that anybody who could copy a simple drawing of a French poodle printed on a matchbook cover probably had the stuff to be an artist. Providing they, too, signed up for a three-year course in the fine arts.

The expanded advisory faculty for this program included several well-known figures, running the aesthetic gamut from Stuart Davis, the designated "modernist" or Cubist, to more representational artists—Ben Shahn, Fletcher Martin, Ernest Fiene, Arnold Blanch—working in a variety of coloristic and stylistic nuances. When completed lessons arrived in the mail, the staff put tracing paper over student drawings and made corrections on the transparencies. Consulting "faculty" criticized the criticisms at regular intervals.[36] All this for $300, payable in monthly installments, plus an estimated $11.55 for basic oil painting supplies. By tipping the scales in favor of the realists, who outnumbered Davis by ten to one, Famous Artists Schools acknowledged the lack of public interest in advanced abstraction and put the focus squarely on a kind of art that was both teachable and illustrative of the effort and the craft that went into it, an art that showed the results of learning the familiar tricks of the trade. Famous Artists art wasn't mysterious or divinely inspired. It was normal, nice—and doable.

Of the new fine arts consultants hired for the amateur course, all but one were closely associated with earlier projects designed to make American artists into mainstream figures, as unlike Stone's erratic Van Gogh as possible. Several were members of Associated American Artists. Most had painted murals to order for public places during the Depression era, in a process that forced the ivory-tower artist to take the taste of ordinary Americans into account. The rest had done occasional assignments for firms which, in the immediate postwar years, sought to add an aura of prestige to their products with ads designed by ranking cultural heavies. Doris Lee, the only woman on the Famous Artists roster, was also one of the best-publicized painters of the day. Her whimsical pictures often graced the pages of *Life*, and she did title, background, and publicity work for the movies and for Broadway.[37]

Lee was a do-it-yourself author of record, too. *It's Fun to Paint*, a beginner's guide to oil painting for enjoyment, appeared in 1947 and stayed in print through the 1970s, probably because Doris Lee's own work, lavishly represented among the models provided for novices, looked so easy to duplicate. The book listed Arnold Blanch, her teacher and spouse, as the coauthor, but the pictorial content was pure Lee: folkish, simple, almost neo-primitive pictures marked by decorative shapes, once-upon-a-time subject matter, and sprightly figures with heads a little too big for their bodies. The sleighing and maypole scenes shown step by step, in various stages of completion, to teach the reader the basics of composition and coloration were quiltlike, childlike in the naiveté of drawing and detail. And almost half the volume was taken up with biographies of self-taught painters and reproductions of their canvases, which looked very much like her own. Henri Rousseau, Camille Bombois, and several other Europeans

Anna Mary Robertson Moses, *Going for the Mill*, 1947. The subject matter of Action Painting was cosmopolitan; Grandma Moses painted an
idyllic countryside, or what the suburbia of the 1940s and 50s aspired
to be.

were discussed, but the lion's share of the attention went to celebrated
American primitives, including Joseph Pickett, Horace Pippin, and
the indomitable Grandma Moses. If Lee did not state outright that
incompetence and amateurism were real artistic virtues, the beginner
was led to believe that the innocent eye would do nicely, after it had
passed over a couple of pages of pointers on perspective and where
to place the easel to get the best view of one's subject. Grandma Moses
didn't use a regular artist's easel herself; she worked at an eighteenth-
century "tip-up" table in the parlor of her Eagle Bridge, New York,

farmhouse. Nor did she examine her motif closely while painting it. "She closes her eyes until she sees a picture," Lee wrote admiringly. Then "she paints [it] with red stable brushes [and] uses a table for a picture rest instead of an easel. That is Grandma Moses' way."[38]

A down-home counterbalance to the aristocratic Churchill and the disturbed Van Gogh, Grandma was America's artist in the 1950s, as wholesome as a country apple pie. "Discovered" in 1938 by a collector who stumbled on a cache of unsold Grandmas in a drugstore window, Anna Mary Robertson Moses had the good fortune to ride a rising tide of interest in folk art. The Depression had turned American attention back to domestic issues, homegrown art, and life's basic pleasures. Later, the A-bomb and the tensions of the Cold War both reinforced a faith in isolationist, pre-technological, and pre-scientific America and in non-experts, who could build their own houses and paint their own pictures. Working at her ancient table by the window, Grandma Moses filled the bill with reminiscent views of horses and wagons, rural feasts and harvests, and winters that used to isolate country people, snug and safe in their cozy valleys until spring. In Grandma's pictorial yesterdays, American living was sweet, slow, and simple—as simple as her embroidery-pattern draftsmanship.

She never had a lesson. She never heard of Pollock or Picasso or Vincent Van Gogh. But she was the hottest ticket in the art world in the 1940s. Praised in Bob Hope's syndicated column. The subject of a popular biography. Holder of a fat new contract to turn her pictures into greeting cards, plates, and drapery fabric. Honored guest of the Gimbel's department store Thanksgiving Festival of 1940 (at which she modestly declined to talk about her art but instead gave tips on home canning). Feted by Harry Truman at a White House awards ceremony in 1949. Truman liked the kinds of pictures Grandma Moses did but he had no use for "the lazy, nutty moderns. It is like comparing Christ with Lenin," he said. Grandma was on the side of angels. Her America was what good American boys had fought and died to preserve.[39]

There was more to it than that, of course. A frail old lady who took up painting at 78 and succeeded was a shining example for hobbyists of every age and station in life. If she could do it, so could Ike—and

Grandma Moses meets the President, 1949. She was a towering national celebrity of the period, and the subject of a 1955 Edward R. Murrow TV profile filmed in color.

so could you. "Anyone can paint if they want to," Grandma Moses declared. "All they have to do is to get a brush and start right in, same as I did." In the 1950s a documentary about her was nominated for an Academy Award. She wrote her autobiography. Edward R. Murrow interviewed her on TV in color, so the few who had the new monitors in 1955 could better appreciate her work. In 1956 Ike's Cabinet presented him with a specially commissioned Grandma Moses depicting the Eisenhower family farm in Abilene, Kansas. And Anna Moses had a special message for the stay-at-home homemaker of the 1950s who was frazzled and crowded by kitchen appliances, the PTA, and the imperative to deliver a husband to the train station in time for the 7:02 to Manhattan. "Women everywhere have the feeling that if Grandma Moses can paint, so can they," wrote one

Top: Ike's Cabinet gave him this Grandma Moses view of the Eisenhower family farm in 1956. *Bottom:* And Ike painted the Eisenhower family home around the same time.

journalist. "Art is the only thing left . . . that is not mechanized, collectivized and regimented."[40]

In Europe, America was widely regarded as a soulless place, a technological wasteland best symbolized by Coca-Cola and skyscrapers. So Grandma Moses's sweet country reveries came as a surprise when her work began to circulate in shows that aimed to introduce postwar Europe to the human face of the United States. American primitives were first shown in London in 1947, and in 1950 the U.S. Information Agency sent an all-Moses show on tour to six European capitals. In both cases, the pictures were well received—to the disgust of some American art-watchers who felt that by praising a backward Grandma Moses the sophisticated European audience was actually rejecting the New York avant-garde. Others thought the paintings never should have been exported in the first place, that it was a symptom of self-hatred to wax enthusiastic over the daubs of a rustic out of touch with the problems and formal experiments of the twentieth century. Still others thought the very lack of avant-garde dogma was what appealed: although museums and government agencies certified that this was art, it demanded no special connoisseurship to remember one's own childhood drawings. Like $1.79 paint-by-numbers pictures from a plant outside Detroit, it was an art for everybody.

Among the influential critics who helped to create the New York School, American folk and popular art had been under mounting attack since the late 1930s. Clement Greenberg dismissed anything representational as "kitsch" while Dwight Macdonald, in a 1958 essay, wondered whether the intellectuals' love affair with Americana—one of the obsessions of the 1950s, at every level of cultural life—had not actually led them to "a somewhat uncritical acquiescence in the American *imperium*."[41] So it was that Grandma Moses, the new sweetheart of the European art world, came to stand for everything the Abstract Expressionists did not. She was 100 percent American; their heritage was European modernism. She was a woman; theirs was a tough, males-only fraternity. She was old and happy; they were young and miserable, and highly critical of a society she patently enjoyed. Albeit a painter of memories and dreams, best seen when she closed her eyes, Grandma stood for realism, the antidote to abstract art or what Harry Truman called "ham and eggs . . . dribble art." Abstraction, said Grandma Moses, was mainly "good for a rug or piece of linoleum."[42]

Ironically, what the so-called primitives did—their spontaneous color-slinging, their happy disregard for inhibiting rules—was not all that much different from what the Abstract Expressionists seemed to be up to. But while pictures of out-of-kilter barns "opened up the joys of painting to fun seekers," in the words of a 1953 investigation of amateuritis, the object was still to paint *something,* not nothing. Nothing was fine for linoleum or a new Formica countertop decorated with gold-and-turquoise shapes that vaguely suggested asteroids or artists' palettes. Nothing may have been what *House Beautiful* and the other home improvement magazines had in mind when they identified a brand new American design principle in 1952: "Free lines and brush strokes, asymmetrical spacing, an abstract, rather than representational, approach." But this so-called "Free Taste," however acceptable to a homemaker in search of a modern look for the kitchen, lost its charm when framed and hung above the sectional sofa. In pictures, as in plastic models of the USS *Missouri,* realism was what sold. As a not-so-subtle contrast to a pageful of spiky, spiny modern sculpture, *Time* ran reproductions of the top calendar designs for 1952—one pretty girl, one idyllic landscape with old mill, one cute kid. Most Americans liked calendar art, "including those who would insist art gives them a pain," read the text. "Although the best calendar art cannot be compared with the best serious painting, it shows far more technical facility and clarity of purpose" than most of what passed for contemporary fine art. Unlike art, calendars were suitable for kitchens, too, and always stayed sunny on the darkest days.[43]

Realism, whether of the calendar, the Grandma Moses, or the paint-by-numbers variety—representational art, that is—drew strength from television, from the sudden intrusion into 1950s living rooms of framed, moving pictures that reduced the objets d'art hanging over the sectional to the status of wallpaper. Like a calendar, television presented images of girls, landscapes, and kids, of real things, in astonishing variety. Like Grandma Moses, it conjured up collective memories of bygone times when, for example, Davy Crockett died at the Alamo (on ABC's Wednesday-night *Disneyland* program during

The difference between the picture hanging over the mantelpiece and the picture on the TV set was merely one of degree.

the 1954–55 season).[44] Like the new paint-by-numbers kits that contained decal transfers for adorning trays, glassware, mirrors, and household furnishings with Dutch, French, or Mexican motifs, or horsy British hunting scenes, television was a picture window on faraway places. It was no accident that Ozzie and Harriet and family, who took up the hobby in one early episode of their TV show, became the celebrity spokespersons for the paint-by-numbers movement. A Chicago company sold paint kits in 1955 under the trade name "Tone-o-Vision," as though its pictures were non-electronic TV sets ("Color-ama!") or frozen-in-place big-screen movies ("Cinerama!" "Vista-Vision!").[45]

On TV, the distinction between picture and art tended to break down in the welter of shifting images: Ed Sullivan juxtaposed Elvis with Charles Laughton, Maria Callas with a troop of jugglers. Everything occupied the same electronic frame. To optimists, all this popu-

A paint-by-numbers tray with a snooty English fox-hunting motif, filled in by the author, circa 1956. Hard use has exposed the numbered areas.

lar art-mindedness—Sullivan's guest list, statistics on sales of tickets and sheet music and highbrow records, the number of amateur artists planted before any given cow on a summer day—spelled the growth and diffusion of culture in America. Alvin Toffler, one of the period's most fervent believers in mass culture, was also, however, one of the first to recommend caution in confusing Sunday painting with true art. Art was infinite in its possibilities and variations, unlike automobiles or number pictures, of which there were a finite number for the consumer to choose from. Art was a one-and-only thing, a cure for conformity, of which a prime example was a picture guaranteed to turn out just like every other puppy painted with a *Twin Scotty* kit. Art was ineffable, difficult, important. It wasn't fun. And somebody else almost always did the painting.[46]

But consumer culture was not as uncreative or second-hand as Toffler assumed. The automobile, for instance, wasn't a finished product, a take-it-or-leave-it affair. Instead, the process of buying a new car in the 1950s was a do-it-yourselfer's dream. Chassis, body style, options, trim: the details were up for grabs. There were two-tone models and finally tricolors, all with mix-'n'-match interiors in "Passion Pink" or "Sunset Pink," "Crest Blue," "Horizon Blue," "Robin's Egg Blue," or any of fifty more tints, like the carefully labeled pinks and blues that came with a paint-by-numbers set.[47] The customer literally created his or her own car from a kit, from a catalogue of standardized components. Given the range of variables, the possibilities were statistically close to being infinite. The only dead certainty was that a Chevrolet would be delivered a few weeks later. And what a Chevy! Painted and bechromed in precisely those areas designated by the owner. A paint-by-numbers project of staggering complexity. A work of art.

Oveta Culp Hobby, Eisenhower's aptly named Secretary of Health, Education, and Welfare, deemed hobbies—art, in particular—essential to the national happiness. "Millions of Americans . . . from the President of the United States down to the humblest person" are turning to art, she observed approvingly in 1954. But why art? Why did messing around with paints fill a special, hard-to-discuss void in American life? The answer lay in the sheer, unpractical creativity of painting pictures. Creativity rounded out a busy career like nothing else, stated a prominent physician-painter. William Whyte, author of the 1956 classic *The Organization Man*, had also pondered the question of creativity and individualism in professional life. The new social ethic of the corporate executive made "the group . . . the source of creativity," he concluded. If great art was what the sociologists dubbed "inner directed"—created out of internalized tastes and motives—then, according to Whyte's thesis, the hobby art of the American business community was quite properly derivative or mass produced from a kit. But in some important ways, the high culture of the 1950s was not radically dissimilar from what the hobbyists were doing. The cool classicism of International Style office towers and the repetitious gesturalism of Action Painting both stressed formal values. The emotional content, when it could be read with any certainty, was detached, generalized, grand. So the inner-directed artist produced large, public objects so formulaic, so reticent in meaning and uniform in manner that they were easily adapted to the boardrooms of corporate America, as trappings of the outer-directed executive. The difference between several thousand all but identical dogs painted from kits and any half-dozen look-alike Pollocks or Rothkos came down to one of degree. Everybody played by creative rules, whether they filled in numbered spaces or dripped paint in patterns circumscribed by the dimensions of the canvas.[48]

Art affirmed the way things were in the 1950s. And a little creativity allowed the Sunday painter to be a participant, to claim that ethos as his or her own, to join a group that included Ike, Sir Winston, Vincent Van Gogh, Frank Sinatra, and Grandma Moses. The American Chemical Society, the Bar Association, the International Ladies' Garment Workers, and the American Dental Association all had affiliated art societies. So did the Junior League, the American Red Cross, and the American Association of University Women.[49] Even paint-by-numbers fans subscribed to newsletters dedicated to their brand of art. Art affirmed one's full membership in American culture, a willingness to be part of an ongoing process of filling in the outlines of postwar society. Ernest Dichter, who psychoanalyzed the American consumer in the 50s on behalf of major corporate advertisers, posited that successful works of art—TV shows, paintings, and ads, of course— involved their audience in a process of participatory re-creation: "A sculpture, a painting, or a poster is better if it is somewhat incomplete, if the onlooker is invited to fill [it] in."[50] By that pragmatic measure, the paint-by-numbers picture was the definitive masterpiece of the period, and the ultimate recreation.

Walt Disney explains the design of his new theme park to his Wednesday night TV audience, 1954. The park and the program were both called *Disneyland.*

Disneyland, 1955:
The Place That Was Also a TV Show

*T*he opening—or openings—of the new amusement park in Southern California did not go well. On July 13, a Wednesday, the day of a private thirtieth anniversary party for Walt and Lil, Mrs. Disney herself was discovered sweeping the deck of the riverboat *Mark Twain* as the first guests arrived for a twilight shakedown cruise. On Thursday and Friday, during gala pre-opening tributes to Disney film music at the Hollywood Bowl, workmen back in Anaheim, some twenty-three miles away, struggled to finish paving the streets that would soon lead to Fantasyland, Adventureland, Frontierland, and Tomorrowland; last-minute strikes had compelled the builders to haul in asphalt all the way from San Diego.[1]

The invitation-only press preview and dedication, broadcast over a coast-to-coast TV hookup on July 17, was a disaster from start to finish. At dawn, with carpenters and plumbers still working against the clock, traffic on the freeway was backed up for seven miles, and gridlock prevailed on the secondary roads surrounding the former orange grove along Harbor Boulevard. Studio publicists had issued twenty thousand tickets to reporters, local dignitaries, Disney employees, corporate investors, and Hollywood stars—including Eddie Fisher and Debbie Reynolds, Lana Turner, Danny Thomas (from the new television elite), and Frank Sinatra. But by mid-morning more than thirty thousand people were already packed inside the earthen berm that was supposed to seal off Disney's domain from the cares of the outside world. Some of the extra invitees flashed counterfeit passes. Others had simply climbed the fence, slipping into the park in behind-the-scenes spots where dense vegetation formed the background for a boat ride through a make-believe Amazon Jungle.[2]

Afterward, they called it "Black Sunday." Anything that could go wrong did. The food ran out. A gas leak temporarily shut down Fantasyland, site of many of the twenty-two new Disney-designed rides the crowd had come to inspect. It was terribly hot, too. Main Street USA melted and ladies' high heels stuck fast in the fresh asphalt. The nervous proprietor (who had spent the night in the park) accidentally locked himself in his apartment above the turn-of-the-century firehouse near the front gate. As the moment approached for the boss to welcome a vast, stay-at-home audience to his California kingdom through the magic of television, Walt Disney was nowhere to be found. And, somehow, ABC's twenty-four live cameras managed to cover all the glitches: the women walking out of their high-heeled pumps; "Davy Crockett," current star of Disney's weekly television series, drenched by a hyperactive sprinkler system as he thrashed about on horseback in Frontierland's western scenery; the regal Irene Dunne showering announcer Art Linkletter with glass and soda water while attempting to christen the *Mark Twain* on televised cue.[3]

Bob Cummings and Ronald Reagan shared the network hosting duties—and a whole range of maddening "technical difficulties"—with Linkletter. Three of TV's most popular and experienced hosts, they handled the glitches with the improvisational aplomb that made live television so engaging to watch. The viewer became an insider who shared the announcer's discomfort when audio and video transmissions winked on and off at will, or when the voice-over described Cinderella's coach at the head of a passing parade while the picture on the small screen showed Roy Rogers and Dale Evans. At one point Linkletter strolled blithely through the portcullis of Sleeping Beauty's Castle and emerged from the other side, seconds later, without his microphone. Walt Disney accidentally appeared on camera ahead of schedule, chatting with the crew and wondering aloud how the show was going.

The *Dateline Disneyland* special had "captured some fun and fantasy, the elements . . . that are supposed to make the place tick," wrote the TV reviewer for the *New York Times*. But despite flashes of honest spontaneity, the tightly scripted ninety-minute program, like the whole Disneyland project, seemed to have serious flaws. It was entirely too Hollywood, according to the *Times:* slick, commercial, star-studded, glitzy. And too reverential, too much like the dedication of a national shrine. Bob Cummings, for instance, had repeatedly assured viewers that cultural history was being made out in Orange County before their very eyes: "I think that everyone here will one day be as proud to have been at *this* opening as the people who were there at the dedication of the Eiffel Tower!"

Park officials had no time to brood over iffy reviews. Monday morning and the *real* opening, for the general public, were less than

Walt Disney faces the TV cameras outside Fantasyland. During the live broadcast on opening day, glitches were the rule.

twelve hours off. A senior from Long Beach State College had stationed himself near the ticket window at 2 A.M. on Sunday, just as the last of the TV crews were leaving and the police began to report abnormal traffic volumes building along the periphery of Anaheim. By 8 A.M., two hours before the posted start of business, eight thousand merrymakers had already cued up behind the weary college kid and the hundred-acre parking lot was almost full. At 10 A.M. Walt Disney appeared and personally greeted the first two children in line.[4] Although the little ones got all the media attention, however, the clear majority of those who followed Disney inside were grown-ups, determined to experience for themselves what they had seen on television the day before. They swarmed over the park, eating everything in sight, dropping garbage everywhere, nearly swamping the *Mark Twain* in their eagerness to board. But they came, they had a wonderful time, and in defiance of strong negative criticism from TV and travel writers, influential columnists, and itinerant intellectuals, they kept coming in enormous numbers, more than a million of them in the first seven weeks alone, exceeding all estimates and giving backers reason to believe their risky, $17 million investment might someday pay off.

Indeed, even before the previews began, speculation about costs and profits all but overshadowed discussion of the park's entertainment value. And while the press did not fail to wax eloquent about chronic traffic tie-ups around Disneyland, most of the first-year complaints came down to dollars and cents. How could pleasure and the bottom-line ethos of corporate America possibly mix? "Walt's dream is nightmare," wrote one particularly disillusioned member of the fourth estate. "To me [the park] felt like a giant cash register, clicking and clanging, as creatures of Disney magic came tumbling down from their lofty places in my daydreams." Other writers on assignment in the park agreed. To them, Disneyland was just another tourist trap—a bigger, pricier version of the Santa Claus villages and the seedy Storylands cast up by the postwar baby boom and the blandishments of the automobile industry. It was commercial, a roadside money machine, cynically exploiting the innocent dreams of childhood. On his second visit to the complex, a wire service reporter cornered

The Jungle Cruise ride in Adventureland was based on the movie *The African Queen*. Critics singled out this attraction for special scorn because the creatures that menaced the little boats weren't real. They were made of plastic.

Disney and asked him about his profit margin. Walt was furious. "We have to charge what we do because this Park cost a lot to build and maintain," he barked. "I have no government subsidy."[5]

Middlebrows continued to carp about the potential profitability of Disneyland, as if capitalism and consumerism were unfamiliar concepts or as if Disney's park, by virtue of its use of characters that all Americans knew and loved from his cartoon features and TV shows, ought to have been in the public domain—free or almost so, like an evening of television, a national park, or a national shrine. With few exceptions, highbrow critics of the 1950s despised Disneyland for similar reasons. Writing for the *Nation*, the novelist Julian Halevy took exception to an enterprise that charged admission to visit ersatz places masquerading as the Wild West or the Amazon Basin. At Disneyland, he argued, "the whole world . . . has been reduced to a sickening blend of cheap commercial formulas packaged to sell." In other words, the sin of commercialism was compounded by the fact that Disney's Amazon was not the real thing. Halevy deplored the empty lives of those who actually seemed to admire the small-screen illusion of "a papier-maché crocodile" sinking beneath the Afro-Indo-Latin American waters of Adventureland. It was "a grim indictment of the way of life for which this feeble sham represented escape and adventure." Alluding to the same specimens of Amazonian fauna, poet John Ciardi dubbed Disneyland "Foamrubbersville."[6]

Disneyland had its champions, too. The science fiction writer Ray Bradbury went to Disneyland in the company of the distinguished actor Charles Laughton (who later introduced Elvis Presley to America on Ed Sullivan's Sunday night TV show). They both loved the place, as much for the fact that the robot crocodiles were made out of plastic as for any other reason. Compared with the genuine article—dangerous and often invisible to the tourists—the toothy Disney version was new and improved: tireless, predictable, and benign, the very ideal of croco-tude on a sparkling clean Amazon in Anaheim, California, adjacent to the freeway. Disney's land as a whole was a lot like that plastic crocodile. It was utopian, perfected—or perfectible. What is most important about the Laughton/Bradbury excursion to Disneyland, however, is the ripping good time the pair had "duck[ing] when pistols were fired dead-on at charging hippopotamuses, and bask[ing] face up in the rain as we sailed under Schweitzer Falls."[7] The Jungle Cruise was a visceral, sensual experience, like stepping, somehow, into the Technicolor confines of *The African Queen* and becoming a member of the cast, bound for some exotic coast in the company of Bogart and Hepburn.

In fact, the ride had been loosely based on the adventure described in that popular 1951 film and on its picturesque river craft.[8] But, in the end, the matinee voyage and the Disneyland cruise were very different propositions. The movie, like all movies, was absolutely perfect: the actors, the director, and the editors reshot and tinkered until they got everything right. When *The African Queen* played in the neighborhood theater, filmgoers saw a finished work of art up there on the big screen—a moving picture, complete, remote, unreal, and detached from themselves despite the implicit intimacy of the darkened room. What Disney's so-called Imagineers added to the film by transferring it in three dimensions to Anaheim was the missing quotient of "reality": running water, gunshots, grinning crocodiles that swam and snapped their jaws to expose pointy plastic teeth. If there were no mosquitoes, no "Montezuma's Revenge," no accidental distractions from the narrative unfolding along the river, there was an abundance of convincing atmosphere to smell and to feel, dripping down one's neck. The once-passive viewer now became an actor, a real-life participant "face up in the rain" as a rackety little boat plowed under Schweitzer Falls. It was better than the movies. More like watching TV, while making a snack and talking on the phone at the same time. But the Jungle Cruise was a lot more fun than that.

During the 1950s, Walt Disney often said that movies were beginning to bore him, because when they were done, they were done. Because it was *real*, Disneyland could never be completed. It was perfectible—and that was the challenge. That was the real fun. The intellectuals who hated Disneyland never reckoned with all that fun. Nor, it would seem, did they share in the genuine pleasure of being only slightly terrified by a plastic (*not* papier-maché) crocodile on a nice, clean Amazon less than three feet deep. Whatever else it aspired to be, Disneyland was an amusement park, a place for good times, for the willing suspension of disbelief. It was not a zoo or a scientific expedition gone awry: it was a place where plastic crocodiles were better than live ones since half the fun came from noticing that the beasts were *almost* real, like fake mink coats, wood-grained plastic TV cabinets, or the plastic film that stuck to the front of the set and made the black-and-white picture look colored. The tension between perfection and reality, between the real and the more or less real, was the primary source of the visitor's delight. The critics, undelighted, saw only plastic and profits in a society hopelessly corrupted by TV, suburbia, tail fins, and too few distinctions of caste and class. "Ours is not so much an age of vulgarity as of vulgarization," wrote a bilious Louis Kronenberger on the decline of American culture in the 1950s: "Everything [is] tampered with or touched up, or adulterated and watered down, in an effort to make it palatable, an effort to make it pay."[9]

The public liked Disneyland anyway. On New Year's Eve, 1957,

TV was a family affair in the early 1950s. Like *Disneyland, Howdy Doody* was a merchandising triumph.

attendance reached the 10 million mark. Statistics further indicated that a hefty 40 percent of the guests had come from outside California, most of them by car. If the interstate highway system and the habit of driving long distances to work and playgrounds were major factors in its success, the outing in the family car was also a key element in the creation story Disney always used to explain how he came to build America's first theme park. In a series of 1956–57 *Saturday Evening Post* articles published under the name of his eldest daughter, it all began with "Daddy's Day," those spare afternoons when a busy father found time to take his two little girls to the zoo or the merry-go-round in Griffith Park. Other anecdotes found the trio bound for some kiddieland or a Ma-and-Pa amusement park on La Cienega

Boulevard. Despite many variations in detail, however, the meaning of the tale never varied. There were two crucial lessons to be learned from the "Daddy's Day" narrative: the importance of family entertainment and the baleful condition of the old, Coney Island–style amusement park. "I would take them to the merry-go-round," Walt Disney remembered, "and sit on a bench eating peanuts while they rode. And sitting there, alone, I felt that there should be something built, some kind of a family park where parents and children could have fun together." There was a crying need for something new, he thought, "but I didn't know what it was."[10]

The urge to build a new kind of family entertainment complex brought the two divergent sides of Disney's personality together for the first time. The Walt Disney of the big, looping signature was the

The car of the 1950s was a *family* car. The freeway and the automobile were basic to the success of Disney's plan for Disneyland.

youngest of the Hollywood moguls, a busy studio head. But he was a family man, too: a typical Los Angeles commuter, a suburbanite with a comfy, unpretentious new house in Holmby Hills. What was not typical was the backyard, where Disney had a ride-on steam train and his daughters played in a cunning replica of the dwarfs' cottage from *Snow White,* complete with picket fence and gingerbread gables, built by the studio shop as a present for Diane and her sister, Sharon. Here, in his own backyard, in the expanding leisure hours that had suddenly become a factor in the life of the nuclear family, the interests of the businessman and the father began to converge. Compared with the average, seedy kiddieland, the Disney garden suggested that he could probably do a vastly superior job of promoting weekend togetherness.[11]

While Disney's interest in family activities began in the 1940s and anticipated the concept by a decade or more, the name for shared parenting and the lifestyle it promoted, or "togetherness," was coined by *McCall's* in the 1954 Easter issue and became the rallying cry of a moral crusade endorsed by anxious editors, clergymen, and advertisers.[12] Togetherness legitimated the new, postwar suburban family—affluent, isolated, reared on a bland diet of TV and TV dinners—by stressing the compensatory benefits of a greater paternal role in the household. Togetherness made fathers into full domestic partners with their wives and provided a healthy male influence in the formation of young psyches. Togetherness meant, in effect, that Daddy occasionally changed diapers, helped with the shopping and the vacuuming, and took charge of the kids on Saturday or Sunday afternoons. And whatever its erotic burden of ornamental chrome, the gigantic American automobile of the 1950s was as large as it was because it was a *family* car, perfect for outings with Daddy at the wheel, Mommy right beside him, and the children squealing with anticipation in the spacious backseat. We're going to Disneyland!

The car offered freedom, "freedom to come and go as we please in this big country of ours," as a Ford ad of the 50s put it. It also liberated the family from the conformity of the suburb, from rows of almost identical houses, rigid social rituals, unspoken rules of conduct for the weekend barbecue, and written rules governing the proper trim-

Disneyland was a powerful antidote to the freeway. It made the family stop, get out of the car, and ride various forms of public transportation instead.

ming of lawns.[13] The car allowed the family to escape the pressures of modern times: out there, on the freeway, it was still possible to play the part of the pioneer, headed bravely off into that unknown America of the presuburban past, in search of adventure and self-exploration. The automobile let the family outrun its fears of recession, of a sudden end to the prosperity of big cars and weekend fun—or its countervailing fears of prosperity and the soulless materialism of which American were so often accused by their intellectual betters.

Early visitors to Disneyland seem not to have noticed any correlation between driving to the park and what they did when they got there. But, mainly, they went for another long ride: on the old-fashioned steam railroad, circling the grounds; on the Model-T–era fire trucks and the horse-drawn trolleys along Main Street; on the *Mark Twain*, coursing through Frontierland; on the Jungle Cruise though Adventureland; on Tomorrowland's rocket to the moon; on the pretty carousel in the middle of Fantasyland. Eschewing conventional shows and walk-through attractions, Disneyland was premised on vehicles, many of them designed to conjure up a faraway, long-ago world of adventure and restless freedom. In 1971 the design historian Reyner Banham became the first to posit that what happened inside Disneyland bore a direct relationship to what was going on outside the gates. Disney's park stood in a suburb of Los Angeles and in that particular environment, Banham concluded, "Disneyland offers illicit pleasures of mobility. Ensconced in a sea of giant parking-lots in a city devoted to the automobile, it provides transportation that does not exist outside—steam trains, monorails, people-movers . . . not to mention pure transport fantasies such as simulated space-trips and submarine rides."[14]

For Walt Disney and his fellow commuters, Disneyland's rides made a daily chore into a treat by isolating and emphasizing the pleasurable aspects of driving. What was a metaphoric escape on the freeway, for instance, became a real or almost real escape aboard the *E. P. Ripley*, the first steam locomotive put into service on the Santa Fe and Disneyland Railroad that circled the park. In a society in which the ticket to adulthood was the driver's license, the Disneyland transportation system permitted regression to childhood through the simple expedient of inviting grown-ups to be passengers, free to daydream and gaze at the scenery. And the destinations were no longer the office, the shopping center, or some sleazy little amusement park. Disney's boats and trains went instead to the places of the heart, to a happy past, to memories and dreams of a perfect childhood.

Mrs. Disney believed that Disneyland sprang directly from her husband's lifelong obsession with the Santa Fe Railroad. The main line ran through his boyhood hometown, Marceline, Missouri, on its way to Kansas City and distant California. As a youngster, Walt Disney had worked as a news- and candy-butcher on the train; he later claimed that he'd invented Mickey Mouse in a westbound Pullman car out of Chicago, somewhere between Toluca, Illinois, and La

The parking lot of Southdale, America's first covered mall. Like Disneyland, the new mall of the 1950s demanded a pedestrian experience.

Junta, Colorado. When financial worries brought him to the brink of nervous breakdown in 1931, he boarded the Santa Fe for a therapeutic trip. In the late 1940s the doctors suggested more time away from the office. A hobby, perhaps. So Walt Disney built a one-eighth-scale railroad on the canyon side of his own backyard at 355 Carolwood Avenue in Holmby Hills, between Bel Air and Beverly Hills. The project grew out of his work. One of the most engaging characters in *Dumbo*, a full-length Disney animated feature released in 1941, was "Casey, Jr.," a determined little engine. While *Dumbo* was still on the drawing boards, animator Ward Kimball bought a full-size 1881 min-

Walt Disney was America's best-known hobbyist. The Carolwood-Pacific Railroad, in his new suburban backyard, was a key prototype for Disneyland.

ing engine and a passenger car and took the boss for a ride on a five-hundred-foot stretch of track laid in his own yard. By 1946 or 1947 there was a Lionel train set in Walt's office. Ollie Johnston, another studio animator, invited Disney to his home in Santa Monica to see his miniature steam trains. "He came out two or three times and he started to get ideas on how he was going to build his," Johnston remembered. "They started building it here in the shop, several months later."[15]

Disney eventually recouped part of the cost of the work done on that first engine by selling duplicate sets of the scale drawings to eager hobbyists. Kimball and Johnston were avid railfans who collected railroad memorabilia in addition to building models and re-storing old trains. This widespread interest in a vanishing industry in the 1940s and 50s was an aspect of a broader concern with "Americana," or not-impossibly-old antiques and commercially made collect-ibles for every pocketbook. These new antiques gave mobile Americans a sense of rootedness; hobbies and crafts also attached leisure activity firmly to the den or the basement workshop of the family home. With his own daughters approaching the stage of roving adolescence, Disney frequently tried to justify his own train set on the grounds that it would keep the girls and their friends close to home. But the distaff side of the family proved indifferent to his hobby and the Carolwood-Pacific line instead served to keep Walt Disney at home.

He invested time and money lavishly in the railroad, relocating power lines and organizing parties geared exclusively to riding the rails. With his own hands he built the little freight cars (one ride-on passenger per car) and a caboose (fitted out with miniature bunks and newspapers printed to scale) in a trackside workshop that was a precise replica of the barn on his father's forty-eight-acre farm back in the Linn County, Missouri, of his boyhood. The geographer Yi-Fu Tuan maintains that the planned and planted garden—or backyard—is, by its very essence, a statement about the dominance of the human personality over nature. The garden imposes order on chaotic natural growth; in that one place, the householder tames and subdues the primal forces of growth, death, and regeneration, the forces of time itself. The suburbanite understands the war against crabgrass in these terms. With twenty-six hundred feet of railroad track circling his backyard, Walt Disney was likewise able to control his environment, and to travel back into a rural childhood perfected by memory. He could make his cartoons come to hissing, chugging, three-dimensional life. Bedeviled by the vagaries of business at the office, here at home Disney was at last firmly in control. Perched atop the cab of a one-eighth-scale steam engine modeled after the Southern Pacific's old Number 173, Walt Disney was master of all that he surveyed, the engineer of his own destiny, firmly in charge of his future and of his own miniaturized and idealized past.[16]

Ollie Johnston saw a direct connection between the Carolwood-

Pacific and the genesis of the park in Anaheim. "The next thing you know, Walt was thinking about putting a railroad around here, at the Studio," he argued. First, Disney talked about buying some used engines that had come on the market. "Then he got to thinking there wasn't enough room here and before long there was a Disneyland." But the Chicago Railroad Fair of 1948 was the crucial event that linked the model train to a new kind of themed amusement park in Walt Disney's own mind. The trip to Chicago was part of Disney's pre-scribed regimen of relaxation. Told to get away from the studio com-pletely, he decided to go to Chicago with Ward Kimball to see what was being billed as a once-in-a-lifetime display of rolling stock and memorabilia in Burnham Park. And when the two train buffs boarded a passenger coach to start their adventure, they discovered that the

The Chicago Railroad Fair of 1948 had a train on the periphery and several "lands," later to be recreated at Disneyland. "Gold Gulch" became Frontierland, for example.

president of the Santa Fe had left an open invitation to join the engineer in the cab. "I had never, ever seen [Walt] look so happy," Kimball said.[17]

The Railroad Fair was sponsored by thirty-eight major American carriers, including the Santa Fe. Ostensibly it honored the centenary of the first steam locomotive to enter Chicago, the nation's greatest rail center. A replica of that first station was built on the fairgrounds. Mrs. Casey Jones, widow of the legendary engineer, rode in the opening day parade. But the Railroad Fair was not an idle exercise in nostalgia. Despite the plethora of railroad relics, the fair was held to drum up business and investment capital for modern-day lines hard hit by competition from cars and planes and burdened with an inventory of equipment all but worn out by hard use during World War II. "Few railroads could sell stock today," the trade journal *Railway Age* admitted as the $2 million extravaganza geared up for the summer on the site of the 1933–34 Century of Progress Exposition. Indeed, the fair took on something of the futuristic flavor of its predecessor, with displays of rolling stock of the 1950s and 60s, including various sleek, domed passenger cars and the Chesapeake and Ohio's mysterious "X" train, designed to compete with the airlines at speeds approaching 150 miles per hour.[18]

But for every train of tomorrow showcased in Chicago in 1948, there were dozens from yesterday. A retrospective mood prevailed by careful design. Statisticians had calculated the number of active railroad model makers at 100,000; most of them were steeped in the arcana of railroad lore, as were the many thousands more who collected "railroadiana," took pictures of rare and unusual sights at trackside, and went on trips under steam power. The total annual investment of these hobbyists was more than $10 million, and organizers of the Chicago Fair were eager to tap their interest, enthusiasm, and goodwill. Besides, as one optimistic rail executive put it, there really were 144 million train buffs in the United States—everybody who had ever dreamed of adventure when a whistle pierced the silence of the night or thought of heading out to L.A. for a fresh start aboard the Santa Fe California Limited.[19]

The fairgrounds were full of old engines. It was the manner in which they were presented, however, that would prove germinal for Disneyland. First, the area was dominated by a working narrow-gauge railroad that separated the exposition from the rest of Burnham Park, as the peripheral rail line at Disneyland would later divide the amusement park from the outside world. Chicago's six-car Deadwood Central was also an important means of moving from one exhibit to another in an environment that made no allowance for the automobile. Second, many of the exhibits re-created in atmospheric detail some exotic vacation spot best reached by train. Leisure, or travel for pleasure and recreation: this was the niche the American railroad was attempting to carve out for itself in Chicago through displays that included a real working dude ranch, transported to the site piece by piece; a mechanical recreation of Yellowstone's Old Faithful that erupted every fifteen minutes (the original went off once an hour) for the convenience of sightseers with other attractions to

The Santa Fe's Indian Village at the Chicago Railroad.

visit; and scenic slices of the French Quarter, an Indian Village, and a sandy beach on Florida's Gulf Coast. "Villages" like these were not new to big expositions. Since the nineteenth century, communities of Philippine tribesmen, native Americans, and other picturesque peoples had been a regular feature of world's fairs, along with reproductions of historic buildings. Chicagoans were quick to compare the scenic bits at the 1948 fair with the popular Belgian Village built for the Century of Progress Exposition fifteen years earlier. In fact, the Railroad Fair occupied the portion of the old exposition layout once devoted to the Alpine Village, the Hawaiian Village, the Spanish Village, a Mayan temple, and a replica of Fort Dearborn. What was different about the Railroad Fair was the coherence and concentration of the experience—the sensation of having dropped in on most of the nation's beauty spots in a single day via a magical train.[20]

Reality rarely intruded. Even dining was apt to be part of the illusion of being in Yellowstone or the Southwest. Thus it was possible to have lunch served by a cowhand from the business end of a chuckwagon and dinner in the dining car of a Rock Island streamliner fitted out as a Mexican hacienda staffed by grandees in appropriate costume. "By dramatizing, . . . by making every exhibit a novelty in entertainment as well as education," the *New York Times* remarked, "the railroads have graphically driven home a realization of how much they mean to our national economy."[21] Although their success in conveying economic data remains arguable, the railroads did make the American scene come alive to the senses. All that was missing was a narrative that tied the stops on the Deadwood Central together: the beach, the Old West, the Vieux Carré, and the transportation technology of the future.

Walt Disney himself became part of the story line supplied by a four-times-a-day play—*Wheels A-Rolling*—enacted by moving locomotives. Spectators sat in a grandstand facing a pair of tracks framed by huge concrete wings, and watched as engines puffed into view and actors stepped down to mime famous tableaux from railroad history, including the passage of Lincoln's funeral train. Dressed as a passenger, in a tall hat and frock coat, Disney played in "a Harvey House scene" depicting a dinner stop at one of Fred Harvey's turn-of-the-century hotels on the Santa Fe route.[22] Designed to encourage rail tourism by providing intriguing destinations for passengers, Harvey Houses used pseudo-southwestern architecture, menus, and gift shops to create an all-encompassing atmosphere of authenticity, like that of the Railroad Fair. Replicas offered predictable quality, safety, and every civilized amenity; dining became an unscripted play, with the tourist-tenderfoot in the starring role. Walt Disney's inclusion in the cast of eight hundred as an actor and sometime engineer was one of the high points of his life. And all the way home, he talked to Kimball about building an amusement park. "Disneyland was already forming in his mind. Of course, he thought [it] should have an almost full-sized steam train that . . . he could have fun operating himself on days when the park was closed."[23]

As it was finally built, six years later, Disneyland owed a great deal to the Chicago Railroad Fair. The Santa Fe and Disneyland Railroad that defined the boundaries of the park. The separate "lands," each with a historic or geographic theme and costumed attendants. Even the kinds of places and concepts singled out for special treatment by the fair's planners—the Wild West, the technological future of railroading, tropical Florida, the age of steam—bore more than a passing resemblance to the constituent parts of Disneyland, from Main Street USA to Tomorrowland. Only Fantasyland was not taken from the prototype. And finally, although Disney did include a Tomorrowland that corresponded to the finale of the Chicago railroad pageant, when trains of the future finally glided into view, the real emphasis in both venues fell on the past—on a culture of railroading that the automobile had all but eradicated. Disneyland would preserve places out of time, bypassed forever by the interstates. Disneyland would have bustling towns, each one with a depot, but no suburbs, no carports. And there were only two ways to reach those pretty little cities: on foot, or aboard an obsolete, doomed-to-destruction railroad train. In that sense, Disneyland was a tacit protest against modern America, on the wrong side of the tracks, to which Walt Disney consigned the cars and the parking lots. Disneyland was old-fashioned and urban. It was everything that L.A. was not.[24]

What L.A. was, according to Disney's own testimony in the late

Walt Disney played a part in a costume pageant held every day during the 1948 season; this scene shows the Golden Spike joining the halves of the transcontinental railroad.

1940s, was dull, a place sorely in need of a tourist attraction for the star-struck: "People come to Hollywood and find there's nothing to see!"[25] But what tour-bus stops did exist also influenced the character of Disneyland. There was Olvera Street, a permanent version of a world's fair "village" constructed in the old historic heart of Los Angeles in 1929 as a Mission-period pedestrian mall, lined with more than seventy shops and cantinas. From the 1920s through the Depression era, the Spanish Colonial style of Olvera Street adorned local buildings that dramatized tourist fantasies associated with the good life in California. Union Station, the amusement piers near Naples and Santa Monica, and movie palaces like the famous Carthay Circle (where *Snow White* premiered): all were lustily Spanish in flavor and denied humdrum reality by translating life as it was lived in California into fabulous, make-believe settings. The pleasures of shopping and dining were particularly susceptible to this architectural masquerade. The 1934 Farmers' Market, one of Walt Disney's favorite weekend haunts, was a let's-pretend midwestern farmscape beneath a windmill. Crossroads of the World on Sunset Boulevard, completed in 1936, invited shoppers to browse through stores housed in a half-timbered Shakespearian village, a lighthouse, and a ship, in addition to the usual early California presidio.

In its upscale manifestations, the architecture of illusion often parted car and driver. The buildings of the past stood for pre-automotive behavior associated with the luxury, ease, and sensuality of premodern times. To shop at Crossroads of the World was to buy the joy of free, unhurried time, the bliss of walking through unfamiliar townscapes, pausing to savor the sensual delights of touch, sight, and smell—or precisely what Disneyland would offer the masses in 1955. But the downscale version of such fantasy architecture—drive-in restaurants shaped like giant shoes or derby hats—could be seen on almost any Los Angeles street corner during the years when Disney was beginning to dream of an alternative to conventional amusement park and city alike. Aldous Huxley, who would soon write the first draft of the script for Disney's 1951 *Alice in Wonderland*, described a typical Los Angeles suburb as a succession of implausible villas in which "Gloucester followed Andalusia and gave place to Touraine and Oaxaca, Dusseldorf and Massachusetts."[26]

History had no dominion over such a world. Time was contingent and malleable. Without a past firmly situated in relationship to the future, there were no beginnings or endings. No death. Storybook architecture rewrote the story of the human condition in California, the Golden State of perpetual youth. Although some commentators have attributed the imaginative vernacular of Los Angeles to sheer, sun-drenched hedonism, most critics see a connection between make-believe architecture and the movie industry. "Motion pictures have undoubtedly confused architectural tastes," wrote the California architect Richard Neutra in 1941. "They may be blamed for . . . half-timber English peasant cottages, . . . Arabian minarets, [and] Georgian mansions on 50 x 120 foot lots with 'Mexican Ranchos' adjoining them on sites of the same size."[27] Neutra's target was the suburbs of Los Angeles but he could just as well have been describing Walt Disney's plans for a little park adjacent to his own backlot property in Burbank.

Public interest in the backlots of the major studios was intense throughout the 1930s and 40s. Where did the moving pictures come

Union Station, Los Angeles, where Walt Disney boarded the Santa Fe. The California Mission style, popular in the 1920s, made the whole of Southern California into a kind of historical theme park.

from? Was this the place? The Disney studio was besieged with requests for tours. But Walt Disney thought that watching animators bent over drawing boards would bore the tourists silly. They wanted a taste of Hollywood razzle-dazzle and magic, not tedious work. They wanted to be a part of the faraway times and places that came to life on the screen. They wanted to be part of the illusion. So when Walt Disney built a new studio in Burbank in 1939–40, he began to think of ways to make the standard Hollywood studio tour more engaging. The first detailed plans for Disneyland coincide, in fact, with the move to Burbank and mandate that a "magical little park" of eight acres be set aside for guests.[28] By 1948, and a detailed in-house memo about the projected park, the concept of theming was already in place, along with a train, a stern-wheeler, a railroad station, a false-fronted Western street, a carnival section with the "typical Midway stuff," and an

Preliminary plans for a Disney park adjacent to the new Burbank Studio in 1948: a glorified, self-guided studio tour with sets depicting the Old West, the Gay 90s, the farm.

old-fashioned townscape that sounded a lot like Anaheim's future Main Street USA.

"The Main Village, which includes a Railroad Station, is built around a village green. . . . It will be a place for people to sit and rest." And there was more: a quaint commercial district with a bookshop and a toyshop and a "restaurant for birthday parties." Linked to the rough-and-tumble attractions of the Western and carnival zones by a variety of trolleys and surreys, Main Village was meant for leisurely strolling and sitting in the shade. It was Olvera Street with an Americana veneer, the pedestrian shopping mall with a touch of fantasy, a whole streetful of backlot, Los Angeles eccentricities of architecture, a model railroad layout enlarged to usable scale. But none of it impressed the Burbank City Council. Ignoring the emphasis on the family, council members quailed at the thought of "the carny atmosphere in Burbank." The acreage was swallowed up by the Ventura Freeway and Disney went back to tinkering with his trains and models.[29]

His pastimes and his plans for the park had become increasingly difficult to separate, in any case. One of the most significant ingredients in the evolving Disneyland of the early 1950s was a plan for a walk-though museum of automata—moving, miniature scenes from his own films and American history—built by Walt Disney himself. A longtime collector of mechanical toys, Disney had already decided to make them in 1951, when he ran into the illustrator Harper Goff in a model train shop in London and told him he wanted to create a touring exhibit called *Walt Disney's America*, to teach youngsters about history. Renamed *Disneylandia*, the project consisted of twenty-four peep-show scenes of salient moments in the American past enlivened by little figures that could actually talk and move. Goff and one of the studio artists were to paint the scenes in great detail, à la Norman Rockwell. Then Disney would go home and build them to scale in his workshop, with some help from company mechanics. "I'm going to do something creative myself," he told an associate, "I want you to draw scenes of life in an old Western town. . . . I'll carve the figures and make the scenes in miniature. When we get enough of them made, we'll send them out as a traveling exhibit."[30] In the end, *Disneylandia* was abandoned: the tiny size of the figures made them

Disneylandia involved automata and working miniatures. It translated Walt's model railroading into the new, robotic dimension essential to the eventual success of Disneyland.

difficult to operate and, at a quarter a head, it would be hard to recover costs. But the idea was folded into the master plan for an amusement park. *Disneylandia* eventually spawned the slithering plastic crocodiles of Adventureland and the flying sprites of Fantasyland.

In *The Lonely Crowd*, a study of the changing American character published in 1950, David Riesman and his collaborators took up the subject of hobbies. The intensity with which the average, middle-class American pursued after-hours woodcarving or outdoor cooking or model making initially puzzled the sociologists because such private interests seemed at odds with the "outer-directed" personality demanded by the times. The "outer-directed" corporate man took his social cues from those around him and remained "a lonely member of the crowd because he never really comes close to . . . himself," the book concluded. But the use of leisure for craftsmanlike activities by nine-to-five conformists seemed anomalous, an expression of autonomy and individual competence that ran counter to the workday norm. In such moments of basement tinkering, the Riesman team suggested, the hobbyist "can often rediscover both his childhood and his inner-directed residues by serious craftsmanship."[31] To make a model—in the case of Disneyland, to recreate the Marceline, Missouri, of a turn-of-the-century boyhood—was to return to those happy, bygone times as a competent adult. To make a model was to construct or reconstruct one's own biography. To make a model of an ideal past was to reject an imperfect present.

In Disneyland, the present—suburban reality, 1955-style—was abandoned in the parking lot, along with the family car. Although ticket buyers would ultimately face a choice between Fantasyland, Frontierland, Adventureland, and Tomorrowland, they were first forced to negotiate a common entranceway defined by the architectural and technological symbolism of an American past that coincided with Walt Disney's own. Here, too, his hobbies displaced the realities of the workplace on a scale that demanded the same "inner-directed" ethos of others. Everybody walked under the railroad tracks and past the station where the old steam locomotive chuffed to a halt. Everybody walked down Main Street USA, under its gingerbread cornices,

An ideal map of Disneyland in the mid-1950s, showing the various "lands," the peripheral railroad, and the controlled access to the park through the stage-set recreation of Main Street USA.

past windows bearing the names of Disney's father and his friends inscribed in gilded letters. It was a working model of Marceline, Missouri, calibrated to the scale of his backyard locomotive.

When measured drawings of that little train were being enlarged to adapt it to Disneyland, the designers determined that a six-foot doorway was just right for a passenger car. As the little freight stations and villages on a railroad layout beneath a Christmas tree are proportional to the engine they accompany, so everything in Disneyland was calibrated from the basic module of the door in the passenger car. "It's not apparent to a casual glance that this street is only a scale model," Disney stated, pointing at the Italianate storefronts that stretched away toward Sleeping Beauty's Castle. "We had every brick and shingle and gas lamp made 7/8 of true size."[32] Actually, it was more complicated. Like the clever set decorators they were, Disney's "Imagineers" built Main Street in forced perspective, with the upper stories much smaller than the lower ones, giving the impression of diminution by distance while keeping the overall height of the cornice lines suburban, unthreatening, and low. The ground floor, in each case, is seven-eighths the size of a "real" turn-of-the-century commercial structure; the second story is five-eighths scale (also used for the various trains and boats); but the top story is only one-half as large as its generic prototypes.

Along with Levittown and places like it, the dimensions of Main Street USA answered Lewis Mumford's call for a postwar "return to the human scale" that made neighborliness and intimacy possible.[33] Main Street was the city's opposite, the antonym of the corporate skyscraper. Its size domesticated, its atmosphere comfy and benign, Main Street evoked the mood of Disney's own small-town movies of the period and the front-porch television tradition that began with *Father Knows Best* in 1954. On Main Street, the grown-up suddenly became a kid again—a Bud or a Betty from TV's fictional Springfield, USA. Main Street's scale captured what most adults experienced when they returned to their hometowns and noticed how small, how toylike the cherished places of childhood had become. Built from the blueprint of memory, Main Street was capable of shrinking the past, stripping away the nasty facts of yesterday—the hardships, the grime, the business failures of Walt's own father—and exalting instead the positive values that recollection had burnished to a golden luster. Main Street was a plaything, a dream at naptime, a TV sitcom better than reality had ever been.

Disney's make-believe Main Street shared much common ground with 1950s suburbia: the sense of uniformity, order, community, and safety, a sort of smiling "I Like Ike" friendliness conveyed by each perky awning. But as a model community, Main Street also stood in obvious contrast to the American city from which the suburbanite had fled. People-sized, organized around the meanderings of pedestrians, it revealed its deepest meaning by its opposition to Los Angeles and to the creeping steel-and-concrete urbanism outside the park. Perhaps, then, Main Street was the real national Fantasyland, since Los

Main Street USA had the uniformity and scale of a suburban residential street of the 1950s. Inside, under its movie-set disguise, Main Street was also a suburban shopping mall.

Angeles and its environs in 1955 constituted the future that had already come to pass for small-town America. Or perhaps, secure from bulldozers and the ravages of urbanization, it was a compensatory monument to Marceline, Anaheim, and all the other vanished Main Streets of the postwar era. Southern Californians, according to one trenchant social commentator struggling to make sense of Disneyland's popularity, habitually "imagine ivy-covered, leaf-strewn squares, and villages clustered around white frame New England churches, and, lacking them in reality, create them in plastic towns to which they go to find themselves." The architect Charles Moore has called Main Street the town square of Los Angeles, an environment of polity otherwise missing from the 1950s city of freeways and housing tracts: "In an unchartable sea of suburbia, Disney has created a place, indeed a whole public world, full of sequential occurrences of big and little drama. . . . [E]verything is as immaculate as in the musical-comedy villages that Hollywood has provided for our viewing pleasure for the last three generations."[34]

Because Main Street USA was built by filmmakers, not by architects, its appearance was calibrated to achieving a desired emotional effect. Form followed function—or script—unashamedly, as it often does in commercial, roadside architecture. "What is Main Street?" asked the Manhattan developer Mel Kaufman after a pilgrimage to Disneyland. "It is an ordinary shopping center where they sell souvenirs, film, . . . ice cream, have a movie house—all functioning as would any ordinary shopping center. Except for one thing. It's a stage set of Main Street circa 1900." It was no ordinary shopping center, to be sure, but Main Street USA was a working commercial district that looked backward to Los Angeles's Olvera Street and forward to Victor Gruen's Southdale, the first fully enclosed suburban mall, which opened in Minneapolis in 1956. Indeed, Main Street was a mall in its own right, since the disposition of the interior space permitted free movement from one shop to another along the entire length of a block. So, by virtue of the controlling position of Main Street in the layout of the park, shopping became a key motif in the iconographic structure of Disneyland. On the one hand, the psychology of the place made for low sales resistance. "Unlike in society's modern cities," a Disney planner boasted, "they drop their defenses [here]. . . . Actually, what we're selling is reassurance." On the other hand, while the ambience created enormous profits, it also exalted the central act of street-corner capitalism—the buying and selling of consumer goods, which went on at a frantic pace behind the lovely facades of what amounted to antique shops in reverse: old-fashioned stores stocked with the latest in Mickey Mouse Club memorabilia. Period decor legitimated consumption by equating the business of Main Street USA with the historical fiber of the nation. Main Street celebrated the pleasures of exuberant postwar consumerism.[35]

A Colonial Williamsburg or a Greenfield Village adapted to the social climate of the 1950s, Main Street USA affirmed that the good life—utopia—was American and middle class: neat, tidy, entrepreneurial. The rest of Disneyland, to which that thoroughfare led,

Southdale, the first enclosed suburban mall, opened outside Minneapolis in 1956.

Up above the shops on Main Street, the windows were adorned with the names of Disney friends and associates, in a kind of architectural autobiography. Elias Disney was Walt's father.

represented a world view grounded in the values of Main Street. Frontierland set forth the story of how the West was made safe for homesteaders—and future suburbanites with ranch houses. Adventureland appropriated the Third World and untamed nature to serve as the new frontiers (and boutiques) of the present, while a high-tech Tomorrowland, full of corporate logos and intent on the conquest of space, was the profitable frontier of the future. As for Fantasyland, its flirtations with the dark and irrational realm of fairytales only served to affirm the ideological clarity with which the progress of the American adventure, from cowboy to astronaut, was described elsewhere in nuances of architecture, cuisine, and gift-shop souvenirs. But Main

Street USA remained the allegorical touchstone for this "Disneyized" history of Cold War America. "It is what America was," writes the cultural geographer Richard Francaviglia, "and provides the bedrock security for what is to be." And so a powerful dramatization of history and destiny, a story geared to the 1950s, arose directly from Walt Disney's own childhood memories. In an act of almost stupefying self-assurance, he made himself—his life, his hobbies, his movies, his TV show—the objective correlative for a whole culture, past, present, and future. In the words of a promotional brochure for the park, "Disneyland reflects Walt's personal experiences, his dreams, his ambitions and special interests which are universal interests."[36]

If not universal, these interests were well known to most Americans through the medium of film. Main Street USA pushed to the foreground the scenic backgrounds of *Lady and the Tramp* (released when Disneyland opened in July 1955). Fantasyland brought back Tinker Bell, Snow White, Pinocchio, and Alice, stars of animated features based on children's classics. Adventureland alluded to Disney's recent True-Life Adventure series of nature documentaries. Tomorrowland, the least developed of the quadrants in 1955, was based on the 1954 film *20,000 Leagues Under the Sea*, a live-action sci-fi thriller loaded with special effects. Hence the characters and themes of Disneyland—or most of them—were familiar to adults who had grown up with Disney cartoons and were now, as parents, taking their own kids to see the latest from the same studio. Everybody knew Disneyana, if not from those movies, then from the products related to them: the books, watches, lamps, toys, clothing, and novelty items—even a line of canned foods marketed under the Donald Duck label.[37] In a pluralistic society, where experiences of church, school, ethnicity, and the like were not apt to be universally shared, Disney motifs constituted a common culture, a kind of civil religion of happy endings, worry-free consumption, technological optimism, and nostalgia for the good old days.

In sheer size, Disneyland's sets invited comparison with those created for the inflated "spectaculars" through which Hollywood in the 1950s hoped to recoup profits lost to television. There was one important difference: Disneyland was a set for a movie that would be made

Spin-off merchandise from the Disney TV empire, 1955: a Mickey Mouse Club "Mousegetar."

only in the mind of the visitor. Turned loose on an ersatz set, the visitor became a temporary Hollywood insider, privy to the secrets of the giant screen. But the intimacy of the backlot also made it the perfect setting for TV and its small-screen revelations of what went on behind the scenes. Walt Disney's first television show, a 1950 "special" broadcast on Christmas afternoon by NBC, made a vast family audience familiar with the doings in his studio during the making of *Alice in Wonderland. One Hour in Disneyland* also gave viewers a look at the Disney family: Diane and Sharon, then high schoolers, appeared with their father. The formula proved so successful that Disney offered another insider's peek at moviemaking in 1951.[38]

Television was the family entertainment medium of choice in the isolated, gadget-happy ranch houses of suburbia, and the commercial benefits of luring those families back to the movie houses with free previews of forthcoming films were enormous. "That telecast should be worth $1 million at the boxoffice to *Alice in Wonderland*," wrote one TV columnist after the first Christmas program aired. But despite its appeal to the swelling postwar middle class, old-line Hollywood moguls and highbrows alike considered television an enterprise of dubious artistic and intellectual merit. The first major producer to join forces with the networks, Disney incurred the wrath of other studio heads bent on ignoring the competition or fighting a losing battle against "the idiot box." His espousal of TV—his intuitive grasp of the potential for profit—gave Disney's critics another reason to consign him to the ranks of the philistines. His sheepish defenders, on the other hand, put forth the curious argument that Disney "demonstrated . . . his inherent contempt for the medium" by using television to create a market for his films—and for Disneyland.[39]

In the early 1950s the Disneyland concept was in trouble. Within the company, Walt Disney had found little support for what many believed to be an excursion into honky-tonk. The planning process continued only because he paid for the work out of his own pocket. And when he approached would-be backers with his idea for a form of participatory entertainment at the furthest remove from television, the business community was inclined to believe rumors that Disney was not quite himself. TV was his last hope. Walt Disney Productions would crank out the weekly series the networks had been angling for in return for heavy cash investments and loan guarantees to see the park through to completion. A written prospectus and a portfolio of Disney site drawings were prepared in a single, frantic weekend, and in late September of 1953 Walt's brother, Roy, went to New York to strike a deal. On April 2, 1954, it was formally announced that ABC— the struggling "third" network—had landed Walt Disney and that Disney, as part of the package, was going to build some sort of "film production center" patterned after the picturesque villages in his movies. The TV show and the center were both called *Disneyland*.[40]

Disneyland, the weekly series, premiered in October of 1954. It played on Wednesday nights at 7:30, the children's hour, and within three months it had reached the top ten. *Disneyland* became a family institution: homework was deferred; sales of TV dinners soared. In Walt Disney's own mind and in its televised format, the popular program was not easily distinguishable from the project now under construction in Anaheim. "I saw that if I was ever going to have my park," he admitted, "here . . . was a way to tell millions of people about it—with TV."[41] And so, every week, the program format introduced the audience to the principal themes of the park. One Wednesday, the topic would be Fantasyland, with the content made up of clips from animated films. Adventureland evenings recycled footage shot for the nature documentaries. But the Tomorrowland segment was perhaps the most revealing in terms of Disney's intentions.

Under the heading of Tomorrowland, the studio prepared a behind-the-scenes preview of *20,000 Leagues Under the Sea*, with an emphasis on special effects technology and robotics. The program won an Emmy, but it was also dubbed "the first 60-minute commercial in the history of TV" and "the longest trailer ever made."[42] Nor did critics fail to notice that three additional Wednesdays were given over to progress reports from the site urging members of the audience to plan future vacation trips to Southern California, much as other telecasts had sent viewers to the drive-in to see a new Disney movie with which they were already familiar before the credits ever rolled. Nonetheless, while *Disneyland* served blatantly commercial ends, the show was also crucial to the creation of the mood or underlying scenario of its geographic counterpart out in Anaheim. Through the medium of *Disneyland*, the American family became part of the process of building the park and acquired an emotional stake in its success. It was Walt's own Williamsburg, his American Versailles, but it was part of the Wednesday-night home lives of countless viewers, too. And by rehearsing the proposed features of the park, the TV show eliminated all grounds for apprehension: Disneyland—the theme park—was just as safe, wholesome, and predictable as the living room setting in which the family gathered every week to watch Walt talk about it. Add a little sunshine and a few hot dogs and going to Disneyland would be just like watching that other *Disneyland* on TV.

Bob Chandler, a television reporter for *Variety*, admired the way in which the show relentlessly plugged the park and the park, in turn, gave permanent form to the transient aspects of Disney's entertainment empire. But the systematic integration of the two arms of the business went further than that. Disneyland's Tomorrowland and Frontierland, Chandler observed, were "tele-creations," or concepts generated for the home screen without much precedent in the existing Disney film archive.[43] In fact, most of the brand-new material produced for the show, including a popular series on space exploration, fell into one of these two categories. Both were important TV motifs of the 1950s.

The Tomorrowland shows always drew high ratings. After a segment called *Man in Space* aired on March 5, 1955, President Eisenhower called from the White House to offer his thanks and congratulations in person. The futuristic hardware explained by rocket scientists (like Wernher von Braun) and animated by the Disney artists was not dissimilar in appearance, however, to the products of American industry on display during frequent commercial breaks: a Ford Fairlane with options and a push-button kitchen range heralded a future of magical ease as surely as any lunar vehicle did. Television suburbanized a future that remained (until Sputnik suggested otherwise) a strictly American phenomenon, a technological wonderland available for purchase with no money down and twenty-four months to pay. The Autopia in Disney's park was a reminder of that consumerist vision of the world to come. Funds ran out before the Tomorrowland precinct was fully realized, but Walt insisted that this one attraction—a replica of the new freeway system that linked America's past with a suburban future—be completed in time for the opening ceremonies. The shiny new cars vroooming past the camera would make for great TV, he thought.

Frontierland embodied both the national past and the most popular recurring theme of the *Disneyland* program, thanks to the Davy Crockett mania of the 1954–55 season. Like Tomorrowland, Frontierland resonated to powerful themes in the suburban imagination. The ranch house, the knotty-pine den, the outdoor barbecue, the search for an acre of crabgrass beyond the boundaries of urban civilization: these facts of American life in 1950s help to explain why the Western genre accounted for more than a quarter of the movies produced in Hollywood and why the cowboy film of the period was so often domestic in flavor, with the tragic hero—Alan Ladd's *Shane* (1953), John Wayne as Ethan in *The Searchers* (1956)—longing for the stability of home and hearth. Because the footage was cheap and available, television developed a voracious appetite for old Westerns in its early years but soon demanded more, made to order for the medium.[44] Disney's *Davy Crockett* episodes—the first one-hour, prime-time Westerns on network television—garnered the highest ratings of the decade (and produced a bonanza of product spin-offs) by validating suburban mobility in the person of the restless frontiersman who waxes nostalgic about home and family as he dies in the wilds of Texas. Those who might have wondered, in a year of recession and economic jitters, about the wisdom of acquiring the push-button appurtenances of Tomorrowland found imaginative comfort in Frontierland's simple, log-cabin past. Armchair frontiersmen uneasy about the nation's postwar transformation into a military-industrial superpower could find solace in the vision of an earlier day, commemorated in their own Early American curtains and wagon-wheel coffee tables. The eye of the camera let the living room viewer travel freely in time and space, backward to the Alamo, forward to the moon. Television was a magical picture window on the world beyond one's own front lawn, and Disneyland was conceived in its perceptual image.

The spatial sensibility of Disneyland comes from television, too—specifically from what media scholars call its "managed gaze."[45] Just as the various segments of the televised *Disneyland* were discrete, self-contained entities, so the "viewer" touring the park could not see Frontierland from Tomorrowland, or vice versa. Disney's theme park planners always used the older, cinematic analogy to describe the way in which the tourist was to be gently nudged from scene to scene (by a "wienie" or attractive object at the end of a vista) in a narrative sequence of edited takes. But in the movies that experience was continuous and unbroken; in Disneyland it was discontinuous and episodic, like watching TV in the privacy of one's own home—each ride a four- or five-minute segment, slotted in among snacks, trips to the rest room, and "commercials" in the form of the souvenir empo-

When Disney's *Davy Crockett* series was the rage on TV, the suburban-rustic style combined picture windows with electrified old-time gas lamps and rugged Early American accent pieces.

riums. "Disneyland . . . is a kind of TV set," writes the historian William Irwin Thompson, "for one flips from mediaeval castles to submarines and rockets as easily as one can move, in . . . Los Angeles, from the plaza of the Mexican Olvera Street . . . to the modern Civic Center."[46] If Main Street USA was a bore, Tomorrowland was just a magical step away. If history or fantasy cloyed, the food and the merchandise were very real. And the family car was in the parking lot, pointed toward the freeway, and ready to roll.

A Motorama-style
automobile ad,
staged in a TV
studio. The car is
motionless sculpture,
safe enough for
Mom to pilot.

Autoeroticism: America's Love Affair with the Car in the Television Age

*T*here's something wonderful, disquieting, and, in the end, embarrassing about America's automobiles of the 1950s: the lunkers, the dreamboats, the befinned, bechromed behemoths that lurked in the driveways of several million brand new ranch houses in the suburbs (because they wouldn't fit in the garage!). They were the kinds of cars, those bloated GMs, Fords, and Chryslers, that Danny Thomas and Ozzie and Harriet drove on TV. They were the kind that Jim Anderson taught Margaret how to drive, thus precipitating the only spat ever to mar the idyllic domesticity of *Father Knows Best*; the expensive standing set for the archetypal Anderson house had a blacktop driveway and attached garage right out in front, making the automobile a prominent part of the dramatic ensemble.[1] They were the kind of car that Ward Cleaver, "The Beaver's" sagacious Dad, parked every week at the curb in front of 211 Pine Street, Mayfield, USA (a suburb of Utopia). The situation comedies were always set in mythical places like Mayfield, part small town, part exotic postwar California subdivision. Perpetually sunny, easy and perfect, the new West Coast way of life soon became the American ideal. The people who lived there apparently thought nothing of driving twenty miles for a routine afternoon of shopping, either. "Their enormous automotive mobility and the decentralization of their shops and playgrounds have tended to make conventional city

Dream cars in the front row, production models behind, at the General Motors Design Center.

life obsolete," said *Life* of the trendsetting Californians on whom the TV families were based. And in prime time, the nation aspired to the condition of these golden, godlike creatures in their insolent chariots.[2]

Andrew Wyeth has a reasonable claim to be called America's first suburban painter: like the Andersons' Springfield and the Cleavers' Mayfield, his world is neither country nor city. But Wyeth's *Young America* of 1950 describes that environment through the image of a boy on a fancy new bike, with whitewall tires and a carrier on the rear fender. Streamers flow from the handlebars. A foxtail tethered to the front axle bobs above his head, a juvenile reprise of the Stars and Stripes that fluttered over six young Marines in Joe Rosenthal's famous World War II photograph of the flag raising on Iwo Jima. The painting is a sort of peacetime icon of security and abundance: unlike the teenagers of 1945, the boy of 1950 is safe and happy, doing what a kid ought to do. Yet there is something old-fashioned and not quite right about the boy on the bicycle, too. In real life, by 1952 or 1953 (if not before), there would have been new houses in the empty field behind him, and new cars in all the driveways, and he'd have been chauffeured to and from his Boy Scout meetings until he passed the driver's test. In real life in the suburbs, Mom and Dad would have cautioned him never to ride his bike along the edge of the highway for fear of being run down by a speeding car. Because it is carless, Wyeth's *Young America* seems sentimental, nostalgic, and false.[3]

It was the urbanist Lewis Mumford, addressing an international congress of city planners in 1957, who derided big American automobiles as killers—"fantastic and insolent chariots," he termed them—and predicted that "either the motor car will drive us all out of the cities or the cities will have to drive out the motor car." By 1957, however, the American family had already piled into the car and headed for Levittown or Southern California. Desi, Lucy, and the Mertzes from the apartment upstairs drove out to Hollywood during

Andrew Wyeth, *Young America*, 1950.

the 1954–55 TV season, and in 1956 *I Love Lucy* moved to Connecticut for the duration. Desi became a commuter; the Ricardo family built a barbecue, met the neighbors, and hobnobbed at the Country Club. Perhaps they were lured away from town by advertising that wrapped up family life, suburbia, and new cars in one neat and appealing package. A 1956 Chevrolet campaign made the case for the two-car family with a scene showing a barbecue in progress on an expansive lawn out in front of a double carport somewhere in exurban America: "Going our separate ways we've never been so close! The family with two cars gets twice as many chores completed, so there's more leisure to enjoy *together.*" General Motors, the company that made the Chevies, was the biggest advertiser of the decade. In 1955 alone, GM spent $162 million to persuade viewers, would-be suburbanites, and the rest of the nation to buy its cars. And in 1956 GM led the Top Ten Advertisers list again, nosing out Ford (number three) and Chrysler (a distant seventh).[4]

The GMs, Fords, and Chryslers of the 50s were the kinds of cars that drove foreigners to exasperated outbursts of envy, so baroque and, well, so *American* did they seem in their excesses of horsepower and gadgetry. Detroit had lobbied hard for passage of the Interstate Highway Act of 1956, but from the other side of the Atlantic the logic of building huge cars to fill up the freeways created to accommodate a growing volume of same seemed a little strained. In the tighter spaces of a Europe in the throes of persistent postwar shortages, the design critic Reyner Banham recalled, American cars looked "like space ships, or visitors from another planet or something." The intake scoop on the 1951 Cadillac was the supreme insult: the Caddy was *air conditioned* at a time when perhaps five buildings in the whole of Britain possessed such amenities. The design historian Bevis Hillier goes so far as to claim that English spies Maclean and Burgess were driven mad by Detroit, that they were propelled into the austere embrace of the Soviet KGB by the sheer garishness of the two-tone family cruiser with 285 horses under the hood. As Europe lay in ruins, the Yanks (who owned three-fourths of all the cars in the world) indulged themselves in a veritable orgy of Naugahyde and power steering. Quite right, what? Any decent chap might turn to espionage under such provocation. "Whilst the Russians had been developing 'Sputnik,'" wrote a disgusted Banham (before his conversion to heavy-duty glitz during an in-depth study of Los Angeles), "the Americans had been debauching themselves with tailfins."[5]

The 1958 model year that followed the launch of Sputnik was a disaster for the U.S. automotive industry. New-car sales dipped to their lowest levels since 1948. The Edsel bombed. The economy slid into a recession. Ike's ad men tried to persuade consumers to step on the gas: "You Auto Buy!" was the official slogan of the government's psychological offensive against unpatriotic, stay-at-home thrift. The White House seemed unsure as to whether the recession had hurt the car business or vice versa. But the Russian Sputnik made everybody queasy about fiddling with annual model changes, color charts, and cosmetic engineering while the enemy was investing in serious rock-etry. The contrast was all the more pointed in that the space rocket had been one of the most prominent motifs attached to the car by advertising. The Olds 88, for instance, was the "Rocket 88," always paired pictorially with a sleek missile zooming skyward overhead. In the early 50s, the car itself still had a dowdy streamlined shape, all curves and bulges, despite a bumper that resembled the intake duct of a jet-interceptor. But the "Futuramic" engine under the hood went from 135 horsepower in 1951 to 202 (a takeoff speed of 110 miles per hour) in 1955: the Olds fed a growing appetite for speed and per-formed like rocket long before it actually looked like one.[6]

One memorable advertisement for the Olds 88 even put Mr. and Mrs. America, hats and purses and all, astride a moon rocket, cartoon style. It wasn't entirely serious. Speed, rocket ships, and their inter-stellar passengers took on an aura of fantasy and fun. And there's a greedy innocence about the pleasure cars *cum* rockets brought to the postwar United States, too, an innocence wasted on censorious En-glish design critics. Rock 'n' roll lyrics caught the mood best, as in Jackie Brenston's "Rocket 88" of 1951 (an R&B song well on its way to rock) and Chuck Berry's 1955 hymn to speed and freedom and the thrill of the chase:

> As I was motivatin' over the hill
> I saw Maybellene in a Coup de Ville;
> A Cadillac a-rollin' on the open road,
> Nothin' will outrun my V-8 Ford.[7]

Berry was pursuing Maybellene down the highway of desire in an old Ford. Behind the wheel of a 1955 Ford, so the catchphrase went, "you become a new man." Buick ads—Buicks were often shown gliding among the planets like garish spacecraft—also strove to attach masculinity and sexual prowess to horsepower. Driving a new Buick, read one memorable line of copy, "makes you feel like the man you are." John Keats, who made a career out of savaging automotive hype in the 1950s, dismissed the wording as "just another way of saying we can't distinguish between illusion and reality, but that buying a Buick will create . . . the *illusion* that we *really are* what we *really are*." But a Ford, an Olds, or a Buick was as much daydream as no-money-down, easy-credit-terms dreamboat. If the cars were complex beyond all telling with their Dynaflow pushbutton transmissions, their power brakes, automatic windows, vacuum ashtrays, retractable roofs, and wraparound windshields, the feelings they aroused in driver/owners were straightforward: after the privations of the Depression, after the hardships and the shortages of a war with no new models, victorious Americans deserved nothing but the best.[8]

Within a year of the Japanese surrender, 12 million G.I.s had been sent home, every last one of them in search of a girl, a car, a new house, and—although they didn't know it just then—a TV set: the American Dream, what sociologists termed "the standard consumer package." In 1945, 200,000 new homes had been built nationwide; in 1950, 1,154,000. In 1945, outside of a few labs, there were no television sets in private hands; in 1950 alone, 7,500,000 were sold. In 1945, 70,000 cars rolled off the assembly line; in 1950, 6,665,000. Between 1945 and 1955, the number of registered motor vehicles doubled; in 1955, Detroit shipped 8,000,000 new automobiles to showrooms.[9] The good life rolled by on big, soft Goodyear tires. It was the car that fueled the new industrial prosperity, created the suburbs where new houses sprouted like dandelions after rain, and shaped the suburban lifestyle whose manners and mores were codified in the TV sitcoms

An Olds "Rocket 88" ad, circa 1950, borrowed for domestic use, in the form of a needlebook cover.

of the 1950s. The car was the new Conestoga wagon on the frontier of consumerism, a powerful instrument of change, a chariot of fiery desire.

Never one to avoid looking squarely at the human emotions invested in the detritus of popular culture, the novelist Stephen King recently turned his attention to the big American car in *Christine*. King's hero, a nerdy tract-house teenager of the 1980s, falls in love with a car—specifically, a red and white 1958 Plymouth Fury. "The new shape of motion! The forward look! Suddenly it's 1960!" hooted that year's TV ads. The bonds of affection possible between man and machine had been extolled earlier, of course. During the 1965–1966 season on NBC, the hapless Jerry Van Dyke found himself the owner of a 1929 auto that harbored the ghost of his late Mom, a feminized, gas-powered version of Mr. Ed.[10] *My Mother the Car* was a comedy (or so the network claimed), whereas *Christine* has sinister, even tragic overtones. So many human feelings have been grounded in the crimson innards of Christine that she becomes an animate being, capable of growing a new bumper at will or sprouting a shiny new grille. But she is also capable of rage and murder and, in a perversion of the symbiotic relationship between car and driver that inspired the designers of the 50s, the emotions of the machine become those of Arnie, her ostensible owner. The possessor is seduced, beguiled, and possessed by the aptly named blood-red Plymouth Fury.

Christine is fiction, but the facts of the car business in 1950s America more than justify the premise. In the 1920s the auto industry had been faced with a crisis: by 1926, according to reliable estimates, everyone who could afford a car already had one, and in 1927 production and sales declined for the first time. The answer was not Fordism—the durable, dependable, unchanging Model-T. No, the solution was Sloanism, or the annual style change named for Alfred P. Sloan, president of General Motors. The object of superficial changes in detail on a yearly basis, Sloan said, was "to create demand for new value and, so to speak, create a certain amount of dissatisfaction with past models as compared with the new one." In practice, then, a business once ruled by engineering took on the trappings of the dressmaker's salon. In the late 1950s, in an effort to appeal to female buyers, the design chief at General Motors actually hired a group of women to produce a fashion show of feminized models for the 1959 season, cars with the distinctive colors of a designer line, fur lap robes, built-in cases for cosmetics, and matching luggage. "Beauty is what sells the American car. And the person we're designing it for is the American woman," said his counterpart at Ford Motor. "It is the women who like colors. We've spent millions to make the floor covering like the carpet in their living rooms."[11]

When Sloanism began back in the 20s, the notion that a serviceable product could be rendered obsolete by appearance alone was transferred from the apparel of the upper class to the single most important industrial product made in America. With the help of the ad copywriter, status and symbolism became compelling reasons for buying a new car, even though the old, black Ford out in the yard still ran like a top. "The automobile tells us who we are and what we think we want to be," wrote Pierre Martineau, director of motivational research for the *Chicago Tribune* in the 1950s. "It is a portable symbol of our personality and our position, the clearest way we have of telling people of our exact position." So the purchaser of an automobile was no longer paying for a mere piece of machinery. He (and, increasingly, she) was buying a brand new life. High style. Sex. Social standing. A rocket to the moon. Dealers observed that members of minority groups, often denied the satisfactions of housing and other property commensurate with their incomes, always bought Cadillacs. "If you've earned it, why hesitate?" asked the commercials.[12]

At first, the ad men of the 1920s balked at selling durable goods on the basis of color and cut. Was the old washing machine no good simply because it wasn't Karnak Green? Was last year's kitchen range obsolete because it lacked the fashionable applied tracery of the 1927 edition? These ethical objections rapidly faded, however, beside the demonstrable results achieved by Sloan. General Motors adopted the annual overhaul in 1927 and the Chevrolet promptly overtook the Ford in sales for the first time. The advertising that moved the new models was evocative and suggestive. It catered to dreams. GM, for example, invented the two-car family: the man who could present the little woman with her own runabout stood to gain a stature unattainable by those déclassé types with one all-purpose buggy. Even Henry Ford finally joined the parade with a Model-A that came in colors. As the author E. B. White later noted in the pages of the *New Yorker*, "From reading the auto ads you would think that the primary function of the motor car in America was to carry its owner to a higher social stratum, and then into an exquisite delirium of high adventure." And a miasma of adventure, sexual and otherwise, did hang over the auto salesrooms of the later 1920s like a cloud of high-octane fumes. There were the opulent settings, the bon-ton hauteur, but there were also the legendary Jordan ads in which the roadster became a wild horse, the parkway the prairies of the untamed West, and the New Woman in the driver's seat a girl who was—ahem—just rarin' to go. Romance, speed, freedom, fantasy: they all came with the easy-payment coupon book.[13]

The car was always a "she," too, even after the old Tin Lizzie gave way to her more glamorous competitors. As William Faulkner once observed (and George Babbitt proved), "The American really loves nothing but his automobile." In 1939 and 1940 the marketing psychologist Ernest Dichter prepared an influential study entitled "Mistress versus Wife" for Plymouth, a new marque intent on finding out why customers picked a given brand and stuck with it. Dichter recommended using convertibles in Plymouth advertising because, although few conscientious husbands and fathers bought sporty models, most longed to drive one. The typical American male looked upon the convertible as a mistress; "The open car was the symbol of youth, freedom, and human dreams." The sedan—the wife—was sedate, practical, and boring. Hedging Plymouth's bets, Dichter urged development of a four-door hardtop, combining the best features of both. But new product design and serious motivational research among the Big Three were put on hold for the duration during World War II, as auto plants churned out steel helmets and aircraft engines and the styling departments, like GM's pioneering Art and Color Section, turned their attention to camouflage.[14]

Nonetheless, it cannot be said that the buying frenzy of the late 1940s, when things finally got back to normal in Detroit, had much to do with compensatory fantasy. Everybody needed basic transportation and everybody bought a car that looked not unlike the streamlined prototypes once displayed at the Century of Progress Exposition of 1933 and the New York World's Fair of 1939. Forerunners of the Las Vegas-style "Motoramas" of the 1950s, the world's fair auto shows of the 1930s had spotlighted "dream cars," models that offered more or less realistic glimpses of future improvements—all in the spirit of making the customer anticipate trading in the model he was still paying for. By today's standards the streamlined dream car was a dignified exercise in modernist design principles, à la Frank Lloyd Wright. Speed was discreetly expressed by thin bands of horizontal fluting applied in triadic clusters. Air was invited to flow smoothly over fluid surfaces that eddied and bulged like the derrière of a Vargas pinup painted on the nose of a streamlined B-24 bomber. If form could not be said to follow vehicular function with any real accuracy, form did help to define function. Auto bodies styled by Raymond Loewy, Buckminster Fuller, and other well-known streamliners of the period (Loewy, Russel Wright, and the major industrial designers were also in demand by advertisers as celebrity endorsers for classy products) intimated that the American automobile was a machine for zooming along toward a crisp, efficient, and thoroughly modern tomorrow.[15]

Many of the theoretical considerations that went into the design of automobiles also determined the shapes of trains, submarines, and airplanes. Thus it happened that Harley Earl, head of the Styling Section at General Motors and a former Hollywood customizer to the stars (he did the bodywork on one-of-a-kind jobs for Fatty Arbuckle and Tom Mix) made friends with an Air Force designer who was testing new fighter planes at Selfridge Field, near Detroit. Shortly before the end of the war, Earl and his styling team (Bill Mitchell, Frank Hershey, Art Ross) were allowed—from a distance of thirty feet, under tight security—to examine the twin-tailed Lockheed P-38 Lightning pursuit plane, with its paired Allison engines (built by GM), fuselages, and stabilizing tail fins. According to Earl, who recalled the event in a first-person article for the *Saturday Evening Post* in 1954, automotive history was made on the spot. "That viewing," he attested, "after the war ended, blossomed out in the Cadillac fishtail

The evolution of the Cadillac tail fin under Harley Earl.

fenders which subsequently spread through our cars and over much of the industry as well."[16]

Although aviation imagery had appeared on cars before—Studebakers and Fords of the 40s had propellerlike gizmos in front, revived in the grillwork of the 1950s; Loewy's 1949 Studebaker would sport engine pods, a prop, and a gun-turret rear window—the pleasing little winglet or hump mounted on the rear fender of the 1948 Cadillac revolutionized the auto business. A housing for the stoplights, it was the first, embryonic tail fin and it was applied to a body that had been roughed out before Pearl Harbor, under the old dispensation of rational, form-follows-function thinking. But subsequent Harley Earl models took their cue directly from the fin. The car became an armature on which to mount a whole panoply of expressive shapes. In time, the car transcended its prosaic function altogether and became a piece of figurative sculpture, a powerful work of art.

The role of the stylist was well understood by the car-buying public and generally appreciated. A *Look* magazine preview of the 1958 models, titled "The Battle of the Stylists," explained the size and shape of Detroit's latest in terms of a twelve-year struggle for supremacy among those who chose the imagery and calculated the proper detailing of the fins. But for all the competition and secrecy, the GMs, Fords, and Chryslers displayed certain common features. "Dramatically larger, broader and lower, our cars are festooned with chrome," *Look* announced. "They have almost as much glass as small houses!"[17] The most interesting feature of the preview was a three-page color foldout comparing the Big Three's tail assemblies in terms of loft, line, and decorative treatment. Function was not at issue. Form was paramount and the reader credited with an expert eye for fin profiles. It was important that, of the major marques, only the '58 Cadillac retained the fin as a radical design element. Design was important, the source of breathless suspense and an insider's pleasure in following the trajectory of a stylistic evolution. Yet *Look* also noted that a small body of critics ridiculed fins, and the stylists responsible for "the luxurious loungemobile," as wasteful or silly, pointing to the recent success of the ugly little Volkswagen, which never changed.

The nay-sayers had a point. By 1959 the Cadillac tail fin had acquired a life of its own: it towered three and one-half feet above the pavement and terminated in multiple taillights, nasty, fearsome red things, shaped like frozen bursts of flame from the afterburner of a jet engine. And as the back end rose, the front end strained forward. After 1953 all Cadillac bumpers were finished off with factory-fresh "gorp" (a.k.a. superfluous embellishment) in the form of "bombs" or "Dagmars" (so called after the reigning late-night TV bombshell with the single name)—protruding breasts that were utterly devoid of utility and impossible to repair after the most minor of collisions. Engineering-proud Chrysler, which had shamefacedly entered the tail-fin-and-chrome derby later than the other automakers, tried to justify the more excessive of its appendages, fore and aft, as being "based on aerodynamic principles [that] make a real contribution to the remarkable stability" of the 1959 models. But the competition made no such apologies for art. Lacking any modicum of functional justification, their added hunks of rubber and chrome existed simply to communicate. They were metaphors, analogs. And sold by analogy, the car of the 1950s—a chorus girl coming, a fighter plane going—was a semiotic anagram of considerable interest.[18]

As the design historian Thomas Hine has suggested, the doctrine of luxury for all—what he calls "populuxe," the postwar American Dream—helped to load down the car with an average of forty-four pounds of surplus chrome for the mid-line Detroit product of the late 50s. Whereas Harley Earl's finny 1948 Cadillac was considered a bit much for the average Joe, by 1955 all of its most gratuitous features were also available on the humble Chevy. The 1957 Cadillac Eldorado Brougham, at $13,074 uninflated bucks, was a mobile seraglio hitched to a dashboard with a built-in tissue box, a vanity case, a lipstick that harmonized with the paint job, and a set of four gold-finished drinking cups. Along with the usual power accessories, deep-pile upholstery, padded interiors, coil springs, and bargelike proportions, the car offered the trappings of kingly ease to a culture that also gave the world the mink-handled beer can opener, the gold-plated charge-a-plate, whiskey-flavored toothpaste (for the morning after), radar-equipped fishing rods, and hair color kits with names like Golden Apricot Delight and Champagne Beige. The cars themselves were the largest hunks of luxury around, but there were other automotive manifestations of the yen for the posh: the pseudo-aristocratic nomenclature attached to models like the "Eldorado," dripping with fevered fantasies of gold; the delicious array of car colors that suggested a lush infinity of choices. In *Lolita*, Vladimir Nabokov ridiculed the illusion of choice. Humbert, his hero, tries desperately to identify a pursuing vehicle on the basis of its particular shade of gray but finds it impossible to tell the difference between "Chrysler's Shell Gray, Chevrolet's Thistle Gray, Dodge's French Gray."[19]

In a 1953 survey of advanced paint-by-numbers kits, with row upon luscious row of color capsules, the design critic Eric Larrabee took note of a trend toward painting trays and wastebaskets and other household items instead of conventional pictures. Like cars adorned with gorp and gold-dipped cups, the kits betrayed a general hankering for decorated surfaces, added embellishment, and visual clutter, a kind of rococo sensibility also tapped by the glittery opulence of Morris Lapidus-designed tourist hotels in Miami, and by multicolored refrigerators "styled" after the prevailing shapes of cars (the classier the appliance, the more closely the decorative metal emblem affixed to the door resembled the familiar Cadillac logo). The refrigerator, in fact, was the closest thing going to the spate of two- and three-toned beauties that George Romney of American Motors dismissed as "Dinosaurs in the Driveway" and that the rest of America bought almost before the latest models had been unshrouded with blood-stirring fanfare every September.[20]

In Harley Earl's informed opinion, fins and Dagmars and the other stuff caught on because they gave customers "an extra receipt for their money in the form of a visible prestige marking for an expensive car." Or, as Thorstein Veblen might have put it, the tail fin was the ultimate emblem of conspicuous consumption. "The cars of the 50s were like nothing that ever came off the assembly line before or since," remarks a sympathetic Detroit-watcher. "They were the stuff of dreams. And the dream was possible for everyone." Humbert Humbert. Chuck Berry. The family up the block, or on TV.[21]

The content of that classless American Dream was not something that was examined closely at the time, a time when Jim and Margaret

The open-plan kitchen of the 1950s encouraged both movement and visual stimulation. Note the liberal application of automotive "gorp" to the large refrigerator and freezer in the form of handles, lettering, and meaningless strips of chrome.

Anderson occupied twin beds and wore visible foundation garments beneath their TV nightwear. Nor has the subject proved compelling to cultural commentators in the thirty-odd years since the Edsel debacle did in the big car for good. In fact, the combination of sex (the bumpers and radiators: one Chrysler exec said he wanted the front of the dowdy Dodge to project the image of "Marilyn Monroe as a housewife") and aggressive, militaristic violence (those fins, with rows of fire-spitting taillights) hints at certain repellent aspects of the American psyche that neither the women's movement nor recent outpourings of national repentance for Vietnam have done much to alter.[22] Sex and violence for all, served up in a flashy chromium package: the Cleavers and the Andersons of the 1950s led secret lives, infinitely richer than anything Walter Mitty might have imagined. And their cars, the ones with the rocket launchers and the 44-D cups, were first and foremost *family* cars. The nuclear family of the Eisenhower years apparently came by that title honestly.

If Harley Earl, Virgil Exner of Chrysler, and George Walker of Ford ("The Cellini of Chrome") could not name the national neurosis to which auto styling catered, they understood the outward symptoms manifested in booming sales figures. In 1927 the industry had first turned to the designer when profits fell. During the first week of August of 1953 economists determined that the postwar sellers' market for cars had finally bottomed out. *Fortune,* in the midst of a self-congratulatory study of the booming marketplace, sounded the first warnings that summer, despite the fact that 1953 had been the second-biggest car year in history. Some dealers were shipping new stock to used-car lots on the sly, the editors reported, and unless families could be persuaded to buy second and third vehicles, a major slump might be in the offing. What terrified those who saw signs of softness in Detroit was recent history. The auto industry had led the nation into the Depression in 1929. Could it happen all over again? Or would gorp make the difference this time around? Would buyers go for hardtops, "extra chrome work, . . . and bumpers to protect your bumpers?"[23]

For the second time, the Big Three called upon the stylists to bail out Detroit with a campaign of "dynamic obsolescence." Fins

Front-end "gorp" on the 1958 Cadillac.

spawned finlets, Dagmars multiplied, and the auto-buying frenzy of the 1950s commenced, as if on signal. In 1955 new car sales totaled $65 billion, or 20 percent of the Gross National Product. While the figures showed that the public was moved largely (and expensively) by aesthetic and imagistic considerations, and General Motors became the first corporation to earn a billion dollars in a single year by catering to such appetites, traditional tastemakers and intellectuals refused to believe the evidence. "What the motivation researchers failed to tell their clients," wrote the semanticist S. I. Hayakawa, "is that only the psychotic and the gravely neurotic act out their . . . fantasies. The trouble with selling symbolic gratification via such expensive items as [automobiles] . . . is the competition offered by much cheaper forms, such as *Playboy* . . ., *Astounding Science Fiction* . . ., and television." But for a decade or so—the lifespan of the two-and-a-half-ton candy-pink steel space rocket with sexual accessories—Hayakawa and his fellow scoffers were dead wrong. Americans were willing, indeed eager, to spend huge amounts of money on objects that were symbols of their desires, reflections of themselves, expressions of their fantasies. On artifacts that succeeded or failed on the basis of appearance. On wheeled statuary, or what Eric Larrabee and David Riesman called "wildly imaginative metallic sculpture." On what can only be described as works of popular art in which the nation freely invested a fifth of the GNP.[24]

In the story of Detroit in the 1950s there is an element of aesthetic self-consciousness, a tacit challenge to the self-righteous rigidity of modernist dogma, and the first stirrings of a postmodern sensibility. Consider, for example, the GM Motorama. An offshoot of the old world's fair car exhibits and the annual luncheons Sloan held for business pals at New York's Waldorf-Astoria during National Auto Show Week, the first full-dress Motorama was presented by Harley Earl in the hotel ballroom there in 1949. Billed as "Transportation Unlimited," the event set off the most evocative of the company's "dream cars" with a thirty-five-minute musical extravaganza. Dancers pranced; singers warbled; an MC extolled the virtues of the GM line. Showgirls pointed at the new Cadillac fin. Mounted on turntables, the autos pirouetted beneath colored spotlights. Until 1961 the Motorama (there were eight of them) served as GM's most effective marketing tool and the scourge of the competition. As Autorama, it traveled from New York to the hinterlands, always greeted by enormous crowds and wild excitement. In 1949–50 the big attraction was a Buick Le Sabre XF-8 with sensors that raised the convertible roof in case of rain and the world's first wraparound windshield. In 1954 Motorama introduced Earl's never-to-be-built Firebird, a literal translation of a new fighter jet. But performance and plausibility were not the issues that kept the crowds coming.[25]

The Motorama was a show, an exhibition, a flashier version of a New York art opening on Madison Avenue, the first of the multimedia happenings.[26] As for the cars, people came to look at them in a museumlike environment, not to drive them or see them being driven (many of the non-production models didn't have motors). They were

The latest General Motors models on display at "Motorama"—the Waldorf Astoria Hotel, New York City, January 1950.

displayed on revolving pedestals which moved not to suggest the open road but to facilitate a minute inspection of a three-dimensional form from every angle. If the critics Clement Greenberg and Harold Rosenberg had their Jackson Pollocks to look at—frozen action; paintings rich in dark, personal meaning—the rest of America (the 2 million who attended every GM show, at any rate) had Motorama, the art of Neal Cassidy and Jack Kerouac: cars that never moved, two-toned chromium-plated statuary larded with primal symbols of war and lust. A parody of the pretensions of American high culture,

Motorama answered extravagant claims for art with outright extravagance, claims for hidden meaning with overt nods to jets and Jane Russell.

The notion of car as work of art was reinforced in other subtle ways and in other media. The automakers were the TV networks' biggest sponsors. In television ads integrated into variety shows ("Drive your Chev-ro-lay, through the USA!" warbled Dinah Shore. "America's the greatest land of all!"), it was often most practical to present an on-stage Motorama in miniature, with gesticulating models and twirling pedestals. A change from the hard-sell formula of radio ads, TV pitches for cars gained stature from their close association with programming, stars, and an artistic ambience. Julia Meade, Lincoln's elegant spokeswoman, appeared in the Motorama format in weekly spots on the Ed Sullivan show, for instance, wearing evening dress, describing cars in measured tones, and running her manicured hands over the upholstery. Singer Pat Boone's standard Chevrolet commercials, filmed on the set of the ABC *Chevy Showroom*, were clearly aimed at a younger crowd but opened with a comparable studio shot of a static vehicle bathed in spotlights. Reviewing the decorative motifs peculiar to advertising of the 1950s, Bevis Hillier has noted the regular use of a picture frame to transfer the importance and prestige attached to a work of art to whatever turned up within its perimeter. The Motorama shot—the car-as-sculpture-on-a-pedestal scene—served the same function on television and, eventually, in magazine ads for Lincoln, too. An establishing shot, it was usually followed by a quick cut to film footage displaying the car in motion, almost as an afterthought, or guilty admission that the work of art was also a means of taking Junior to the orthodontist.[27]

Julia Meade was not a typical suburban Mom, either. She was as classy as a Lincoln, as tastefully turned out as any diva on Sullivan's guest list. And Lincoln made her a celebrity, if not a star, the object of intense viewer interest. In 1953 a *Look* profile disclosed her behind-the-scenes aspirations to a Hollywood contract, her years of study at Yale's drama school, and even her annual salary for walk-ons and commercials ($16,000).[28] Meade was also noteworthy as the first example of a TV personality wholly identified with a single product;

Top: The classy car ad, laden with prestige and high-art overtones: Julia Meade, wearing evening dress, pitches Lincolns and Mercuries on Ed Sullivan's Sunday night show. *Bottom:* Manicured fingers caress the luxurious upholstery.

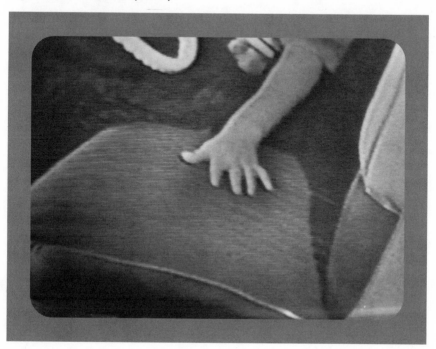

A studio shot like this one was followed by action film of the car on the open road. This amounted to a guilty admission that cars actually moved.

Betty Furness's association with Westinghouse products and James Mason's soap testimonials on *Lux Video Theater* would come later. But her greatest claim to fame was her stately presence behind the wheel. It is noteworthy that, in Julia Meade's segments for Ed Sullivan, location footage of cars rolling down a new California freeway or a suburban cul-de-sac succeeds in making motion virtually motionless. Cars never bob or weave. They never start or stop with visible effort. Only the changing landscape convinces the viewer that Meade and her mink stole are actually speeding toward the Beverly Hills Hotel or some other tasteful destination for the end of the commercial. In part, this technique appeals to a strong customer preference for the heavy, "mushy" car that denies any kinship with the surface beneath it. In part, the gliding motion refers to aerodynamics. The car seems to be a plane, liberated from earthly potholes and sharp corners. But the motionless motion demonstrated was also the aesthetic ideal embraced by the stylists who created the American car.

There were several kinds of TV car commercials on the air in the 50s: the Motorama type; the abbreviated domestic drama (of which more later); the pseudo-documentary; the ersatz "lecture" by an expert (often Truman Bradley, the scholarly-looking host of *Science Fiction Theatre*). What all these genres have in common is an obsession with design, and specifically with a set of artistic principles the audience is presumed to understand and appreciate. One of Truman Bradley's outings, a documentary-format ad for the 1956 Chrysler line, contains a sequence in which the driver stops at a suburban golf course and a supermarket. In both venues, ordinary citizens burst into spontaneous tributes to Chrysler styling. It has "The Forward Look of Motion—even when it's stopped!" exclaim the duffers, while the bag boy at the store notices that the shape of the rear deck derives from the aft end of a jet plane. But even more to the point is the automotive chalktalk invented by Ford Motor. Julia Meade's husband, a professional illustrator, occasionally appeared with her on the

A two-toned Chrysler: "The Forward Look of Motion" in suburbia.

Sullivan show, drawing pertinent details of Lincolns and Mercuries. The series culminated in the illustrated lectures by Professor Tom Foldes, "artist, author, educator," that sold the 1955 Ford.

In these ads, Foldes shows precisely how draftsmanship—design—can make a static form move. Speed lines (the old technique of streamlining) are additive and superficial, he contends, whereas good contemporary design bends the form as a whole toward the image the stylist wishes to create. "The expression of motion though design is the goal of all automotive styling," he says: this means visor headlights surging forward, a raked-back tail assembly, and a highlight running from bumper to bumper in a smooth, unbroken arc. "When the design of a car expresses its functions forcefully and imaginatively, we derive more pleasure from owning and driving it," Professor Foldes concludes.[29] The Ford commercial is a stunning fragment of 50s television. For one thing, it is long by today's standards. Network

The TV styling lecture by Professor Tom Foldes explained the finer points of automotive design.

time was cheaper in 1955 and the audience still had a reasonable attention span. But even given a cultural willingness to stay on the couch, Foldes's presentation is a remarkably detailed and sophisticated slice of Art Appreciation 101, with its distinction between superficial embellishment and form, and its assumption that genuine aesthetic pleasure is accessible to everyone—and available in the form of mass-market, manufactured goods. Detroit knew that it was selling sculpture and hired experts, like Professor Foldes, to distinguish good art from bad.

This kind of pop-cultural artiness infuriated real sophisticates. While the Abstract Expressionists, by and large, ignored the whole vulgar spectacle and bought foreign cars (though Pollock met his death in an Olds V-8 in 1956), pioneers of industrial design like Raymond Loewy fulminated against the so-called stylists and their "Forward Looks." In 1955, shortly after his dismissal from Studebaker, where he had been lead designer since 1938, Loewy blasted the industry in an address to the Society of Automotive Engineers. Widely quoted and reprinted, his jeremiad detailed the case against Detroit, whose latest models Loewy called "jukeboxes on wheels," aesthetic aberrations that masked the workings of the machine beneath layers of tinsel and cheap "flash." Much of what Loewy said made ethical sense. The weight of increased ornament and big, smooth autobodies had led to over-horsed engines, rising costs, ruined roadways, and huge fuel bills (although the critic failed to ask why Americans still loved their big cars despite such drawbacks). But Loewy's real objection to the 1955 models was their shape. "Is it responsible," he asked, "to camouflage one of America's most remarkable machines as a piece of gaudy merchandise? Form, which should be the cleancut expression of mechanical excellence has become sensuous and organic."[30]

Designers like Loewy hated stylists: the very term was a profanity that smacked of crazed whimsicality, of superficial facelifts, of tinkering with decor and the fripperies of fashion while neglecting the deep-down, permanent beauty of art. Henry Dreyfuss, designer of the standard black handset telephone and General Electric's clean-lined 1930s refrigerators, condemned the artificial obsolescence created by stylists of the 50s as manipulative and wrong because it worked by "embarrassing people into buying." Automotive styling was a special case, however, because cars were so costly and so vital to the nation's economic well-being. "The engineer has had to take second place to the 'designer' and the market researcher," Eric Larrabee sputtered in his reprise of the 1955 models, "while the auto itself has come more and more to conceal its ancestry in surface transport and to engross a panoply of hitherto unrelated images—of a living room, a jet plane, or even (in certain hard-top models) a bathroom." "Never has it been so easy to identify a make or model, and never has it been so hard to see the basic structure of a car," fumed *Industrial Design* when confronted with the same crop of Detroit iron. "In defense of [the] riot of color one can say that the '55 automobiles look very much like what they really are—not necessities of life but expensive toys."[31]

When Detroit replaced designers with stylists, the automobile changed in a fundamental way. It became a "new entity," wrote Larrabee, "which would embody impermanence, escape, mobility. . . . There was no prototype for this kind of design." It lost its machine-like properties, its own reality. The principle was tacitly accepted that nobody really knew what a car looked like any more, either, so it could assume virtually any form that signified speed, modernity, and a ponderous luxury. The conflicting desires for bulk and for speed gave the automobile an increasingly neurotic flavor as the decade wore on. The messages became unclear. The sensory systems overloaded. And like any business dependent on style and mass taste, the auto industry ran the risk of consumer satiety, boredom, or disgust. Fashions in merchandise change. In the aftermath of the ascetic Sputnik, the sensuous and organic shapes that had seemed so enticing in 1955 looked pretty silly on the 1958 Edsel.[32]

That single phrase—"sensuous and organic"—had revealed Loewy to be a design puritan, morally superior to the herd, the monklike disciple of a Modern Movement which had tried, without much success, to convince people to live in pure white cubes and commune with pure geometry. Although corporate America occasionally succumbed to modernist austerity in the interests of economy and an efficient image, Americans resisted the incursions of modernism into their private lives, into the places where their hopes, desires, and fantasies grew lush, convoluted, and profoundly sensuous. They liked the new, efficient rectangular dinnerware best when it was enlivened with flowers or boomerangs of turquoise and gold; the squared-off ranch house on a slab when it was warmed up with Early American accents (Ozzie and Harriet had an American eagle emblazoned on their TV fireplace); portable TV sets with two-toned cases; a car when it came with a built-in vanity, a matching lipstick, Dagmars, and fins. They liked complexity, lots of stuff, expansive scale, everything but the kitchen sink. In a backhanded way, their taste was closer to Jackson Pollock's than to Raymond Loewy's. And the car was its most public expression.

Detroit, or its hirelings in the ad game, appreciated the humor of the "loaded" model: the multicolor bus, a home on wheels, with extra exterior detailing and every interior amenity—everything *but* the kitchen sink. That sink is the visual punchline of a drawn-out commercial for the 1955 Dodge station wagon that takes the form of a situation comedy, an episode of Danny Thomas's *Make Room for Daddy*. The family finds itself in the woods for the day, although Daddy would prefer to be back in town showing off the new car to the neighbors. The children, Rusty and Terry, pick wildflowers and discourse precociously on the new styling features of the Dodge. Finally, Daddy decides to load up on flowers, too, to bring the excursion to an end, and winds up with an armful of poison sumac. But he has the last laugh as he opens the back of the Dodge and out pops a big, double sink.

Even when the Danny Thomas show is not the point of reference, the car is still shown in a familial context, closely related to the conventions of the sitcom. A 1954 commercial titled "Family Argument" pits the typical American Dad—bluff, stubborn, smarter than he lets on; a Stu Irwin type and a veteran of earlier campaigns for wall-to-wall carpeting and a fur stole—against the wiles of his nearest and dearest. The family gathers for a council of war around the console-model TV in a suburban living room. Junior is adamant, Sis seductive, and even Martha (solid old Martha) is convinced that the time has come to put "Jezebel" out to pasture. So they all go, en masse, to pick out an automobile that becomes part of the family unit, a statement about its status and its collective self-image. And it is tacitly assumed in the ad that everybody will drive the car, a factor which may contribute to the babble of symbolism loaded on its rapidly swelling chassis.

The Thunderbird and the Maverick achieved later success at smaller scale as *personal* vehicles, like the British or Italian sports car, whereas throughout the 50s, the standard American car was a family car. Foreign models became chic in the mid-50s, as second cars. Before the decade was over, a million small autos had been imported and sold, many to successful men in gray flannel suits who parked them at suburban train stations by day. Or to readers of the new *Playboy* (founded in 1953), a magazine obsessively concerned with jazz, hi-fi sets, and hot sports cars.[33] But American cars eschewed both the playboy image and any exclusive sense of identification with men. Rarely, in fact, do stereotypical heads of households drive cars in commercials, and when they do, Dad shares time with Mom. Putting a woman behind the wheel—her usual motoring outfit, which consisted of a hat with a veil, gloves, and a crisp print shirtwaist, was exactly what June Cleaver wore to PTA meetings—justified the purchase of power steering and power brakes. "I drive just as well as my husband in our new Olds," chirps the perky housewife in a make-believe TV interview with "Roving Reporter" Bob Lamont. "You certainly look lovely after a whole day of driving around town," he coos. The perennial hat, generally worn in a convertible model, was there to show that the new car dispensed with every hazard, every inconvenience, including the errant breezes.

In an otherwise damning look at the American car, the British social commentator Ashley Montagu did concede that the big auto "compensates for the weakness of the driver while endowing him with power that he can obtain in no other way." But the most graphic expression of this automotive omnipotence was not the King of the Road ensconced behind the wheel. It was the image of the little woman in her hat and gloves, with one dainty foot on the accelerator and a finger on the push-button transmission, bound for the shopping center, or parallel parking like a man with the help of power steering. Jokes about women drivers became a staple of television comedy as

Bob Lamont conducts a fake interview with a typical suburban housewife on the rigors of driving.

housewives were forced to commute long distances themselves to run the family errands. Detroit dimly sensed that women played a major role in the purchase of their products. GM's 1954 Motorama included kitchen appliances as a sop to feminine interests, for example, and all the automakers implied that color and design changes catered to the ladies' eye for fashion. No wonder the car was a "she," especially when contempt for the annual model change was on the agenda. John Keats compared the "sow-fat" American passenger car of the 1950s car to a nagging wife who, "with all the subtlety of a madam affecting a lorgnette, . . . put tail fins on her overblown bustle, . . . lifted her face—expensively—from year to year; incessantly demanded new gauds and different colors, developed ever more costly eating habits, [and] threatened to break the family budget."[34]

Teenagers, whose schemes for extracting the keys to the Plymouth Fury from Dad's pocket formed a staple of sitcom humor, rarely appeared in advertising because, it was thought, they neither bought new cars nor (except for Sis) determined the family's buying preferences. There were singular exceptions, however. Chevrolet's 1955 V-8 was the first domestic model pitched as a "hot car" to a youth market made up of boys with hot dates.[35] Pat Boone, the wholesome, all-American alternative to Elvis Presley, did a weekly TV show for Chevy in the late 50s, when the automotive slump had forced complacent carmakers to look for new buyers. Teens with afterschool jobs and the college crowd were worthy targets, as Volkswagen had proven with its witty, deglamorized emphasis on economy and reverse snobbery. And in time, research proved that adolescents were important family trendsetters, with a relish for the slightly unconventional. Given half a chance, any California teenager would chop and stretch an old prewar Ford until it looked like new Valiant with a hangover. In *Rebel Without a Cause* (1955), set in Los Angeles, James Dean drove a customized 1949 Merc, "channeled" almost beyond recognition. A souped-up version of adult tastes for gold, plush, and sparkles, the aesthetic of the rebel ran to chrome, furry dice, leather, and candy-coated paint jobs. Dean died in a little car, a foreign car, a month before the movie opened. It was a silver Porsche Type 500 Spyder, customized with racing stripes and the words "Little Bastard" painted on the rear end.[36]

The Dean smashup might have served as a warning against putting too much stock in kids' fascination with little cars. Instead, the wreck became a teen icon that portended the eventual smashup of the family gas-guzzler. But the big car did not succumb to its own wastefulness, as might have been expected. No. It was a shift in taste and aesthetic judgment—the perception that American cars were ugly—that did in the loaded model with fins in 1958. The industrial designer Carl Sundberg quipped that "panning the American automobile has become a pastime that threatens to replace baseball as a national sport." George Romney of American Motors, which was tinkering with smaller cars, could not "recall a period when . . . car design was subjected to as much lampooning in newspaper and magazine cartoons." The ugliest of the lot was the 1958-model Edsel, unveiled on September 4, 1957, after an unprecedented media blitz. Rumor had it that Ford spent $10 million on "tease" advertising for its first all-new car of the postwar era. There were planted "news" stories designed to whip up interest, too. The sociologist David Wallace, director of market research for the Edsel campaign, let the *New Yorker* publish his thirteen-month correspondence with poet Marianne Moore in aid of a suitable moniker (she suggested "Mongoose" or "Pastelogram"; the company eventually named the vehicle after the founder's son). Three million gawkers turned up at Ford showrooms all across America on opening day and 6,500 cars were sold. And then the ridicule began. Car thieves wouldn't steal one, they said. The distinctive oval grille looked like an egg, a toilet seat, an unmentionable portion of the female anatomy. The Edsel looked like an Olds sucking a lemon.[37]

It *was* ugly. Or it failed to communicate much of the "personality" Wallace had endeavored to attach to the design through consorting with poets: brash, ambitious, highly visible. Or, perhaps, those were the very qualities that had begun to offend the discriminating eye in the fall of 1957, when the Edsel and the sack dress were both greeted with hoots of derision. In Wallace's mind, the Edsel was the ultimate family car, neither masculine nor feminine, "the smart car for the . . . professional family on its way up." The car that "Looks Expensive But It Isn't," in the words of a slogan that baldly acknowledged the importance of status seeking. But by seeking to appeal to everybody, in a showy flourish of chromium ovals, the Edsel satisfied no one in particular. Teenage girls adored Elvis and the sack dress and boys in VWs, the sports car became the hallmark of youth and freedom, but the Edsel was just a blob of colored steel that added little panache to a trip to the supermarket. It was dull and ugly.[38]

The era of the family car was over, and its heyday is still a puzzlement. But it seems to have stood for family, house, and aspirations, all at the same time, with its welter of additive features. In contrast to the personal vehicle that came to replace it, the big multipurpose car pointed to a moment of real communal sensibility and a concern for making public statements about one's private life. Thanks to Maidenform bras, women looked a lot like the cars they tooled around suburbia in, and so did the penile rockets being tested by Chuck Yaeger and America's future astronauts—two sets of gender markers for every family car. His 'n' hers. Male and female, sensuality and violence, domesticity and high adventure, entertainment and economics, waste and technological efficiency all came together in blatant, unprecedented, and highly original configurations in gas-powered symbols that were the objects of minute scrutiny. The average American had never taken a greater interest in how *anything* looked, and why. In how it made the people who owned it and used it feel, and those who only watched it from the curb.

Or saw it on TV. When Elvis appeared on Ed Sullivan's show for the third time, in January of 1957, he thanked his fans profusely for the cache of birthday and Christmas gifts he'd recently received and joked that he'd like to have given each one of them a new Lincoln in return, "but they wouldn't sell us that many." The remark was a graceful nod to Sullivan and his longtime sponsor. But there was more to it than that. Cars and their imagery, the display of the car, and the act of buying an automobile (and then giving it away, sometimes) had an abiding significance for the young King of rock 'n' roll. His "old" car, according to a 1956 article in *Life*, had been a Lincoln, fresh from the assembly line. He drove it for three weeks, parked it on a Miami street, and came back to find the pastel paint job covered with messages scrawled in lipstick by teenage girls. So Presley traded the dirty car in on a Continental Mark II and the Lincoln ended its days in the front window of the dealer's showroom, still encrusted with love notes.[39] Earlier that year, at age 21, he had already bought three Cadillacs—a canary yellow one, a convertible in pink and black to match his current wardrobe, and an all-white Eldorado—and a new tract house for his parents; the acquisitions attested to his success in a highly specific way, given the aspirations of families everywhere for a seven-room suburban ranchhouse and a big, new car. Despite the obvious prestige of Julia Meade's Lincolns, the Cadillac was the big-car paradigm, the pinnacle of luxury and "visible prestige marking" to which all the others feebly aspired. The boy who bought a Cadillac, or three of 'em, had made it in terms that respectable American mothers and fathers and their offspring could understand.

Elvis Presley wanted class from his pink dream Cadillac.

The number of Cadillacs that stood in the Presley driveway at any given moment in 1956 was difficult to ascertain. Some counted four, from which fans surreptitiously harvested the dust. Others thought they saw five, plus the Continental. One of the only times Elvis did anything impolite or less than respectable in his very public private life of 1950s stardom was a scuffle with a Memphis service station manager who told him to move his $10,000 Caddy because a crowd collected when the singer stopped for gas. Edd Hopper, the irate gas jockey, emerged from the fracas with a $25 fine and a black eye. It wasn't smart to mess with Elvis Presley's cars. They drew crowds wherever he went, but they meant something personal and private to him. On September 3, 1956, after he signed his record contract with RCA and made his debut appearances on network TV, the first thing Elvis bought with his newfound wealth was a pink Cadillac.[40] Back at Sun Records, a year earlier, he had recorded a song about a poor country boy with an upwardly mobile girlfriend. Like Chuck Berry's Maybellene, observes the cultural historian Warren Belasco, Elvis's girl in "Baby, Let's Play House" is in the process of running away. Maybellene drives a Cadillac Coupe de Ville. Presley's "Baby" is making her escape in a pink Cadillac, just like the one he would shortly buy. Women and cars were both elusive prizes, just beyond the grasp of a singer who drove a truck for a living. The pink Cadillac is a blatant, look-at-me symbol of having made it. It is also distinctly feminine, a love object, a sign of a ravishing desire to succeed, in the most conventional of ways. Elvis had lots of cars, and they came in outlandish colors, but numbers and colors were all that distinguished the quality of his longing from anybody else's. This wasn't life in the fast lane, either. Gladys Presley didn't drive, so the candy-pink Fleetwood sedan he bought for his mother with his first big paycheck sat in the driveway, like a car on a pedestal in a TV ad, going nowhere in fact, but bound for dreamland nonetheless. A two-tone love trinket with white sidewall tires. A testimonial to love and sex, money and home—and family. A beautiful statue. A monument to the tragedy of dreams come true.[41]

Elvis in 1956, his long hair barely
held in check under a layer of oil.

When Elvis Cut His Hair:
The Meaning of Mobility

*I*n the spring of 1958 word reached the nation's newspapers that Elvis Presley had cut his hair—twice in the past week, a little shorter each time. Known as much for his rococo pompadour as for his pelvic pulsations and rock 'n' roll music, the 23-year-old singer was apparently trying to ease his way gently into the standard G.I. buzz cut. For early on the morning of March 24, a Monday, accompanied by his parents, a crowd of weeping teenage girls, and his manager (who passed out balloons inscribed with the title of the inductee's upcoming film), Elvis braved a drizzling rain to report to Local Draft Board 86 in Memphis, Tennessee. Along with eleven other potential privates, he took the oath and left for Fort Chaffee, Arkansas, and a rendezvous with an Army barber. Although the sideburns of the young man bearing serial number U.S. 53310761 had mostly vanished already, there was enough coal-black hair left in his modified crew cut to elicit spirited bidding for the clippings.[1]

Back in '58, teen legend had it that Elvis actually tooled up to his Army physical in a great big Cadillac convertible, with a Las Vegas showgirl snuggled up beside him, his ducktail rippling luxuriantly and defiantly in the breeze. But later rock critics and historians view the rainy morning of Elvis Presley's induction as the beginning of the end. Playing Delilah to young Presley's Samson, the Pentagon cut off his hair and thus delivered him up to the Philistines. "Military con-

Elvis gets an Army haircut at Fort Chaffee, Arkansas. "Hair today, gone tomorrow," quipped the star.

scription tamed and revealed him for the dumb lackey he always was in the first place," Lester Bangs argued in 1977. The day of his Army haircut—the clippers were wielded by James Peterson as a *Life* photographer looked on—was also the day *real* rock 'n' roll died.[2] By the time Elvis finished his tour of duty in Germany in 1960, he had lost his edge. He came back vowing never to let the famous sideburns grow out again. And he made his first public appearance in a tux on Frank Sinatra's TV special, singing sedate duets with that middle-aged idol of the World War II generation. Many critics probably agreed with the *New York Times* pundit who called Presley's "recent liberation" from the Army to co-star with Sinatra "one of the most irritating events since the invention of itching powder." But most of them had precious little to say about the music. The hot news was that Elvis's hair now stayed demurely in place when he sang.[3]

The old Elvis had a head of hair that made decent men cringe and maidens yowl: it flopped and fluttered and fell across his face, requiring constant adjustment. Back at Humes High in Memphis, rumor had it that he went to a ladies' beauty parlor, that he had a permanent wave. In 1954 Elvis was almost blond. A year later his locks were a smoky brown and getting darker by the week. There was something perverse about boys who fussed with their hairdos like girls, although the young Elvis Presley was by no means the first teenager to seize on a hirsute symbol for generational rebellion in the Eisenhower years, when baldness stood for presidential wisdom and authority. Unorthodox styles with sculptural ducktails (known in less elegant circles as the "duck's ass," or DA cut) were a sign of spring in the high school set in the mid-50s.[4] The names varied from region to region. Brooklyn's "Cavalier" became a "Princeton" in the Pacific Northwest. But the use of wave-set lotions and intricate sectioning and layering were universal. Neighborhood barbers charged an average of 25¢ extra for the time and the aggravation involved, if they consented to do DA's at all. Tints and permanents were often administered furtively at home, by a helpful girlfriend.

It was tempting to read a deeper significance into this particular form of boyish vanity during a period in which Audrey Hepburn's short, gamin hairdo amounted to a national craze. With their poodle cuts and Italian boy looks, girls were appropriating manly prerogatives of grooming while robust males were spending more time and money on their long, wavy hair (which required frequent applications of "control wax") than their dates or their mothers did.[5] Was this tonsorial androgyny a sign of social decadence, of some awful moral lapse? Or was hair simply the last frontier between carefree youth and sober maturity?

A judge in Tacoma, Washington, sentenced a young offender with sideburns and a crown of curls to ten days in jail or "a man's haircut." Respectable professional men on Madison Avenue wore short crew cuts with their gray flannel suits. And Army regulations expressly forbade "extreme civilian haircuts [of the] 'Hollywood Ducktail' type." Grownups and organization men conformed to certain rigid stylistic norms: they were, in the parlance of the sociologist David Riesman, "outer-directed." But in teenagers of both sexes, the protest against the inevitable coming of age was liable to go straight to one's head. Some high school girls showed their devotion to Elvis in 1957, as discussion of his draft status turned serious, by getting haircuts just like his, "slicked back with a lank hank over the forehead and a grippable tuft in front of each ear." And even before Elvis came on the scene, wrote correspondent Harrison Salisbury from Moscow that same year, rebellious Soviet teens (who had listened to bootlegged Sinatra records until Presley tunes began to circulate on used X-ray plates) showed their disdain for gray Russian conformity by wearing sideburns and DA's.[6]

A survey of the most popular men's haircuts of 1957 noted a general preference for close-cropped styles based on the standard G.I. clip. In older men, the crew cut (also known as the "Ivy League") reflected a certain nostalgia for a lost youth. Parted and brushed, the inch-long variant worn on Madison Avenue amounted to a mark of membership in a professional caste. But new, longer looks, imported from the Continent, had a theatrical panache thought appropriate for those in the entertainment industry. Barbers had taken to calling the old DA an *"Elvis, . . .* all hair and a mile high, hanging over the temples, deliberately, and with a long slashing sideburn"—but it was still strictly for kids. Boys bound for the service were urged to try a transitional "post-Elvis" with "normal" sideburns to lessen the pain of the inevitable shearing.[7]

Elvis's own hair was transgressive in a particular way, however. Normal kids fiddled endlessly with their "dos," sculpting each glistening, pomaded lock into place. Presley's hair was almost never neatly coiffed. The first barrage of Elvis Presley photos, published by the picture weeklies in the summer of 1956 after a series of television appearances made him a household name among adults who didn't play 45 records, used his disheveled hair as a kind of visual signature. The Elvis wannabes and rivals pictured alongside him have perfect, monolithic DA's while his hair is invariably disarranged by performance or by the sheer force of personality. Whether he sings or smooches fans or just sits and listens quietly to records in the new $40,000 ranch house he bought for his parents, long, single strands of hair escape from the network of comb tracks above his forehead to fall forward, over Presley's face. Even when he's riveted to the spot, the effect is of a man in motion, of a moving body just barely come to rest. The issue of *Life* that carried the pictures of Elvis and his trademark hair also included a story on the death of the rebel artist Jackson Pollock, the father of Action Painting, who had run his Olds convertible off a Long Island highway. The painter and the singer had both made mobility into an American art form. Pollock traced his own ritual movement across the canvas in drips of paint. In Elvis's case, the trajectory of the swinging, bristling, dangling locks of way-too-long hair became the means by which the still camera conveyed the shock of a live rock performance.[8]

His clothing enhanced and amplified his movements. In one of the most frequently quoted television reviews of the decade, Jack Gould of the *New York Times* said that the Elvis who appeared on Milton Berle's show in June of 1956 was nothing but a male "hootchy-kootchy" dancer "with no discernible singing ability." But Gould also took exception to Presley's physical appearance—to the sideburns and, most especially, to "the familiar oversize jacket and open shirt which are almost the uniform of the contemporary youth who fancies himself as terribly sharp." According to the rock dress code in force only a decade later, Elvis's jacket-and-sports-shirt ensemble seems remarkably tame. If his stage costume was an ironic comment on respectable street clothes, it was a mild one, conveyed through the exaggerated scale of the coat. In physical terms, however, his performance dress both permitted movement and enhanced its effects. As video recordings of the early TV appearances show, his heavily interlined jackets did not follow Presley's twists and turns of position. Instead, by retaining a stiff, rectilinear shape, especially across the front of the body, they called attention to the fluid wrigglings of the wearer contained cocoon-wise within. His trousers were big, too, especially loose in the hips and legs (although pegged or tapered at the ankle) so that ripples and billows of fabric allowed each twitch of his notorious left leg to register dramatically, in the distant recesses of the balcony. It was precisely this outfit—big jacket, big pants—that appeared on the poster for his famous Jacksonville concert, in the summer of 1955, at which overheated fans, swept away by the sheer sensuality of the show, charged the stage and ripped off his shirt, his suit coat, and his shoes.[9]

This was, to be sure, the look or *a* look for less than a year in the mid-50s. At the time, Elvis shopped almost every day and confirmed his reputation as a distinctive dresser by showing up for concert dates in unfamiliar combinations of things: on one noteworthy occasion, for instance, he wore a multi-colored cowboy shirt with cherry-pink slacks and a black tuxedo jacket. This outfit came toward the end of a memorable "pink-and-black kick" (there were fleeting interludes of red and black, too) detailed by Elvis in May 1956, which had him matching Cadillacs to shirts to the decor of his own bedroom, until he pronounced himself thoroughly "sick of it." Back home, they called Elvis Presley the "Memphis Flash" for the zoot suit drape, the pink sport coat with the black velvet collar, and the pegged pants with darts up the legs that fell open to reveal a pink lining, all bought at Lansky Brothers, where white kids rarely ventured.[10]

His taste in clothes suggests a fine disregard for impediments to social movement across lines of class and race. Indeed, the standard explanation for his contribution to American popular music is that Elvis brought a black rhythm and blues sound into the white mainstream and in the process, created the hybrid known as rock 'n' roll. But the characteristics of his wardrobe in the 50s, the obvious pleasure he derived from clothes, on stage and off, and his frequent fashion shifts (by 1957, for example, he was wearing tight black satin pants under sequined gold boudoir jackets and a $10,000 gold lamé suit from Nudie's of Hollywood) invite a more complex reading of the issue. The "Memphis Flash" earned his name for styles—black *or* white styles—that literally flashed across the field of vision like a two-toned Rocket 88 from Oldsmobile: high color contrasts, lots of shiny buckles and buttons, hidden details suddenly disclosed in motion, reflective and textural fabrics that engaged the sense of touch even as they caught the play of light. They were "Hey, look at me!" clothes, excessive and theatrical, even before Elvis cut his first record; movie costumes for real life, or vice versa.[11]

Jac Tharpe recalls Elvis's days as a teenage movie usher who spent

The young Elvis in performance, wearing a big jacket and an unbuttoned shirt. His open mouth and facial gestures were as offensive to his critics as the twitching of the Presley pelvis.

his paycheck on fancy duds and suggests that this overblown wardrobe provides a key to a personality in which the line between adorning and concealing was beginning to blur. Discussing his musical style, Greil Marcus calls Presley a "blues-singing swashbuckler

He loved wild clothes. Contrasts in color and texture delighted him.

[whose] style owed as much to Errol Flynn" as to black R&B artists. The clothes were a technicolor Hollywood fantasy from the beginning. If his hair moved and his taste often zoomed freely across the boundaries of social decorum, his dress propelled him toward a stunning transcendence, a mobility beyond mere hip-wagging motion. A boy in cherry-pink pants and cat boots with floppy tongues must really *be* somebody. A pirate. A movie star. The King of rock 'n' roll.[12]

Elvis's regal dandyism was the most extreme example of a new male fascination with color and finery. Nineteen fifty-five was "The Peak Year for Pink," according to *Life:* the popularity of pink apparel began with a Brooks Brothers shirt, suitable for Ivy League men or women, first introduced in 1949. But the delicate pink of the buttondown, Oxford-cloth shirt (always worn with gray flannel), and the ladylike pink of *House and Garden*'s 1953 "House of Ideas" were pallid blushes in comparison to the hot, sizzling hues favored by the young Elvis, whose pinks were overheated further by tonal juxtapositions with clashing reds, complementary greens, and the coolest, blackest of blacks. Elvis was not quite alone in his fondness for pink and Hollywood gold, either. The middle-class man in the street was also wearing louder colors in the mid-50s: at work, the occasional pastel shirt; at home, sports shirts in busy prints and multicolored appliqué. The association between leisure and the freedom to adopt brighter, more expressive color as a sign of the personal, non-corporate realm was strong. Market research noted an upsurge in the sale of colored sports shirts in the suburbs where leisure-time rituals, like the barbecue, clearly demanded new forms of attire. Men—or the wives who shopped for them—seldom resorted to the prewar expedient of reusing old items of business garb for in-home activities, however. Leisure was informal, festive, and fun: so were the clothes that demarcated work from play. New clothes were inherently pleasurable, also, like the weekend itself. And color announced the onset of enjoyment, just as surely as the sobriety of gray flannel defined a Monday in the workplace.[13]

In that sense, Elvis's outlandish get-ups represent feelings of personal liberation and pleasure in a visual language already understood by the culture at large. In an essay on Elvis and "The Myth of

America," the pop music historian Timothy Scheurer suggests that Presley's "greaser" look—the hairdo, the flashy outfits—posed a serious challenge to the work ethic. If a kid in a hot pink shirt and sideburns could earn enough to buy his Mom a new house in the Memphis suburbs just by twitching and looking strange, what use were all those moral lessons about hard work, grit, and pluck? But insofar as the costumes and colors were souped-up versions of contemporary leisurewear, Elvis's outfits celebrated the same values to which the suburban Dad subscribed when he took off his suit and put on a shirt printed with pictures of little pink flamingos or flying barbecue accessories. Freedom; sensual enjoyment; play; an inchoate sense that the guy who drove a truck or wore a suit on Friday afternoon might become a wholly new person by Saturday night—a pirate or a movie star.[14]

Color was the bright side of the leisurewear picture. Denim was the somewhat sinister reverse. While social critics made fun of men who wore flamingo shirts, they were a little suspicious, at first, of the fellow in blue jeans. In the 1950s denim began the slow transition from work clothes—the sailor's dungarees, the farmer's overalls, the cowboy's jeans—to play clothes. From *Shane* (1953) to TV's *Davy Crockett* (1954), the western hero enjoyed unprecedented popularity as a symbol of the freedom and individuality also associated with modern leisure. And while the durability, washability, and low cost of denim favored its adoption by men at their leisure, jeans entered suburbia first as ranchwear, or the adult equivalent of Hopalong Cassidy suits for children. Denim pants were the costume of choice for make-believe cowboys with quarter-acre ranches and picture windows.

The movies did provide an alternative iconography for blue jeans. That was the twitchy adolescent, the "crazy mixed-up kid," the biker, the mumbling method actor of the James Dean and Marlon Brando school, who wore rolled-up jeans, a black leather jacket, and a t-shirt. While Elvis almost never appeared in anything so commonplace and casual as denim trousers, his age, his on-stage demeanor, and even the quavering, bluesy delivery of his lyrics evoked Dean—and blue jeans. Among the first lines of special teen merchandise marketed under the Presley name were distinctive "black . . . jeans with emerald green stitching [and] Elvis' signature stamped on a leather patch pocket." The president of the Amalgamated Clothing Workers of America deplored the whole jean fad and blamed it squarely on Elvis: the under-dressed, he argued, were generally under-educated, and neither bought quantities of the fine garments his constituents made. Manufacturers, meanwhile, worried that Elvis jeans would go the way of the Davy Crockett hats currently piled up in warehouses thanks to a fad that faded overnight. But 72,000 pairs of emerald-trimmed jeans were snapped up even before the 1956 Christmas shopping season arrived: unlike their younger brothers and sisters, who had to beg indulgent grandparents for coonskin caps, high schoolers had plenty of their own money to spend on clothes with overtones of rebellion against the gray-flannel establishment.[15]

Like their fathers (and Elvis himself), they were also suckers for color and for the concept of self-expression through dress. Although nobody arrived at a coherent explanation for the menswear revolution of the 1950s, everybody sensed that the inner man was somehow struggling to emerge. To a well-known psychologist, garish sports shirts were modern-day equivalents of the silk waistcoats and high-heeled shoes worn by the founding fathers. Modern-day design had robbed the American man of the "emotional outlet" once provided by highly individualized costume and muffled him "in a gray cloak of anonymity." With his leisure garments, he was trying to regain his personal authenticity. To an eminent economist, clothing had lost its primary function as protection from exposure to become "like plumage, almost exclusively erotic." Clothes still made the man—but they were making him very sexy.[16]

Entertainment critics, youth experts, and guardians of public morals all felt uneasy about Presley's sexual persona. At a convention of high school principals held in Washington in 1957, for instance, members voted to suppress blue jeans, ducktail haircuts, and Elvis Presley records at future sock hops in the interests of decency: kids who dressed like their rock 'n' roll hero were practically certain to come to a bad end.[17] But the educators managed to pussyfoot around the real issue, which was the way Elvis moved. In cities where he appeared live, local reviewers were quick to condemn "Pelvis Presley" for lewd on-stage movements. A St. Paul columnist responded to his Midwestern tour in May of 1956 with an open letter calling the singer "nothing more than a male burlesque dancer . . . [with an] unnecessary bump and-grind routine" and told him to clean up his act. In a virulent review of the Presley spot on the Milton Berle show, TV critic Jack Gould dubbed him "the virtuoso of the hootchy-kootchy. His one specialty is an accented movement of the body that heretofore has been identified with the repertoire of the blonde bombshells of the burlesque runway." A rival television writer was even more explicit in his condemnation of the "'grunt and groin' antics of one Elvis Presley . . . [who] gave an exhibition that was suggestive and vulgar, tinged with the kind of animalism that should be confined to dives and bordellos." *Look* found his abdominal gyrations (and phallic byplay with the guitar) in shocking "bad taste."[18] Catholic Cardinal Spellman joined a choir of clergy voices condemning his "suggestive dancing" on television as a symptom of a new teen "creed of dishonesty, violence, lust and degeneration."[19]

Presley's "strip-tease behavior" was particularly repugnant to TV watchers because his performance style was, in some perverse way, ideally suited to the new medium. The moving image was supposed to separate television from radio yet much of the standard programming in the 1950s showed static or almost static pictures to illustrate a sound track. Announcers and talk show participants sat rigidly at desks. On variety shows, the location of microphones kept singers and comics frozen to their marks. In drama, the small screen favored close-ups of faces over motion or action; bulky cameras, not easily adapted to location work, confined what action there was to a small set on the studio floor. The use of a portable camera by host Dave Garroway in 1950 to visit a dentist's office and let the viewer peer into a patient's mouth was widely hailed as a historic innovation, but even at that early date Garroway's admirers were forced to admit that the medium was failing to live up to its promise.[20]

Until the advent of Martin and Lewis, the comedy team that virtually owned the airwaves in the early 1950s, TV remained little more than radio accompanied by black-and-white photographs. But Jerry

Lewis helped to change the aesthetic of television. While Martin (a romantic crooner much admired by Elvis Presley) stood still, in the prescribed manner, Jerry Lewis stomped around him, arms and legs akimbo, shouting, aping, and mugging the camera with mad abandon. Established chiefly by erratic movement, Lewis's emotional intensity was sometimes compared with method acting. More remarkable than the histrionics was the effect of his physical movements on an audience that howled in transports of unrestrained delight as Lewis circled his suave and motionless partner. Like Elvis, Jerry Lewis seemed rebellious because he wouldn't stand still; he both projected and aroused strong emotion through motion. When Elvis—the sex-hot, jelly-kneed, thigh-slinging Elvis who couldn't seem to stand still either—appeared opposite Ed Sullivan on Steve Allen's show in July 1956, it was the first time since Martin and Lewis had aired in the key Sunday night time slot that Sullivan's ratings were topped.[21]

Steve Allen was another bold explorer of the medium. Although he has been roundly condemned by Presley partisans for demeaning (or de-twitching) the singer by making him stand still during his act—the script also called for him to croon "Hound Dog" to a live basset hound and impersonate a cowboy/hillbilly in a silly skit—Allen's format was an ironic commentary of sorts on TV's presentation of Elvis to date. Elvis Presley's first national exposure had come on the *Tommy and Jimmy Dorsey Stage Show* in the spring of 1956. Despite the name, the *Stage Show* belonged to comedian Jackie Gleason. A means of lightening his own on-air duties, it extracted a half-hour of variety and musical numbers from Gleason's usual sixty-minute format to serve as a lead-in to his popular *Honeymooners* sketch. Convinced that he was "a guitar-playing Marlon Brando," Gleason booked Elvis over the objections of the Dorseys especially to cater to younger viewers: "He had the same sensuous, sweaty, T-shirt-and-jeans animal magnetism," said the star. As Ralph Kramden, bus-driver hero of *The Honeymooners*, Jackie Gleason had brought working-class culture to prime-time television. Elvis, he thought, might appeal on the same earthy grounds.[22]

In six appearances alongside acrobats and ventriloquists, Elvis did a dozen numbers in his usual style. Audience reaction to Elvis's manner and to the new rock 'n' roll music was intense—so strong, in fact, that the conservative Dorsey Brothers threatened to walk out if Gleason made good on his intention to bring him back. So Presley's next network engagements came on what would be Milton Berle's two final shows. Because Berle was "Mr. Television," the first great star of the small screen; because he agreed to pay Elvis the princely sum of $50,000 per week; and because Ed Sullivan, the new king of variety television, had publicly vowed never to let Elvis on *his* stage, the Berle performances were closely watched. Because Berle himself was desperate to hold onto his series by making a splash, he deliberately exploited Presley's unconventional "dancing," first, in a series of head-to-toe shots broadcast live from the deck of the USS *Hancock* (as Elvis ground out "Shake, Rattle, and Roll"), and second, in a series

TV sets began to move in the 1950s, with the invention of the portable. So why not the performers who filled the little screen?

of suggestive skits, discussing Presley's animal magnetism (actress Debra Paget came on stage and screamed like a teenager at the mere sight of him). Packaged to direct attention to Presley's uninhibited movements and their electric effect on female fans, it was the Berle performances that finally brought down the wrath of the critics. The male answer to Marilyn Monroe. A peep-show dancer. A "sexhibitionist," in *Time's* snide coinage. A corrupter of youth. And all, essentially, because he moved on TV. "Ah don't see anything wrong with it. Ah just act the way Ah feel," Elvis told *Look* in the face of mounting outrage.[23]

Rock 'n' roll and television were made for each other. In dancing blips of light, television registered the bobbing hanks of hair, the swinging jackets, the swiveling hips. Detail wasn't important: on the little living room screen, motion—new, exciting, and visually provocative in its own right—was the distilled essence of Elvishood. In that intimate setting, too, it became doubly shocking, as if a family friend had begun a series of bumps and grinds in front of the sofa. TV, suggested one cynical Presley-hater, was the real reason teens were so crazy about Elvis; having witnessed their parents' stunned disapproval at close range, over a TV dinner, kids figured he must be worth liking, if only to annoy their elders. But another channel-watcher, trying to reassure adults that Elvis-worship was just another adolescent fad, saw television as a major threat to the continued survival of rock. "You can easily foresee the process of absorption and standardization at the prevailing level," John Sharnik told the nervous Moms and Dads who flipped through *House and Garden* during commercial breaks. The culture of television bred a kind of solemn puffery: phony sets and production numbers, melodramatic lighting, and big bands. Eventually, after "a few more shots at guest starring," Elvis would have learned the drill. He'd wear a fancy costume and stand still—and rock 'n' roll would start to sound like Rodgers and Hammerstein.[24]

That was the point Steve Allen was making when he dressed Elvis in white tie and tails, took away his guitar, plopped him down on a set full of pseudo-classical columns, and had him serenade a dog while standing perfectly still. In a critique directed as much at the pretensions of the medium as at his hapless guest, the cool, under-stated Allen parodied the inertia of artsy, big-ticket television by deep-freezing the hottest act ever seen in prime time. "Allen was nervous," wrote John Lardner in *Newsweek*, "like a man trying to embalm a firecracker. Presley was distraught, like Huckleberry Finn, when the widow put him in a store suit and told him not to . . . scratch." Diehard fans never forgave Steve Allen. But Ed Sullivan noticed that Allen had trounced him in the ratings with the help of Elvis Presley. Suddenly, Sullivan's earlier moral reservations melted away. Suddenly, finding nothing objectionable in Presley's act, he signed him for three upcoming dates.[25]

Elvis had not been redeemed by one stationary appearance in respectable evening wear, however. Nor did Sullivan apparently grasp the significance of Allen's satirical staging for, on the first two Sundays, he let Elvis rock his way through "Don't Be Cruel" and "Ready Teddy" in full, unobstructed view of the nation's living rooms. But when the critics started in again—Jack Gould attacked not only the familiar body language but certain "distasteful . . . move-ments of the tongue" visible in closeups—Sullivan told the camera-men to shoot Presley strictly from the waist up during the last show, on January 6, 1957. And then he told the studio audience what an exemplary young man this quiescent, half-an-Elvis was: "A real de-cent, fine boy."[26]

By some estimates, 82.6 percent of the American viewing public saw Elvis on the *Ed Sullivan Show*. And critiques of the programs assumed that the Presley appeal was strictly telegenic—not vocal. Jack Gould, who led the charge to immobilize Elvis, was convinced, for example, that he had "no discernible singing ability," beyond an undistinguished whine sometimes uncorked to juice up the rhythm. But fans who never saw Elvis on TV bought his records and re-sponded to the same qualities that electrified (or offended) viewers on the basis of sound alone. His vocal style, in fact, was every bit as mobile as his hips. Since most of journalists on the Elvis beat denied him any artistry, his two-and-one-third-octave range was never men-tioned and the music itself was rarely analyzed.[27] There were happy exceptions, however. An early Elvis story in *Coronet* went beyond the usual list of dress code violations and possible obscenities to posit a

Ed Sullivan defined the spectrum of American culture for 1950s TV: guests ranged from opera stars to black bluesmen, from circus performers to Elvis Presley.

direct connection between his stage actions and an "irregular stress on syllables" that gave the typical Presley song "an urgent jerkiness" identical to the visual aspects of the performance. Others detected a breathless urgency, a freedom in his phrasing, the impatient syntax of a young man going someplace in a terrific hurry. Or a whole vocabulary of howls, mumbles, coos, and cries, of drawn-out, bisected, and broken notes that made the music lurch and twitch and thrust like— well, like Elvis Presley! When he sang, the melody picked up speed and barreled along like a freight train on a midnight run to Memphis, like a pink Cadillac bound for glory: "Ah-h Wa-ha-hunt Yew-who, Ah Nee-hee-heed Yew-who!"[28]

Of all the ink spilled over Elvis Presley in the 1950s, only one article—by James and Annette Baxter—credited Elvis with prodigious musical talent and a growing sense of how to manipulate his vocal pyrotechnics "into an organic whole." Published by *Harper's* in 1958, as most other journals were gearing up for heavy-handed Elvis-gets-a-haircut stories, the Baxter essay concentrated on shifts in mood and timing and twists in tonal quality, or what might be called the mobility of Presley's voice. Later students of rock have labored to show precisely how these techniques propelled his singing and ultimately shaped his performance mode. Thus the musicologist Richard Middleton detects an off-beat quaver in Elvis's interpretation of certain lyrics of the mid-50s; the unexpected accent produces cross rhythms and syncopation virtually demanding physical movement. In other words, his slurs and mumbles, his split syllables—all the linguistic tricks that made Elvis an easy target for parody—inject extra notes into the melodic line. The result is a sort of jittery vibrato simulating effort and speed. This rhythmic boogification has its lyrical equivalent in the delicate burps of appoggiatura heard in "Love Me Tender" (over the word "never" in "Never let me go . . .") and other crooner ballads. The sound waffles and quavers and slithers and slides. It moves. And Elvis moved with his music, a sign, a symbol for a new and problematic American mobility.[29]

The supposed transformation of Elvis from the rockin' rebel of the 50s to the mainstream entertainer of 1960 was always couched in terms of movement, or the absence thereof. Hence the *TV Guide* review of Presley's "comeback" television appearance focused on motion to underscore the contrast between Ed Sullivan's X-rated Elvis and the glossy pop idol who traded quips with Frank Sinatra on ABC three years later. "Presley wiggled off to military service," wrote columnist Alan Levy, but "comes marching home . . . shorn of his sideburns and behaving the way a sedate, serious-minded youngster should." Not that clean-cut American youth had fared particularly well on the home screen in the years of rampant Presleymania: there was, for instance, the sad case of Charles Van Doren. A tweedy young Columbia University instructor with a passable haircut and impeccable egghead connections, Van Doren debuted on TV in November of 1956, in the lull between Elvis's second and third Sullivan spots, as a contestant on a quiz show. Pitted against a swarthy, surly fellow from Brooklyn in a cheap, ill-fitting suit—the Elvis or James Dean of this real-life melodrama—Van Doren sweated, stammered, and bit his lip in a glass booth (supposedly soundproof, it was a visual guarantee of the fairness of the proceedings) and emerged the winner. During his own long reign as the *Twenty-One* champ, Van Doren accumulated 129,000 pretax dollars and became a television celebrity, eventually signed to a contract with NBC, as cultural correspondent for Dave Garroway's *Today* show. Then, in 1959, after years of rumors, the whole thing came apart. A congressional investigation revealed that Van Doren had been coached on the answers and had lied about it repeatedly under oath. He lost his post at Columbia and his new NBC job too.[30]

In the aftermath of the quiz show scandal, sideburns and wiggling began to look pretty wholesome. But at the height of his popularity, Charlie Van Doren had provided an almost irresistible contrast to Elvis; he was articulate, conservative, neatly barbered—all the things Elvis appeared not to be. Unlike the sensual, some would say downright dirty Elvis, he was cool, restrained, and cerebral, the perfect hero, it would seem, for the American teen in the age of Sputnik. Van Doren himself waxed sanctimonious in the media about the good influence of quiz shows in promoting an "increased respect for knowledge" and education. Yet *he* didn't watch TV, Charlie confessed in the pages of *Life*, nor did he know anybody who owned a set. On the contrary, before his own prime-time duel to the death with Herb Stempel, he'd been afraid of television: "I thought it could hurt people, that it could corrupt them, perhaps." Van Doren's own corruption gives his reservations about television an ironic wrinkle. He was by

Charles Van Doren, the eggheads' idol, confesses his televised misdeeds to Congress, 1959. Note the short hair and trim, conservative suit.

no means alone in his skepticism about the TV set, however—a wariness the quiz show scandal helped to expose and define.[31]

The quiz show format came to dominate television in the mid-50s for several reasons, not the least of which was the whole rags-to-riches premise, the idea that *anybody*—an Elvis type or a Charles Van

Doren—could strike it rich in America.[32] On some shows, the consolation prizes for the losers were shiny new Cadillac convertibles![33] In a backhanded way, the programs also affirmed the prestige of the expert or the increasingly hierarchical and bureaucratic structure of the workplace, but the experts on *Twenty-One* and the other hit shows were often comic-opera versions of professionals; the psychologist who knew everything about boxing and the Marine gourmet challenged the rigidity of conventional job descriptions at the same time as they exalted the purposefulness and seriousness of leisure. But it was the apparent lack of contrivance that won the quiz show its widest following. Unlike a movie or a dramatic show, this was real life, unrehearsed and spontaneous, fluid: what television was meant to be (and what a Presley appearance, coincidentally, always delivered). The isolation booths twirled around on stage to show that there were no hidden wires. The contestants perspired and grimaced and wrung their clammy hands. It all added up to immediacy and authenticity, a reality inside the picture tube that matched the tension and mumbling and fidgeting in the American living room, on the other side of the glass.

That all was not as it appeared to be, that what looked so real on TV could be contrived and false, was a terrible blow to viewers' faith in the medium. More than the duplicity of any given quiz show hero, the failure of television itself was what caused the public outcry in the Van Doren case. In the wake of the *Twenty-One* investigation, CBS executives even castigated Ed Murrow's at-home interview show, *Person to Person*, because the format aimed to preserve some sense of spontaneity even though it was obvious that cumbersome cameras, lights, and microphones did not, as Murrow retorted testily, "just wander around" a celebrity's house. The problem was as much aesthetic and structural as it was ethical. Gilbert Seldes, the most persuasive apologist for early television, thought TV was inherently different from the other public and popular arts. "The novel says: 'He walked,'" Seldes wrote, while "television says: 'Look, I am walking.' Perhaps the movies say: 'He was walking.'" The presentness of television was a function of its location, in the home: events witnessed there became part of the continuum of daily life, making it almost impossible to believe, for example, that what was happening on screen might have occurred before the viewer saw it.[34]

Fraudulent by nature, the illusory presentness of the moving image was one of several factors that made TV dangerous, especially to the young. From mid-decade on, the baleful effects of television on American life became a national obsession. Polls, surveys, and experts all agreed that something terrible was happening. People stayed in the house more and read good books less. Kids were glued to the set for three or four hours a day. The content of programming aroused "morbid emotions in children," stirred up "domestic quarrels, . . . loosed morals and ma[de] people lazy and sodden." The Kefauver Subcommittee of the Senate Judiciary Committee issued a report late in 1955 suggesting that TV caused juvenile delinquency by inuring teenagers to lawless and violent behavior.[35]

The mechanism whereby clean-cut teens suddenly turned into blue-jeaned mobsters while watching TV was not specified in the report; perhaps moving pictures induced criminal restlessness in unformed characters. As the historian Merle Curti has observed, however, one consequence of World War II and the rise of the totalitarian state was to convince Americans that anybody could be manipulated by appeal to the non-rational self. Confirmed by the "brainwashing" of captured troops in Korea and by the plots of science fiction movies in which germs from Mars turned average citizens into obedient zombies in the twinkling of an eye, this insight formed the basis for much postwar advertising. The flirtation between Madison Avenue and the behavioral sciences climaxed in the summer of 1957 when ad executives tried out subliminal pitches—"Drink Coca-Cola!" and "Hungry: Eat Popcorn!" flashed over the picture for one three-hundredth of a second—in a selected group of movie theaters, and reported sales increases of 50 percent. The results were disputed, debated, and ultimately discredited, but the brouhaha about subliminals, motivational research, and the application of psychological voodoo to ad campaigns left the lingering suspicion that people were regularly induced to act against their own best instincts by what they saw. In 1957 and 1958 the acceptance of the sack dress by teenage girls was often cited as a prime example of how images—of Paris chic, of something wild and new—could turn a whole class of consumers into mindless fashion robots wearing garments of an unprecedented hideousness.[36]

At issue was the change from an accepted style to something unfamiliar, from the Saturday matinee to weeknight TV, from crew cuts to ducktails and sideburns, from Dean Martin and Charles Van Doren to Elvis Presley. Change. Speed. Movement. Presentness. What made Elvis transgressive on television and inseparable from it. The annual *Look* award for the best variety show of 1957 went to the editions of the Sullivan program on which he was featured, in all his subversive, subliminal, syncopated glory, twisting and twitching like a Waring blender full of testosterone. The essence of motion, Elvis was, in the words of a brand new hit recorded a week after his last Sullivan gig, "All Shook Up." In the abstract, at least, the cultural style of the 1950s tilted toward motion and away from stasis. Drive-ins, Oldsmobiles with jet-plane tail fins, the interstate highway system first proposed by the Eisenhower administration in 1954; Vladimir Nabokov's determination to put "the geography of the United States into motion" by visiting every tourist attraction his guidebook had to offer; Jack Kerouac, driving from Denver to Chicago in seventeen hours ("not counting . . . two hours with the police in Newton, Iowa") in a borrowed Cadillac at a mean speed of 70 mph; the lyrics of *all* the best rock and proto-rock songs, beginning with Willy Love's "V-8 Ford Blues" of 1951: to move was to live and breathe, to be an artist in America in the 1950s. The national spirit was all shook up even as the body politic reposed inert before the picture tube, waiting to be zapped by secret signals from networkland.[37]

In 1955 designers at Chrysler Motors retooled the whole product line, lowering auto bodies, raking tail fins backward, extruding front bumpers in the opposite direction. McCann-Erickson, Chrysler's New York ad agency, called it "The Forward Look" and waxed poetic in TV commercials about the sort of car that had the "forward look of motion—even when it's stopped." Plymouths and Dodges became symbols as much as vehicles, signs of a new cultural engagement with movement. But just how the concept could best be marketed on television became a major problem. In 1956, utilizing the latest in electronic techniques for testing audience reactions, the Central Research Department at McCann-Erickson conducted an in-depth study of actor William Lundigan, incumbent host of Chrysler's two weekly shows, *Climax* and *Shower of Stars*. The study disclosed that Lundigan was perceived as a passive figure, identified more closely with what he was—an actor, a personality—than with what he was doing for Chrysler. In Madison Avenue terms, he was a "soft sell," largely because he stood still while the product moved. The agency therefore recommended a whole range of changes to correct this "basically *inactive* impression." Lundigan was given stage business to do whenever possible—"more active chores as part of the commercial."[38] The non-active announcer, whom the viewers surveyed preferred to the hard-sell type (Lundigan got fan mail!), was not as effective at actually moving the family toward the auto showroom, the ad men concluded. The act of movement alone, with no change in dialogue or content, was the psychological key to selling "The Forward Look" on TV, with nobody the wiser.

While Elvis and Bill Lundigan were moving the audience by sheer movement, the viewers themselves were shifting positions within the home. Lynn Spigel and Cecelia Tichi, in recent studies of television and domesticity in the 1940s and 50s, have both noted the disruption of traditional patterns of household space by a set that needed to be visible from a number of unobstructed vantage points. The television crept into many homes disguised as a kind of electronic version of the colonial fireplace because it invited the same radial arrangement of seating; period cabinets on some early sets helped to integrate a new technology with the time-honored repertory of chairs and sofas standard in the American living room. But it is also clear that televiewing entailed movement that called wholly new kinds of furniture into being. The TV tray-table is one good example. Manufactured by several companies, of which Cal-Dak of Illinois was the industry leader, the highly portable, fold-away, stackable, over-the-knees table for one first appeared in national advertising in 1952 and 1953: it was, read the copy, "Perfect for TV dining."[39]

Those were the years in which Mamie and Ike usually ate supper off matching tray-tables in front of a bank of special TV consoles built

The TV tray-table: perfect for eating in the living room, in front of the set—and so easy to move.

into one wall of the White House family quarters. Ordinary families followed suit: TV trays were inexpensive to purchase and frequently available as premiums. Niblets brand canned corn offered a pair of them, decorated with Norman Rockwell scenes, for just $1 and a label, in a supermarket promotion in the spring of 1953. The tray-tables had a recessed center well to secure the plates. This feature made them handy and useful but it also meant that the form of the table mimicked the configuration of a TV screen. So the snack table was telecentric in its very shape, like a long list of other products, beginning with Swanson's TV Dinners, that capitalized on the attraction of the new medium. And it joined a whole family of home furnishings designed exclusively to be moved into positions close to the set: Servel's Electric Wonderbar, a "refrigerette" on casters, "so handy while watching TV!"; a roll-around "television plastic dinette set" from Virginia House in a choice of three woodgrain finishes; electrified serving carts of every description.[40]

All these new furniture types made a virtue of necessity by bending the metallic legs into eccentric forms that tended to dominate the

New, perambulating furniture of the 1950s, adapted to the TV set, included pieces on wheels.

overall design. This artistic strategy expressed the altered function of a fixed piece suddenly on the move and the properties of nontraditional materials, such as steel tubing. But the leggy look in tables and chairs had already posed a real problem of clutter for high-style furniture designers in the postwar era: "modern" rooms by Charles Eames, George Nelson, and the other arbiters of home fashions for highbrows often looked like cocktail parties attended by swarms of long-legged insects because all the horizontal surfaces were borne aloft by thin, expressively angled supporting members.[41] Such environments were virtual symphonies in legginess and potential movement. But, in a way, the wobbly little TV table in the average "colonial" living room carried the greater symbolic weight, since those spindly sawhorse legs had so little competition from the stodgy wooden cabinetry all around them. Their message was bold and plain: things associated with television moved, or looked as if they could and should go prancing across the room. And under the weight of a bowl of chip-dip, they wiggled like Elvis himself.

Many familiar appurtenances of domesticity took on a new mobility in the 1950s when television entered the picture. Teamed with a serving tray and four individual glass snack trays, Toastmaster's reliable old electric toaster became "Television's Twin." The idea was that "while the show is on," the hostess did not need to miss a minute of the fun if she whipped up toasted treats right in front of the set. Even simple serving bowls acquired hinges and ball bearings, so that a whole meal could be dispensed from a single unit that slid open to disclose hidden casserole wells and pop-up side dishes.[42] The immediate consequence of all this movement in the living room was a radical change in American table manners and patterns of entertaining. Stiff, formal service, with everyone pinned in position by place cards, was replaced by the party at which hosts and guests moved as a matter of course: the stand-up cocktail party, the patio barbecue, or the TV party, with its moveable tables, portable bars, twirling lazy-susan servers, and viewers making their own meals buffet-style during the Lincoln commercials on the Ed Sullivan show. The television set itself helped to break down rigid patterns of social propriety. An agent of movement and change long before the rock 'n' roll images

Even the toaster became a TV accessory.

flashing on the picture tube shook up America, TV was the perfect medium for a kid from Tupelo, Mississippi, on the move.

During his last appearance on the Ed Sullivan show, Elvis Presley thanked his fans for the carloads of birthday and Christmas presents (including 282 teddy bears) which had recently inundated his Memphis home. "I'd like to tell you that we deeply appreciate it," said the uncrowned King of Rock, invoking the royal plural. "We're sorry we couldn't give every one of you a new Lincoln, but they wouldn't sell us that many," he joked, with a genial bow to Sullivan's sponsor. The automobile industry was a dominant presence in television advertising. The medium showed off cars to best advantage in filmed motion sequences. But automakers also used television to associate their products with certain ideas and personalities. By sponsoring Sullivan's Sunday night variety package, for instance, Lincoln positioned itself near the middle of a sliding scale of taste that included performing chimps at one end and opera divas at the other. In that particular context, the car seemed elegant yet perhaps affordable some day, not so pretentious as to be irredeemably snooty but nice enough to make the neighbors take notice. It wasn't quite a Cadillac—that remained the Cinderella car, the give-away car of choice in contests and sweepstakes—but it was an acquisition that announced a major change in status, a big climb up the ladder of success. Bill Lundigan's Chrysler ads associated the "Forward Look" with established stars and "quality" drama, showing that progressive taste need not be too new for comfort. Automotive advertising coupled movement through space—driving to work, a Sunday spin—with precisely calibrated movements in social position and values. In that sense, the folks at Lincoln were probably relieved that Elvis had thus far bought only Cadillacs in quantity (he owned one purple Lincoln Continental and five brand new Caddies in January of 1957). Despite his off-the-cuff endorsement, Elvis Presley was too radical, too *fast* for Lincoln's middle-of-the-road image.[43]

In 1955 Chevrolet marketed a special V-8 model "to create the image of a 'hot car'" and specifically to attract the young buyer. Research further suggested that even when the teen was not the owner, he or she was likely to be the taste-maker with the greatest influence in the selection of the family car. As a result, Pat Boone, Elvis Presley's main pop rival, became the TV spokesman for Chevy. In 1956 and 1957 oddsmakers in the entertainment business were betting that the well-barbered balladeer, who was the father of three and a direct descendent of frontiersman Daniel Boone, would soon inherit the crown of "Top Singer." He was a perfect gentleman on stage. His most radical dress statement was a pair of immaculate white buck shoes. He didn't have sideburns. And adults seemed to like his music almost as much as teenagers did. Pat Boone was the perfect pitchman for an inexpensive, family car like a Chevy because he wasn't Elvis Presley. Boone gave the Chevy a youthful flair, beamed directly at the teen arbiter of car taste, but he was the essence of wholesome, family values—the rock without the roll, or a living denial of the several kinds of mobility (physical *and* social) that car commercials usually exploited. No wild teenager would ever speed to her doom in a car endorsed by Pat Boone! But neither would one of Boone's Chevrolets do much to enhance the rising status of the family that owned it.[44]

Elvis Presley, on the other hand, was all about a rapid rise to fame, fortune, and whatever unmistakable marks thereof lots of new money could buy. The rock critic Simon Frith concludes that Elvis was the media archetype for a long line of working-class idols to come, "the poor Southern boy who escaped a life of truck-driving by remaking American music."[45] Elvis affirmed his success by buying garish pink and lemon-yellow Cadillacs, vehicles at the opposite end of the transportation spectrum from the trucks he used to drive for Crown Electric. He reaffirmed it in March of 1957 by buying Graceland, a two-story limestone mansion in suburban Memphis with a pediment over the front door and a brace of stately *Gone With the Wind* columns instead of a porch. As big houses went, Graceland was on the puny side. But it showed, with its screen of columns, that Elvis had moved beyond the ordinary American dream of a nice, new home in a good neighborhood toward a far grander vision of antebellum posh. Elvis's neighbors at the first house he bought with his windfall riches—his Ozzie and Harriet ranch house on Audubon Drive—complained about the flocks of intrepid girls who dipped cups of water out of the swimming pool and knelt with their ears pressed to the clapboards, hoping to hear their master's voice. Yet Elvis's choice of Graceland, with its spacious grounds and enclosure wall, seems influenced less by thoughts of fan control than by a hankering for rolling lawns and tall white columns. People who lived on Audubon Drive were Pat Boone or Ed Sullivan sorts of people: if they were headed up the long, steep road of status, they weren't going to make a big noise about it to the neighbors. Elvis Presley was different. He was bound for glory in a fleet of Cadillacs and wanted the whole world to sit up and take notice.

Elvis went too far, too fast, in the opinion of many. A media watch for signs of an impending plunge back into obscurity began in 1956, when speculation about Presley's draft status first made headlines. In November 1957 *Time* thought it sensed the "beginning of wilt [in] those poodle-wool sideburns," and a whiff of cautious austerity in the purchase of "a black, bankerish Cadillac limousine." To the consternation of those who wished him ill, however, Elvis simply added movie stardom to his list of accomplishments and kept on rockin'. But even his well-wishers thought that the rock 'n' roll might eventually have to go. Interviewed by *Variety* in the summer of 1957, as the draft loomed large, a noted dance expert predicted that Elvis would need to adapt, to tone things down in order to survive: "Much of [his] popularity can be attributed to teenagers, mostly girls. Elvis will last but he'll change his style. Before long, I think you'll find, he'll swing to ballad style stuff. If he does that he'll be around for years and years." After all, by the time Elvis Presley got back from Army service in Germany, his teenage fans would be all grown up and married and settled down. They'd have Chevy station wagons, babies, and Pat Boone albums.[46]

The Army was as nervous about a Presley hitch as Elvis was about a G.I. haircut. More than a year before his scheduled induction, military officials were said to be holding secret conclaves to plot the logistics of protecting a buck private from invading squadrons of fans. "Not since Eddie Fisher served his stint has the Army faced the star problem, and at that time Fisher was nowhere near the celebrity that Presley is," *Billboard* reported. The larger question was whether Elvis could safely be used as a Cold War bargaining chip. He was no answer to Sputnik, of course, but his lack of restraint and enormous appetite for consumer goods could make Elvis a sort of pop paradigm of freedom, American style. Freedom and a frightful power, worth calling to the attention of allies and enemies: like America's nuclear arsenal, Elvis was "an atomic-age phenomenon . . . hotter than a radioactive yam."[47]

The notion of making Elvis a NATO agent or unsecret weapon in Europe gained plausibility from Eastern Bloc hysteria over American teen culture. In 1958 Radio Moscow condemned excessive movement of the hips by women, blaming suspicious undulations recently seen in Russian streets on decadent Western practices: "This may be good training for girls of fashion abroad who shamelessly indulge in rock 'n' roll with its hideous stamping, wriggling and somersaulting but this is not at all suitable for our girls." When it was announced that Presley was bound for the U.S. base at Friedberg, the East German Communist Party accused the United States of plotting to undermine the morals of Red youth. To show that this act of provocation would not be tolerated, party boss Walter Ulbricht ordered the arrest and imprisonment of fifteen teenagers who marched through the streets of Leipzig in 1959 shouting, "Long live Elvis Presley!"[48]

In the end, however, Elvis served the interests of Cold War strategy best by his virtual invisibility. He piloted a tank, stood guard duty,

Elvis (who liked the stuff) was as liquid as Silly Putty, a 1950s invention marketed through the pictorial evocation of a TV set.

drew his pay, and maintained no overt ties to his former show business life. With the exception of raucous press conferences at the beginning and the end of his military adventure, Elvis did what every other American soldier on duty abroad did, by the book. The man who had once moved like a scalded cat did not so much as twitch a muscle unless ordered to do so. G.I. newspapers in Europe speculated that Operation Elvis had been formulated at the very top: "Advance word from Washington ordered the military to keep Presley under restraint. [The division] was given the word not to go all out for him—no guest appearances, no Presley platter parties, etc."[49] Managed in this way, Pvt. Presley offered an object lesson in dramatic reversals: a khaki uniform instead of a gold tux and blue suede shoes, a crew cut instead of a head of hair that looked like a built-in Davy Crockett cap, an $82 paycheck instead of a mansion, and temporary restraint as the price of freedom. In a democracy, everybody was equal under the law, commoners and rock 'n' roll kings. The moral of the story was that Elvis Presley was perfectly wholesome, too, an all-American boy underneath the hair and the spangles and the wild wiggling. His Army service validated the most threatening aspects of Elvisness and American popular culture by treating them as expendable matters of style.

There was some objection to the perfect-little-Private-Presley plan because it seemed to be an egregious waste of Army resources. Why not put Elvis in an entertainment unit and let him tour Europe as a goodwill ambassador? Why not have him perform for the troops at hardship bases in Lebanon and Turkey? But backroom scuttlebutt from Hollywood blamed Presley's manager for keeping him out of Special Services. Interviewed in his suite on the Paramount backlot, the cagey Colonel Tom Parker was quoted as saying that "a sure way to debase your merchandise is to give it away." Gossip columns also had Parker renegotiating existing movie contracts on the basis of the fact that Elvis Presley's exemplary conduct in the Army would pay off in greater boxoffice "appeal to adults."[50]

In a way, however, the immobilization of Elvis completed by Parker and Uncle Sam began in 1956, in the publicity department of Twentieth Century-Fox, just after the release of his first movie, *Love Me*

Tender. In that costume piece, Elvis impersonated the youngest brother in a Civil War-era family, betrayed by a faithless wife. The part was romantic and conventional but the musical numbers added to appeal to the teen market spotlighted the difference between the dangerous rock 'n' roller and the benign role he played. As one savage review of *Love Me Tender* put it, there was Elvis, grotesquely enlarged on the big screen, doing 1956-style "bumps and grinds to raise money for [a] new school" in a make-believe old South. And because his on-screen movements in the darkened confines of motion picture theaters fed fresh fears of teen lawlessness and libidinousness, the studio opened discussions with Parker aimed at remaking the cinematic Elvis "into an influence for the good." How this was to be accomplished was outlined only in the vaguest of terms. Publicists were told to accent Presley's strong family ties and churchgoing background. There was talk of a Presley-sponsored charity for juvenile delinquents. Of a mild infusion of Continental culture with an eye to better overseas ticket sales. And special tutoring to support "his maturing orbit." So, before Draft Board 86 ever made a move to slow him down, a newer, calmer, quieter Elvis was in the works. An Elvis "hellbent on the mainstream," in the words of Greil Marcus. An Elvis who would, of his own volition, get two haircuts in preparation for a new role as a shining satellite in the fixed orbit of American stardom.[51]

In January of 1958, after his local board announced a brief deferment to permit Elvis to finish another movie, a draft official in Kentucky resigned in a huff, charging that stars were getting favors denied to ordinary boys in his state. How did rock 'n' roll stack up against the national defense? If a movie about a kid singer sweeping floors in a Bourbon Street nightclub was sufficient reason to put off induction, "then the Sputnik . . . age isn't as serious as represented," he reasoned. When Elvis came home from Germany, however, his handlers made the most of his status as a Cold Warrior, guarding the frontiers of freedom. Paramount sent a crew to Europe to film authentic backgrounds for *G.I. Blues,* the thinly disguised autobiography of a young American tank driver/singer stationed in West Germany; publicity hit hard on the many parallels between Elvis and the fictional "Tulsa McLean," who attains a new maturity from his tourist's-eye-view of Germany. *Life* showed him in costume (uniform)

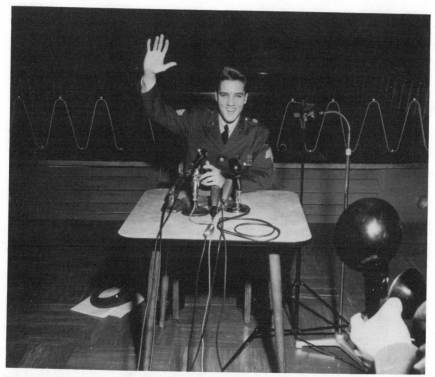

March 1960: Elvis comes home from the Army, a Cold War hero in a uniform.

tending a baby that figured in the flimsy plot. Perhaps the real Elvis—the one who had "come back from the Army easygoing, unassuming, fatherly . . ."—had traded rock for rock-a-byes, too. The *New York Times* met Presley on the set, looking and sounding as relaxed as Bing Crosby, the very model of the successful singer/actor. And in the telling, at least, *G.I. Blues* sounded like an old Bing Crosby musical. Of the eleven songs slated for the picture, only three or four had a rock beat. "If things change," said the young star, "I'll change too. You have to. That's show business." Show biz to the core, he was dating Frank Sinatra's ex-girlfriend, according to the trade papers. "The Army made an adult of him," his producer was quoted as saying. "This film will show people a grown-up Presley."[52]

The new, adult Elvis had all but lost his Southern accent; he sounded like a movie star, like a pre-packaged American idol. He was

The new, respectable Elvis tends a baby in *G.I. Blues.*

When Elvis got his hair wet, in this beefcake scene from *G.I. Blues,* it wiggled in the old Presley style.

still wearing the regulation Army "convertible cut," flat on top, a little longer on the sides, and didn't intend to change that coiffure much once the movie was finished. Meanwhile, between takes, he wore a hat: no matter what he did, not a hair was supposed to move. Neither was Elvis, for that matter. "I can't change my style," he complained to an interviewer the day they shot the star-in-the-shower scene for *G.I. Blues.* "If I feel like moving around, I still move."[53] But a director told him when to do it now. The camera looked at his soapy head in close up and ignored the rest. They used fake steam and cold water in the beefcake shot so as not to ruin his makeup. And it made his hair stand up in stiff, evocative spikes that wiggled, just a little, under the icy spray.

Friendly, competent
Betty Crocker as redesigned
for the 1950s by artist Hilda Taylor.
She reassured the suburban housewife that
it was possible to perform kitchen miracles
under her maternal, step-by-step guidance.

Six

Betty Crocker's Picture Cook Book: The Aesthetics of Food in the 1950s

*F*rom its first publication in 1950, *Betty Crocker's Picture Cook Book* became a perennial favorite and the gift of choice at bridal showers, especially in the deluxe, ring-bound edition that originally sold for a mere $3.95 (or $3 with premium coupons from cake-mix boxes). Second on the all-time culinary bestsellers list—it noses out *The Joy of Cooking* (1931) and *The I Hate To Cook Book* (1960)—the familiar red-and-white volume with the old-timey, Early American design on the cover broke records that first year when it outsold *Kon-Tiki*, *The Lonely Crowd*, and Hubbard Cobb's *Your Dream Home*, a do-it-yourself guide to building a Cape Cod cottage for less than $3500. In the spring of 1951 delighted General Mills executives presented the millionth copy to the American Mother of the Year and the distributor, McGraw-Hill, shipped another 950,000 units to retailers. A year later, with the book in its seventh printing, sales had passed the 2 million mark and there was no end in sight.[1]

Although General Mills functionaries expressed a becoming surprise at the commercial success of their cookbook, its popularity was neither unexpected nor undeserved. In September of 1950, when the volume was being test-marketed, business analysts were already predicting a publishing coup: in downtown Minneapolis, headquarters of the giant milling and food-processing corporation, women lined up for hours at department stores to buy the preview edition; grocery

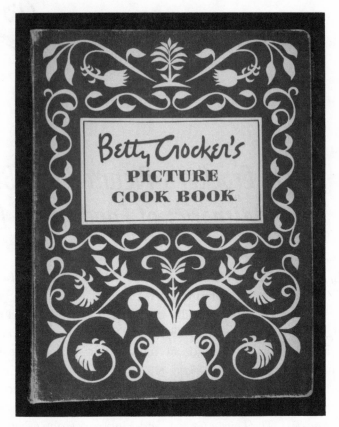

The first loose-leaf edition of Betty Crocker's bestseller.

and drug chains were besieging General Mills with pleas to carry the book; and the initial print run was said to be "three times as large as any first order . . . ever given in the United States."[2] And, thanks to ten years of kitchen testing by home economists and housewives, the quality of the finished product earned the kudos of the most demanding food critics.

The *New York Times*, for example, after quibbling with the appearance of sugar on the list of ingredients for French dressing, went on to praise the lavish use of instructional photographs (633 step-by-step photo essays on culinary technique, printed in black and white, and 36 full-color glamour shots of the finished dishes) and the simplified recipes, consisting of a single, basic formula followed by several more sophisticated but equally easy-to-follow variations. Margaret Gram, writing in the *Saturday Review,* found the recipes precise and "accurate . . . with all the fine details as to performance so essential for the

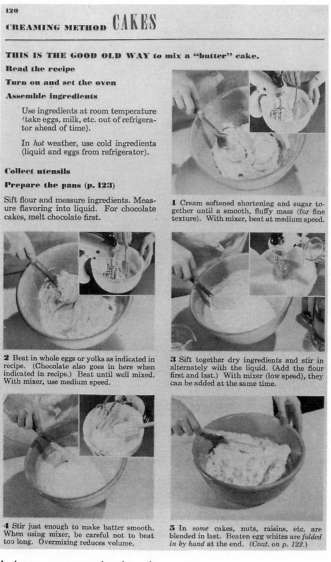

120

CREAMING METHOD CAKES

THIS IS THE GOOD OLD WAY to mix a "butter" cake.

Read the recipe

Turn on and set the oven

Assemble ingredients

Use ingredients at room temperature (take eggs, milk, etc. out of refrigerator ahead of time).

In *hot* weather, use cold ingredients (liquid and eggs from refrigerator).

Collect utensils

Prepare the pans (p. 123)

Sift flour and measure ingredients. Measure flavoring into liquid. For chocolate cakes, melt chocolate first.

1 Cream softened shortening and sugar together until a smooth, fluffy mass (for fine texture). With mixer, beat at medium speed.

2 Beat in whole eggs or yolks as indicated in recipe. (Chocolate also goes in here when indicated in recipe.) Beat until well mixed. With mixer, use medium speed.

3 Sift together dry ingredients and stir in alternately with the liquid. (Add the flour first and last.) With mixer (low speed), they can be added at the same time.

4 Stir just enough to make batter smooth. When using mixer, be careful not to beat too long. Overmixing reduces volume.

5 In *some* cakes, nuts, raisins, etc. are blended in last. Beaten egg whites are *folded in by hand* at the end. (*Cont. on p. 122.*)

A photo-essay on creaming shortening.

beginner and so satisfying to the experienced homemaker." A Chicago daily called it "the finest basic general cookbook that has ever been published . . ., superlative in the fields of breads, cakes, cookies, pies and pastries." The preponderance of quickbreads and desserts—at the expense of meats, salads, and vegetable dishes—was duly noted by the food authorities but readily excused on the grounds that General Mills, after all, sold flour and Betty Crocker was the humanized, feminized, wise, and kindly face of the corporation.[3]

The *New York Times* was telling no secrets when it explained that "Betty Crocker" was actually the forty-eight women who made up the Home Service Department of General Mills. The largest customer-service division in the food industry, the staff fielded an average of 2,000 letters a day from homemakers asking for help in matters ranging from planning a buffet (suddenly popular in the 1950s) to preventing sogginess in layer cakes. Since 1921, the name Betty Crocker had stood for sound housekeeping advice dispensed first by mail and later by a long-running radio show on the NBC network.[4] Given visible form and personality in a portrait commissioned from the cover illustrator Neysa McMein in 1936, her competent-looking, dignified, neither-young-nor-old ("an ageless 31," said one publicist) self began to grace packages, especially those containing the new convenience foods developed as a result of wartime experiments in dehydration and factory preparation. A trademark now as much as a symbol for service, she also appeared in ads, in recipe columns, and on the boxes containing small appliances manufactured by General Mills in the plant in which it had briefly turned out gunsights for the Navy and other military hardware. A company survey cited by *Fortune* in 1945 revealed that 91 percent of all American housewives knew who Betty Crocker was—and 56 percent correctly identified her with General Mills products.[5]

Betty's success spawned a whole sisterhood of look-alike household experts: Mary Lee Taylor of Pet Milk; Aunt Jenny, the "Spry" shortening lady; Jane Ashley (Karo syrup and Linit starch); Mary Lynn Woods (Fleischmann's yeast); Kay Kellogg (Kellogg's cereals); Martha Logan (Swift meats); Anne Marshall (Campbell soups)—and Ann Pillsbury from Minneapolis-based Pillsbury Flour, General Mills's

The real Betty Crockers: home economists at work in the Polka-Dot Test Kitchen at General Mills, 1951.

chief competitor and rival. The fad was by no means limited to the food business, either. Airlines and manufacturers of ranges and television sets also adorned their advertisements with head-and-shoulders cameos of crisp professional women endorsing the wares offered for sale. Monsanto Plastics identified the "Marion Palmer" whose signature was affixed to ads for vinyl floor coverings and easy-wash TV trays as a "modern living consultant." Modern living had something to do with the proliferation of female experts, both real and make-believe, and the use of their pictures to soften the image of corporate America.[6]

Big business was a male preserve (Dr. Lela Booher, chief nutritionist for General Mills in the late 1940s, was the exception), and the factory a venue that stood in sharp contrast with the home, especially during

This New Photo-Method tested and perfected in the Occident Home Baking Institute,
Minneapolis, Minn.

"Virginia Roberts," a Betty Crocker look-
alike of the late 1940s.

World War II, when Rosie the Riveter went to work, and shortly
thereafter, when she was abruptly sent back to the kitchen. But female
trademarks did more than take the curse off the consumer industries
that would transform the postwar definition of domesticity. In their
choice of visual symbols, such ads also addressed the specific nature
of the new American household and the losses it had incurred. The
Betty Crocker of the cookbook years, for instance, wasn't a whole,
living person. She was only a head, a graceful bust delimited by the
implicit oval outline of a locket or a colonial portrait. By her manner
of presentation, she evoked the past, a heritage, a disembodied memory, maternal authority. These were the elements lacking in the lives
of the college girls and peripatetic war workers who moved to Levittown and settled down with ex-G.I.s in the late 1940s and early
1950s—girls who, according to General Mills research, missed "the
apprenticeship of the stove" which had once equipped their mothers

and grandmothers and great-grandmothers before them with basic culinary skills.[7]

The historian Harvey Levenstein blames the breakdown of the familial chain of expertise on the big food processors, who turned the mass media into the most attractive sources of culinary advice in the 20s and 30s.[8] Whatever the role of industry in the change, however, the flour business suffered acutely in the immediate postwar years, before commercial baked goods became the norm. One of the most compelling reasons for issuing a cookbook in the first place was to reestablish the profitable tradition of home baking—a tradition stretched to the breaking point as modern brides moved to the suburbs and left their mothers with their old-fashioned ways and complicated ethnic recipes behind them in the cities. Out went the *kleppas,* the *kolaches* and the *klenater;* by 1950 General Mills was already giving more ad space to prepackaged Bisquick easy baking mix than to Gold Medal Flour. In an atmosphere of uncertainty and change, Betty Crocker's pictorial evocation of womanhood and history provided a welcome sense of reassurance. Modern living had isolated the homemaker in suburbia, without the skills necessary to duplicate the fabulous new meals pictured in the magazines, and with little sense of how the vast array of boxes and bottles and frozen bricks of food on display in the new supermarket might constitute a family menu. With kindly expertise and a never-fail recipe for Chiffon Cake, Betty Crocker became the substitute mother to a generation of motherless exurbanites.

The importance of that image to the 1950s is demonstrated by General Mills's collective anxiety about Betty Crocker. In the mid-40s, for example, Betty's official portrait—rose-colored dress with an unfrilly pleated ruffle at the neck, flecks of gray in the hair, a serious expression—was shipped back to Neysa McMein "to be sharpened up a little," ostensibly for the sake of better reproduction in magazine layouts. This revised version, with a tentative smile, appeared in the series of recipe-bearing ads that led up to the release of the cookbook, but Betty's likeness was nowhere to be found in that volume or in the 1950 Christmas Gift Box of pans and mixes offered to stockholders and employees. Ninety-seven percent of American women now rec-

The supermarket was the showcase for the new postwar food technology.

ognized the Crocker name. And it was her name alone (and her easy-to-read signature) that suddenly constituted her graphic symbol.[9]

Television seems to have been one major reason for Betty Crocker's temporary disappearance. On the radio, Betty could be played by anybody with a good script and a little natural warmth. In her pre-network career on the airwaves, there were multiple Bettys broadcasting from Minneapolis, Buffalo, and a dozen other cities. The listener's imagination supplied a picture of a home economist with a chatty side to her personality or, after 1936 and the McMein portrait, connected the voice with the picture in the ads. As a visual medium, however, television threatened to change the pictorial relationship between audience and corporate symbol by exposing the agreed-upon fiction of Betty Crocker. Since there was no real Betty—no one at General Mills who looked just like McMein's painting—the trademark lost ground with account executives working on prime-time commercials for *The Lone Ranger, Life with the Erwins, Live Like a Millionaire,* and the other ABC shows sponsored by General Mills. Adelaide Hawley, the current radio Betty Crocker, moved to Saturday afternoon TV in the fall of 1952, in what the company called an experiment. Although the camera was often focused on Hawley's hands rather than her face and the current hiatus in pictorial ads minimized the imagistic disparity between brunette Betty and the stunningly blonde Miss Hawley, General Mills wrote off the show as a million-dollar mistake and quit the home screen after the second season.[10]

An early TV cooking show: how to bake cookies. The pictorial technique was duplicated in *Betty Crocker's Picture Cook Book.*

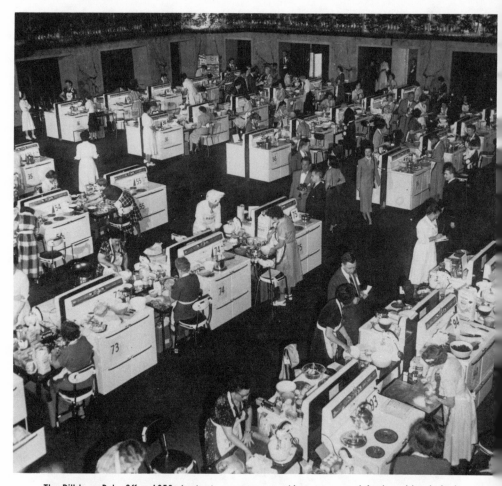

The Pillsbury Bake-Off, a 1950s institution, put home cooking on an equal footing with televised sports and encouraged the use of mixes. It also helped to put a human face on a big, impersonal corporation.

Market research, in the meantime, was telling the firm to clarify and strengthen Betty's image and to put her back at the center of the consumer effort. This was especially true of a pair of in-depth psychological studies using the new techniques of motivational research undertaken independently for General Mills by Dr. Burleigh Gardner of Chicago and Dr. Ernest Dichter of New York. Dichter was a great admirer of Betty Crocker. Her continuing popularity, he believed, proved that Americans still hankered for individualism in an age of corporate monoliths. She took the edge off the impersonal transaction between the homemaker-customer and General Mills. The man who later claimed credit for the decision to leave powdered eggs out of General Mills cake mixes in order to give the housewife a sense of making a creative contribution to the process, Dr. Dichter advised all his food-industry clients to aim for a balance between creativity and the scientific efficiency of the home economist. But he was obsessed with the iconography of baked goods. Although the psychologist realized that home-baked cakes were being reduced to obsolescence by the supermarket, they retained a disproportionate symbolic importance because baking still gave women a powerful emotional satisfaction, a womanly feeling, and a sense of being needed in the automated prepackaged home. To present one's husband with a homemade cake was an "act of love," he rhapsodized. It was a gift of self, a talisman of fecundity. By that logic, Betty Crocker—a warmer, more womanly Betty Crocker; a wifely, motherly, less starchily professional Betty Crocker; "a woman's woman," associated with the home, young housewives, holiday entertaining—was General Mills's greatest potential asset. And so Betty was redesigned for the 1950s.[11]

In 1955 six famous artist-illustrators, including Norman Rockwell of the Famous Artists School, were invited to submit fresh interpretations of the McMein portrait to a jury consisting of 1,600 women chosen from General Mills customers across the country. The winning entry, by Hilda Taylor, banished the dated cupid's-bow mouth and the marcelled hair. If Betty Crocker was still a home economist, wearing a simplified version of the old red-and-white coverall uniform, she was more open and accessible now, with a broad smile—or the same blend of home expert and happy, creative cook, of science and art, that Dichter and his colleagues looked for in designing new food products to mediate successfully between industry and the American home. Her temples had grayed markedly, too; this was an older and a wiser Betty Crocker, a woman fully capable of giving the kind of household advice that mothers used to give. Her whole demeanor, according to the company's squad of Freudian consultants, seemed to ask, "What can I do to help you?"[12]

That, of course, was the message of *Betty Crocker's Picture Cook Book,* despite the absence of a comforting likeness to ask the question in person. And the graphic medium used to render assistance to the homemaker was almost as personal and intimate as learning how to cream sugar with shortening at a mother's elbow. The photo-essay technique, borrowed from the magazines in which General Mills advertised, taught the novice how to perform each operation by duplicating the actions of a pair of hands seen from the point of view of someone sitting or standing directly across the countertop from a woman with polished pink fingernails wearing a white, long-sleeved coverall. The reader, or viewer, in other words, was placed in close proximity to the cooking instructor and saw the inside of the bowl or the markings on a measuring cup from the same angle of vision as Betty Crocker did. For surely it was Betty—the almost invisible Betty of the early 1950s—who offered up the innermost recesses of her bowls and pans to the scrutiny of the nervous bride.

Photographic cooking instruction did not begin with Betty Crocker, although it was apparently perfected in Minnesota milling circles during World War II, as a home-front version of the Army training manual. A recipe booklet demonstrating a simple "photo-method" for cake-making was issued in 1944 by Occident Flour of Minneapolis, under the authorship of Virginia Roberts, another fictional cooking expert who looked a great deal like Betty Crocker. But the numbers of photos in the *Picture Cook Book* and the emphasis on vision—on the picture over the written word—also link the enterprise to the television set which, by 1950, was as much a desirable feature of the suburban home as the washer, the dryer, the electric range, or the General Mills pop-up toaster. The culinary historians Jane and Michael Stern observe that television turned out to be "a fantastic way" to sell the new home appliances and the products meant to be used in conjunction with them because the actual properties of electric skillets, Juicerators (endorsed on camera by Johnny Carson, Merv Griffin, and Bess Myerson), and the Hotpoint all-electric kitchen (in which Louise Leslie, perky hostess of the afternoon *Homemakers Exchange* on CBS, whipped up everything from prune cupcakes to sherbet) could be demonstrated in convincing close-ups right before the homemaker's eyes. Besides, airtime was cheap: commercials ran on

158

CHIFFON CAKES Once upon a time we had a secret . . .

Read recipe   Assemble ingredients
Collect utensils   Preheat oven
Sift flour and measure ingredients

2 Beat with spoon (or electric mixer) until smooth.

1 Sift flour, sugar, salt, baking powder into mixing bowl. Make a "well," add in order: oil, egg yolks, lemon rind, and flavoring.

3 Add cream of tartar to egg whites. Beat until they hold *very stiff* peaks (stiffer than for meringues). Do not underbeat.

4 Pour egg yolk mixture in thin stream over entire surface of egg whites, gently cutting and folding in with rubber spatula.

5 Fold gently . . . bringing scraper across *bottom* of bowl, up the side and over. Turn bowl and continue until completely blended.

6 Pour into ungreased pan. Bake until surface springs back when lightly touched. Invert pan immediately. Let hang until cold. Loosen with a spatula. Turn pan over and hit edge sharply on table to loosen.

7 Frost and trim cake as desired. This is the Peppermint Chip Chiffon, *p. 160,* with a cooked white frosting and crushed peppermint candy sprinkled over it. Chiffon cakes are delicious unfrosted.

The *Picture Cook Book* put the reader in the bowl; the shot resembled a TV closeup.

and on. In addition to selling appliances, they taught techniques housewives could not have learned elsewhere—and convinced them that the foolproof pushbuttons they saw in action on TV would never let them down.[13]

By making cooking look both effortless and dramatic, like the shows they interrupted, some TV commercials gave a boost to new convenience foods. The *Kraft Television Theater* stopped periodically in the 50s to let a pair of disembodied hands, derived from the Betty Crocker format, prepare TV snacks or quick, one-dish dinners in a "jiffy" with the company's processed cheeses, as a cheerful off-camera voice (male!) chuckled with amazement at the sheer simplicity of it all.[14] The ads strongly implied that the viewer could cook along with the program, at the same breakneck speed, and get the essential housework done during commercials. That was the message, too, of

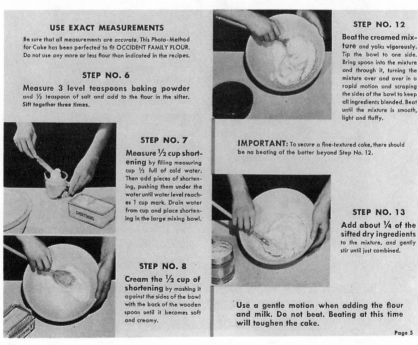

USE EXACT MEASUREMENTS

Be sure that all measurements are accurate. This Photo-Method for Cake has been perfected to fit OCCIDENT FAMILY FLOUR. Do not use any more or less flour than indicated in the recipes.

STEP NO. 6

Measure 3 level teaspoons baking powder and ½ teaspoon of salt and add to the flour in the sifter. Sift together three times.

STEP NO. 7

Measure ½ cup shortening by filling measuring cup ½ full of cold water. Then add pieces of shortening, pushing them under the water until water level reaches 1 cup mark. Drain water from cup and place shortening in the large mixing bowl.

STEP NO. 8

Cream the ½ cup of shortening by mashing it against the sides of the bowl with the back of the wooden spoon until it becomes soft and creamy.

STEP NO. 12

Beat the creamed mixture and yolks vigorously. Tip the bowl to one side. Bring spoon into the mixture and through it, turning the mixture over and over in a rapid motion and scraping the sides of the bowl to keep all ingredients blended. Beat until the mixture is smooth, light and fluffy.

IMPORTANT: To secure a fine-textured cake, there should be no beating of the batter beyond Step No. 12.

STEP NO. 13

Add about ¼ of the sifted dry ingredients to the mixture, and gently stir until just combined.

Use a gentle motion when adding the flour and milk. Do not beat. Beating at this time will toughen the cake.

Page 5

Virginia Roberts's "photo-method" for baking cakes was one possible prototype for the Betty Crocker format.

Father Knows Best, The Adventures of Ozzie and Harriet, and the other family comedies that featured fully equipped kitchens in which the stars often appeared to make and serve meals during the course of the half-hour time slot, without so much as mussing their aprons.

If the TV was not yet permanently ensconced in the corner of the living room or in the pass-through between the kitchen and the multipurpose space that opened onto the patio, the set was a staple fixture of the ideal home in *Better Homes and Gardens* and the *Ladies' Home Journal* in 1950, when the Betty Crocker cookbook appeared. The TV was the mark of modern magic and the good life. And so, despite the traditional cakes and pastries that her surrogate hands prepared in easy-to-follow photographs, Betty Crocker's volume was very much a part of the consumer paradise of the 1950s, in which pictures—of cars and ranch houses, appliances and gorgeous cakes made in a jiffy from a miracle mix—diagramed the floorplan of carefree suburban living, in how-to-do-it steps. The General Mills model kitchens illustrated and described in the color section at the very beginning of the book announced the modernity of the enterprise: the Terrace Kitchen with its sleek, rounded corners, color-coordinated cabinet front, and "every known home-type convenience"; the gaily decorated Polka Dot Kitchen "with stainless steel counters and a laundry cart"; and the Kitchen of Tomorrow, whose every push-button and easy-care surface was already being advertised on prime-time TV.[15]

There were ultramodern recipes, too, suggestive of changing patterns of eating and entertaining. The color spread on appetizers, for instance, pushes the various fruit cups and vegetable juice cocktails of formal, sit-down dining to the corners of the page and gives the middle over to fingerfood, to trays of crackers, chips, and vegetables surrounding bowls of what the text calls spreads or "dunks" reputed to have originated on West Coast—the forerunners of the famous 1954 Lipton California onion-soup dip for potato chips.[16] The self-service canapé, laid out on the coffee table or the patio, was "easy, informal, and fun," and it suggested a new kind of suburban gathering, where guests drifted at will through an unstructured series of spaces, nibbling and chatting as they pleased, in contrast to the prewar pattern of seating charts and a rigid order of courses. Betty Crocker's friends

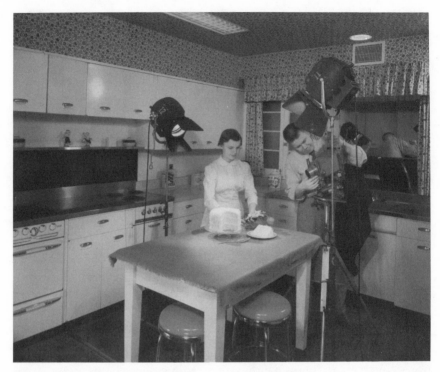

Betty Crocker's Kamera Kitchen in 1955, with a photography session in progress. The countertops are stainless steel and flow without interruption into adjacent cooking surfaces.

were more likely to wind up in the backyard, enjoying an impromptu "Supper in the Garden" (as the *Picture Cook Book* termed it) consisting of hot dogs, baked beans, and salad, or what the West Coast had already begun calling a barbecue.[17]

Heavily promoted by the beef industry and manufacturers of outdoor furniture, the barbecue boom showed that postwar cooking had become a chore readily shared with the man of the house, who was expected to preside over the family's new Weber kettle grill. In his cowboy/outdoorsman's mode, Dad saved Mom the drudgery of cooking another big Sunday dinner, said *Esquire*'s 1953 gentlemen's guide to outdoor hospitality. Since cooking was as time-consuming and difficult a task for women as it was for their husbands, convenience foods came into their own in the postwar era. *Fortune*'s 1953

Quick frozen—for quick serving

An old-fashioned fried chicken dinner

with fluffy mashed potatoes

A barbecue without the fuss, from the TV Dinner folks at Swanson's.

analysis of spending on groceries found that, contrary to the usual economic rule of thumb, the percentage of the average American family's income spent on food was going up as total income rose because consumers were willing to pay more for processing. By 1954, for instance, the value added to the cost of food by processing was 45 percent above 1939 levels.[18] And the ingredients that went into the dips and picnic-table menus were likely to be "short-cut foods," frozen, packaged, canned, ready to serve with a minimum of fuss, like the prebaked Brown 'n' Serve rolls introduced by General Mills in November of 1949 and discreetly recommended by the cookbook.[19]

Nicely browned dinner rolls, towering cakes, and pies rich with jewel-tinted fruit photographed well in color and gave the baked goods that accounted for the majority of Betty Crocker's recipes both an added eye appeal and a posh, luxurious hint of tomorrow. Except for the wealthy few who owned prototype sets, television was a black-and-white experience in 1950, in a world that openly craved color. Color was an index of status and fashion in the 1950s. It signified a break with the sameness of the military uniform, an answer to the drabness of hard times, a visible sign of a car or a set of kitchen cabinets bought brand, spanking new. Color was an extra, a mark of futuristic technology at work, of miracle fabrics and plastics in a thousand unimaginable rainbow-tinted hues. So everyone talked about color TV, although nobody had it until the mid-1960s, a decade after the NBC peacock signaled the beginning of regular color programming.[20] Competing with television, Hollywood went Technicolor, spelling the doom of the cheap B-movie and the double feature. In a darkened theater, color exuded a kind of lavishness, a sensuality lacking in the grainy, small-screen dramas and sitcoms that played nightly amid the clutter of the typical suburban Cape Cod.

This appetite for strong color made the ads more appealing than the articles in most magazines. Even in *Look* and *Life*, where the balance had already been tipped away from text and toward the photo-essay, the cheap color gravure of food ads all but overshadowed the black-and-white news shots that had riveted a generation of readers. Nor was this color natural, by today's standards. Each object was garish and bright and most pictures redoubled the effect by the use of forced contrasts between one item and another, between object and background. Colorized appliances came in blinding primaries, like so many Jell-O molds. In *Betty Crocker's Picture Cook Book*, a pink-and-white cake reposed loudly upon a green satin tablecloth, in the company of another confection adorned with orange and purple flowers. The Betty Crocker feature cake of 1951, widely promoted on TV, was called the "Colorvision" and was made by tinting the standard Partycake mix with packages of red or green or yellow gelatin.[21]

It would be logical to conclude that some accident of time and lithography had distorted the coloristic content of cookbooks and ads of the period were it not for the evidence provided by films, clothes, vintage cars, and even the bottled maraschino cherries that adorned everything from Manhattan cocktails and grapefruit halves to two of the most impressive cakes in Betty Crocker's published repertory.[22] Along with crimson refrigerators and two-toned shoes, these artifacts reveal a cultural preference for loud, clear color, often enhanced by the calculated use of complementary contrasts (between a pink cake, for instance, and a pale green tablecover; between orange and purple cake decorations). Applied to comestibles, this interest in tonal quality meant that the aesthetic character of a cake or a canapé was at least equal in value to older criteria of excellence, like taste and texture. But the two-dimensional universe of the food advertiser, the realm of pictures and the *Picture Cook Book*, put the emphasis on appearance alone—on shape, on surface gloss, on dazzling color.

The influence of such factors on American cookery in the 1950s can be gauged by the vehemence with which the aesthetic approach was denounced. In a passage written in 1949, M. F. K. Fisher, perhaps the leading food writer of the day, ridiculed the spate of recent recipes concocted for their visual appeal alone, without any consideration for the palate, or what she called "the onslaughts of marshmallow-vegetable-gelatin salads and such which smile at me in Kodachrome from current magazine advertisements." Perhaps, as later critics of the American diet have charged, taste became an acceptable tradeoff for convenience in the 1950s: the pleasure of the eye was meant to compensate for the loss incurred by the tastebuds. But the strategy was not unopposed. A widely used home economics text deplored the practice of dyeing foodstuffs for holiday menus and went on to detail other instances of misguided creativity, including a fad for a kind of food sculpture—"a chicken croquette molded in the shape of a chicken, a mock duck made from a leg of lamb; and a peach salad supposedly resembling a jack-o'-lantern." A mock duck (fabricated from a five-pound shoulder of lamb), a fake T-bone steak (modeled in ground beef and Wheaties breakfast cereal, with a strip of carrot inserted to resemble a bone), and ersatz chicken drumsticks were all included, in fact, in Betty Crocker's slim section on meat, and she did not stint on the food coloring elsewhere in the volume.[23]

Sometimes called "decorative cooking," this style of cuisine went back to the late nineteenth century and to reform-minded cooking schools that aimed to elevate the feminine work of the kitchen to a science—or a fine art. The artfulness of table presentations, it was thought, stimulated the salivary glands and thus aided digestion. But ducks manufactured from table scraps and all-green or all-white meals also asserted the homemaker's control over her environment at the same time that they ennobled the base animal function of appetite. And, according to the first systematic anthropological study of American foodways, published in 1952, such labor-intensive dishes gave a strong "impression of trouble [taken] in preparation."[24]

The radio voice of Betty Crocker in the late 1940s harped on a new "Design for Happiness," or ways "to create happy new homes." Ministering to the family through good food was "the age-old way to express love and concern for their welfare," Betty Crocker further noted in her introduction to the *Picture Cook Book*. The simple equation between love, happiness, and home cooking was complicated, however, by the allure of ready-to-eat foods and mixes. Relentlessly advertised (even by Betty Crocker's corporate bosses) and powerfully appealing on grounds of novelty and prestige, such convenience products seem to have been most readily accepted by the housewife as ingredients in recipes that added the love quotient—lots of time and fuss—and thereby took the curse off the promised ease of preparation. Canned soups became the basis for intricate casseroles. Equipped with boundless imagination and a single utensil, wrote the author of the 1951 *Can-Opener Cook Book*, "I become the artist-cook. . . . It is easy to cook like a gourmet though you are only a beginner."[25]

Even the new frozen main dishes introduced in the wake of Swanson's revolutionary TV Dinner of 1953 were often described, in recipes printed on the packages, as starting points for other, time-consuming gourmet treats. Stuffed into a pie shell, a pepper-half, or a tomato, with appropriate seasoning and embellishment, a single flash-frozen entree could serve for dinner, luncheon, or a party supper.[26]

If the recipes supplied to women's magazines by the food industry are any indication, color, "fancy compositions" for the table, and inconvenience often went hand in hand. Although there is no proof that any wife and mother actually made deep-fried pastry cups in the shape of magnolia blossoms especially to hold individual servings of canned fruit cocktail, Del Monte strongly suggested she do so in a full-age ad in *American Home* in 1954. "Blossom out with this stunning new dessert," urged the copy. It might take the better part of the afternoon to make, and make mockery of the real reason for buying pre-sweetened, ready-to-serve canned fruit in the first place, but this was the ideal way to present a product distinguished by "sparkling clear colors [and] trim, tidy cuts." Each one topped off with a piquant, too-red cherry half, the pale golden cups showed off the golden hues of pineapple, pear, and peach to best advantage.[27]

Chicken à la king, a party favorite of the 1950s (when chicken was still a Sunday-dinner luxury item, rarely packaged in manageable portions) was another feast for the eye. It was also providentially easy to freeze and thus led the march of frozen entrees to the American dining table. If made from scratch, it required long hours of advance work, simmering, skinning, and boning the bird, preparing a lumpless white sauce, slicing and gently sautéing the vegetables that set the dish apart from mere creamed chicken. But whether home-cooked or merely thawed, chicken à la king was supposed to be arranged in or upon edible cups, timbales, or decorative rings of pastry that did require lots of fuss. The results, however, were stunning—a visual symphony in purest white, accented by grace notes of scarlet pimento and green pepper. In the classic 1950s presentation, chicken à la king looked like Abstract Expressionist color drips applied to a dinner plate, so completely were its properties as food overwhelmed by its pictorial charm.

The cake—the centerpiece of *Betty Crocker's Picture Cook Book*—was the ultimate in aesthetic fare. The cake was food as sculpture, frosted in living color. It was a test of mother love and womanly competence, the battleground between packaged mix and mastery of the culinary arts, between modern ease and old-fashioned, time-consuming kitchen drudgery. The most heavily promoted food icon of the 1950s in the forms of mix, bakery product, and made-from-scratch talisman of Crocker-style "Home Life," the cake emerged from the oven laden with personal and collective anxiety and a thick icing of symbolism. One of the overnight hit records of 1950 was a silly, vaguely sexy novelty tune called "If I Knew You Were Comin' I'd've Baked a Cake," in which the cake stood for feminine hospitality.[28] Beginning in 1937 the nation's commercial bakeries had urged sons and daughters to observe Mother's Day with a white "Roses-in-Snow" cake topped by a wearable corsage of artificial flowers (this had become a plastic lapel pin by 1950); Valentine's Day was similarly marked by a heart-shaped "Sweetheart Cake" tricked out in bows and cupids. Heavily promoted by General Mills in the interest of selling more flour to bakers, both campaigns were linked to the Betty Crocker tradename in the 1940s—and to the concept that mothers and best girls were somehow to be equated with cakes, as recipients of the love fetishes that women used to make in their own kitchens. Cakes were, according to Dr. Dichter and his Institute for Motivational Research, gender-specific by virtue of their appearance. Male chefs naturally gravitated to meat and drink. But "the shapes of desserts and their prettiness, colorfulness, and playfulness," he concluded, "embody symbols of femininity. . . . [The woman's] concern with . . . eye appeal . . ., her ability to impart the telling decorative touch, the qualities of lightness, delicacy and grace all symbolize her essential femininity."[29]

Brainstorming sessions on cakeishness, held in a special room at the Madison Avenue offices of Batten, Barton, Durstine and Osborn (painted yellow to stimulate creative thinking), produced a slew of footnotes to Dichter's core insight. Cakes were female indulgences, the ad executives decided—markers of social ostentation or added attention. Like the popular new home freezer—12 percent of all American households would have a deep-freeze by 1953—the cake stood for maternal abundance, for having enough to eat, and all the

A labor-intensive, aesthetic food ad of 1954. Far from simplifying household tasks, convenience foods seemed to demand ever more elaborate decorative forms of presentation.

extras, too. Because cakes hinted at any number of deep-seated needs and psychological gratifications, for which they served as substitutes, admen were reluctant to show them being consumed in TV and magazine pitches; they were meant to be contemplated and appreciated, like works of art, but eating an icon of American womanhood was tantamount to sacrilege.[30]

Cake baking presented two big problems for the women who were supposed to enact that highly charged ritual of gender. One involved fear of failure; the other, a lack of time. A study issued in 1950 by the head of the Institute for Family and Community Living at Vassar College showed that over 8 million wives, or approximately one in every four, held a job outside the home. Although the author of the study disapproved of careerists who "thwart[ed] motherhood to maintain false standards of living," most working women needed their paychecks to make the monthly payments on the freezer and counted on labor-saving devices to take up the slack on the domestic front. With time in short supply, products that promised to achieve results quickly and effortlessly won a following. Early favorites included Minute Rice, Readi-Whip, one-dish meals (like Betty Crocker's 1949 proto-frozen pie, the "Dinner-in-a-Shell"), and TV snack foods that could actually be cooked in small tabletop appliances during station breaks. It was in this atmosphere of overheated domesticity, where the pressure to produce a token of femininity was exacerbated by the shortage of free time for housewifely pursuits, that the cake mix came into its own.[31]

In a sense, popular demand for a fast, foolproof cake pushed food chemists into inventing mixes. The Double-Quick method, first introduced on the Betty Crocker Cooking School of the Air in 1944 in honor of its twentieth anniversary, was a revolutionary way of mixing batter, with the wet ingredients—including cooking oil in place of solid shortening—added to pre-measured amounts of the dry ones. The closely guarded process had been invented by a Hollywood caterer known as "the baker to the stars," who sold it to General Mills in 1943 for a reported $5,000. That technique, in turn, spawned the "mysterious and provocative" Betty Crocker Chiffon Cake—"the first really new-type cake in 100 years," claimed recipe-ads in *Look*, the women's magazines, the trade journals, and the leading dailies—in the spring of 1948. A Double-Quick formulation with stiffened egg whites folded in at the last minute, the Chiffon Cake was a light, lofty creation baked in a tube pan, "a whopping big cake with the delicacy of angel food, the richness of pound cake, and freshness lasting for days."[32]

The archetypal 1950s cake was all those things, and more: rich, big, tall, complex in shape—a vast canvas for acres of colored frosting and trimmings; a showstopper; a culinary feat that looked harder to make than it actually was. It was a modern recipe by virtue of its quick-and-easy features, but one that produced a cake somewhat reminiscent of the taste and texture of old-time cakes that mother use to bake. Above all, it was impossible to ruin. Despite the weather, the season, or the mood of the cook, it turned out the same way every time, eliminating any remote possibility of failure. And the housewife's fear of failure, concluded the psychologists who worked for the food business, was the key to understanding how to make a profit from cakes. If the cake was a litmus test of femininity, a sexual symbol in which height and perfection of shape stood for a successful birth, then the possibility of disaster in the kitchen was fraught with enormous personal consequences.

The Chiffon Cake was one early response to this syndrome. But the perfect solution was the cake mix, with Betty Crocker's guarantee of quality emblazoned on every box. Ernest Dichter told General Mills that "most women refused to bake cakes because of 'fear of failure' and bought cake mixes to eliminate mischance rather than to save time." The cake-mix cake allowed Mrs. Average American to enjoy the creativity of pseudo-birth without the labor pains. "The success of ready-mixes," Dichter added, "arises from the unusual promise they offer the modern woman":

> For the first time she has the possibility of compromise; mixes not only save time, but permit [her] to be creative in new forms. If saving time were the only factor of importance, then it would be best to advise the woman to buy . . . her cakes from the bakery. Instead, modern ready-mixes permit her to bake at home, but in an easy fashion which assures her success.[33]

Indeed, by the time she finished adding the eggs (or parts thereof) and the various flavorings and extra ingredients suggested on the back of the box for those who preferred an individualized cake, the process had probably taken longer than the made-from-scratch version. From General Mills's perspective, the gain was a loyal and satisfied customer, dependent on Betty Crocker for assured performance and for a sense of accomplishment. What the cake mix whispered to the housewife, as she steered her shopping cart past the home-baking section in the local supermarket, was a siren's song of sweet reassurance: "You are a wonderful cook. Our cake mixes will permit you to use your wonderful talent without drudgery. You are the one who does a remarkable job. We only furnish the tools."[34]

So cake mixes multiplied on store shelves and, General Mills insisted, "banish[ed] cake failure completely." Gingercake Mix. Devils Food Cake Mix. And the Partycake Mix that could yield a golden cake when made with egg yolks, a yellow cake with whole eggs, a white cake with egg whites, and a spice cake with whole eggs plus a few kitchen condiments: sixty-four separate possibilities in every package, if the assorted frosting recipes printed on the box were stirred into the equation. More than a billion cakes were either made or bought in the United States every year in the late 1940s, but the statistics also showed that only 2.2 percent of the total volume of flour used in the home came in the form of cake mixes. The potential market for products that combined convenience with an ironclad guarantee of success was enormous, and the new mixes answered that demand. The first food-marketing triumph of the postwar boom, mixes tripled in sales between January of 1947 and August of 1948 alone. *National Grocers Bulletin*, summing up the status of the new flour-based grocery items in 1953, noted that "cake mixes have done in six years what pancake mixes did in twenty." The First Family ordered mixes for the White House pantry. The American family, on average, now took home two boxes of Partycake Mix or a competing brand every single month.[35]

There were limits to the amount of creative fiddling around with a mix that the modern woman would tolerate, however. The advertising critic Vance Packard recounted the cautionary tale of the ad

Reading the boxes in the supermarket: the possibilities seemed endless, as baking mixes edged out flour on the eye-level shelves.

agency which, in the early 1950s, determined to take advantage of Jell-O's color and the shimmering shapes it could assume by picturing the product "in beautiful, layered, multicolor creations with elaborate decorative touches." The ads were spectacular but sales plummeted because homemakers took the tempting photographs as prescriptive and began to wonder if gelatin was worth that much trouble. When the company went back to showing a simple, one-flavor Jell-O mold in 1956, profits rebounded immediately. In 1953 *Food Field Reporter* ran an editorial pointing out the disparity between time-saving advances in food technology and the corporate promotion of convenience foods through recipes for pretty concoctions that consumed vast amounts of time "not only in whipping up the dishes but in cleaning up afterwards." Weren't the overblown recipes and the gorgeous pictures

Crisp Vegetable Salad

Dissolve 1 package Lemon Jell-O in 1 cup *hot* water. Add 1 cup cold water, 1 tablespoon vinegar, and 1 teaspoon salt. Chill until slightly thickened. Fold in ¾ cup diced cucumber, ½ cup thinly sliced red radishes, and ½ cup thinly sliced young onions. Pour into individual molds, or 1-quart mold. Chill until firm. Unmold on crisp greens. Makes 4 to 6 servings.

JELL-O IS A REGISTERED
TRADE-MARK OF
GENERAL FOODS CORP.

This ad ran in women's magazines in 1950: salad as do-it-yourself art!

that accompanied them out of step with the fast pace of modern life and "valuable only to that minority whose enthusiasm matches that of the home economist who formulated the recipes in the first place?" Apparently not. Figures cited in the same trade paper noted an escalating demand for illustrated recipes: home magazines sold out in days on the strength of new ideas from the kitchens of General Mills and General Foods, and grocers struggled to keep up with customer requests for the free recipe cards that manufacturers dangled from the fronts of the shelves that held their mixes. Only the psychologist could explain it, sighed the editors.[36]

Yet even if the recipes and the lovely photos in the women's magazines are regarded as food fictions, as kitchen dreams never actually meant to come true, they still help to explain the perverse popularity of *Betty Crocker's Picture Cook Book* in the golden age of the cake mix and the frozen dinner. By depicting exquisite homemade cakes, the cookbook established an ideal—an ideal of lush, moist, decorated cakeness—that could be approximated in a variety of other, easier ways, including the use of a mix. Despite the easy-to-follow pictures, or perhaps because of their sheer numbers, the cookbook proved that home baking was a long and demanding task and made alternative methods of achieving results similar to those set forth in the color photographs all the more appealing. The *Picture Cook Book* was the best possible advertisement for the brightly colored boxes of cake mix stacked high on the grocer's shelves.

Color sold packaged goods to women in self-service stores, according to the latest research in food retailing; they tended to reach instinctively for red boxes (Betty Crocker's book was red, too).[37] Studies commissioned by executives in other, unrelated industries also indicated "that color was an apt loosener of middle-class purse strings." The luscious color pictures of finished, frosted cakes on boxes of mix made the imagination leap forward to the finished product: wishing and dreaming eliminated the work of preparation until the shopper could no longer resist the urge to pay a little extra for a gigantic, mouth-watering, thoroughly modern cake, somehow compressed into a cardboard cube bedecked with photographs.[38]

Because it gave the advertiser one last crack at the consumer at the crucial point of sale, packaging was the subject of intense scrutiny in the 1950s—especially the cartons and wrappers used in visually competitive situations, like cigarette kiosks, supermarkets, and television spots. In search of a telegenic image that would translate readily from the small screen to the freezer case, for instance, Sealtest hired the legendary industrial designer Raymond Loewy to redo the makeup of its trademark circus clown, Ed McMahon, along more distinctive lines. Other firms, including meat packers and breweries whose stodgy labels dated back to the nineteenth century, were converted to the view that vivid color was associated with "pleasure and gaiety" and thus belonged on beer cans, cardboard overwraps, and the cellophane wrapping on hot dogs. Food and grocery trade journals were quick to equate more colorful packaging with recent trends in daily life. If furniture, men's clothes, cars, refrigerators, and bedsheets all came in pink and lime green, if color TV was due in the lime-green and turquoise American living room at any moment, then surely color had a place on coffee cans, milk cartons, and cake-mix boxes. "All this rage for color is based on the fact that it attracts attention, pleases the eye, emphasizes the best features of the goods, and sells, while fixing the brand in the buyer's mind," *Progressive Grocer* concluded in 1954.[39]

The best case for building a product around packaging and food aesthetics came from Swanson's of Omaha, Nebraska, and their stunning success with the "TV Dinner," introduced in October of 1953 at a national convention of food editors meeting in Chicago. Frozen dinners, complete with meat, potato, and vegetable, were nothing new. They were civilian byproducts of rations developed for fliers during the war. Several East Coast concerns had begun to market precooked meals on a regional basis, beginning in 1951 when Frigidinner of Philadelphia offered ten "variety platters" for home consumption through a self-service laundry chain that also rented TV sets and repaired shoes.[40] Stouffer's of Cleveland and Quaker State of Pittsburgh weighed in with dinners of their own, packed in segmented aluminum trays, several months in advance of the Swanson announcement.[41]

What set the original TV Dinner—turkey, gravy, and dressing, whipped sweet potatoes with a pat of butter, and peas—apart from the rest was its appearance. The tripartite foil container presented the meal in a pleasing way: the meat course in the larger bottom compartment, set off by the bright green and orange of the side dishes nestled in the smaller sections placed above and around the focal point of the dinner. And thanks to the divided tray, it looked like a scientifically balanced meal, or the kind of big, square meal hungry

An early precursor of the TV Dinner.

servicemen got at boot camp. The turkey dinner had been chosen to test the concept because it usually was a big meal, a festive, once-or-twice-a-year meal when served at home, a menu associated with the holidays and good times, and a labor-intensive meal that showed off the convenience of a frozen entree to best advantage. But the fact that the traditional turkey dinner with the trimmings contained a preponderance of richly hued foods cannot have been wasted on a company that took pains to make sure portions being prepared for freezing looked appetizing, with the butter pats precisely in the center of the vegetable servings and the slices of light and dark meat stacked just so. And the overwrap of the TV dinner carton, consisting of a six-color sheet of printed cellophane laminated to tissue parchment, was the wonder of the industry because it reproduced the contents with such stunning, lip-smacking fidelity.[42]

REVOLUTIONARY NEW FOOD TREND!

"The over-$4,000 consumers . . . want not only good food, but convenience built into the food as well; and they are prepared to pay for whatever services the food industry can provide."   *Fortune Magazine, October, 1953*

—and Here's Swanson's Answer!

Swanson TV Dinners

A complete quick-frozen turkey dinner ready to heat and serve

Just what housewives want—no work, no thawing needed. Out of the box into the oven—25 minutes later a hearty turkey dinner ready to eat on its own aluminum serving tray.

Swanson TV Dinners contain:

Thick slices of juicy turkey with rich, real turkey gravy and cornbread dressing. Whipped sweet potatoes, tender garden peas both with Swanson's country butter. Swanson's famous old-fashioned goodness!

A BIG BOLD SWANSON SMASH CAMPAIGN IS SPREADING THE NEWS LIKE WILDFIRE

It's the "hottest" item ever handled in a frozen foods department. Get in now. Call, write, wire your Swanson Frozen Food Distributor.

C. A. S W A N S O N & S O N S • O M A H A 8 , N E B R A S K A

QUICK FROZEN FOODS   28   JUNE. 1954

The first industry ad for the TV Dinner, 1953. The arrangement and colors of the food were as important as the ease of preparation.

The TV Dinner as advertised on TV *was* a TV set.

The iconography of the carton was important, too. The full-color dinner was positioned so that it constituted the picture on a wood-grain TV set, complete with two prominent tuning knobs (the one on the left carried the USDA inspection seal and the one on the right was blank, to accommodate the retail price at the point of sale). By associating the turkey dinner with color TV, Swanson managed to suggest that the product was modern—even futuristic—but very much at home, nonetheless, in front of the tube in the average living room. The relationship with television further allowed buyers to excuse any change in dining habits represented by the purchase of heat-and-eat cuisine; if it was okay to eat in front of the set, then it was socially acceptable to eat turkey dinners somebody else had prepared. The TV dinner was as easy as turning a dial, too, an important consideration, Swanson thought, at a time when over half of the nation's jobs were held by women. The busy Mrs. America could even throw away the dirty dishes after her family had dined in the company of their favorite TV stars!

So the lion's share of the advertising budget for the frozen meals was expended on sponsorship of popular, low-key, family television shows: Ted Mack, Bob Crosby, Robert Q. Lewis. This was an unusual food-marketing strategy in the early 1950s and helped to identify the product even more closely with the values attached to television, including delight, lack of effort, and pictorial pleasure. In industry discussions of the TV Dinner, in fact, the last of these outweighed considerations of taste and nutrition by a wide margin. Swanson's turkey dinner was expected to meet "certified standards of eye appeal to the housewife," wrote one food commentator: "Thus, everything possible is done to make certain that when [she] takes the aluminum cover off . . . she sees a product that is not only delicious but appetizing and eye appealing as well." While other companies were quick to adopt the TV theme—Armour put out "TV meals" in cans; Dupont came up with a multipart carton to hold a single serving of cake, ice cream, and strawberries called a "TV Dessert" with a look-alike TV-set wrapper; TV Time Popcorn's tubes of kernels and hardened cooking oil afforded a glimpse of the contents through a window shaped like a picture tube—none shared Swanson's determination to make an exact match between the picture on the TV screen and the contents of the box, or vice versa.[43]

This aesthetic preoccupation first came to public attention in 1955. A year earlier, after a resounding success with the first "flavor," Swanson had introduced a fried-chicken dinner, also packed in the familiar, TV-style box printed with the Fidel-i-tone color process. But the hue of the chicken pictured on the box was found wanting—no small matter when processors were competing for customer attention in the recesses of the new open-top refrigerated cases in supermarkets, and counting on tantalizing color close-ups of sizzling chicken to spur impulse sales. In an effort to achieve the brighter yellow tones Swanson wanted, the packaging manufacturer resorted to a powerful solvent that leached through the outer wrap into the paper box and penetrated the air sealed inside the trays. Tests conducted in Omaha found the smell "all but undetectable," yet 300,000 solvent-treated dinners were packed up and dumped on the market in Florida at giveaway prices. Word of a possible health hazard eventually appeared in local newspapers: tests on sample dinners revealed the presence of bacteria, origin unknown. Since the potatoes in the chicken dinner were topped with cheese, which contains its own natural cultures, the investigation probably fueled needless fears of infectious disease. And, because Swanson agreed to pick up the medical bills (and refund the price of the product), Floridians quickly came down with all manner of ailments, directly attributable to the consumption of TV Dinners.[44]

The great TV Dinner scare of 1955 was quickly forgotten. It does, however, highlight the importance of certain new precepts in the preparation, promotion, and packaging of foods for a modern America. Disposability, portability, evidence of advanced technology, and freedom of choice were all important themes in the frozen-food industry. But color, pictorial verisimilitude, and visual enjoyment—the real keys to the success of Swanson's TV Dinner—were also the hallmarks of wide-awake marketing for a variety of other foods, including canned and boxed goods. So widespread had the color-photo label become by 1953 that what had begun as a daring experiment in stimulating desire for new products ended up being an annoying cliché. That, at any rate, was the conclusion of the industrial designer Martin Ullman of New York, who returned from Europe predicting the demise of six-color photogravure along the supermarket aisle. Nowhere had he seen "a realistic picture of the contents" on European packaging. The continental method was to put the emphasis on the trademark, or what ought to distinguish one box of cake mix from another. The 1953 convention of the National Flexible Packaging Association also heard designer Jim Nash denounce overreliance on appetite appeal for destroying brand identity. As Nash saw it, the current packages for cake mixes and flour had turned the store shelf into an art gallery of beautiful pictures in which "unfortunately, few brand names stand out boldly." That penchant for beauty helps to explain the stunned fascination with which Europeans regarded the American supermarket. At the Zagreb Trade Fair of 1957 and other such expositions, the U.S. government routinely re-created the supermarket to show off the high standard of living possible under the American economic system. But the ranks of pictures on boxes were clearly as startling and interesting to that audience as any subtle

Pictures were the key to successful packaging in all products, from canned goods to frozen dinners.

ideological point about capitalism. And in supermarkets back home, the aesthetic of the aisle upset old economic rules. The advantage often went to the newcomer, without the support of brand loyalty: any upstart could have a set of pretty pictures taken, hire a printer, and compete on equal terms with established firms. What counted was the color, the razzle-dazzle.[45]

The designers' fears were more than justified by the cake-mix wars of the mid-1950s, when the battle was joined by General Mills, Pillsbury, Duncan Hines, and a host of lesser-known competitors, all using magnificent picture boxes. Although Betty Crocker had the advantage on paper—a high degree of name recognition, a reputation for service to the homemaker, a threefold increase in sales since

1949—General Mills's market share of the total cake-mix business had begun a slow decline. To regain the lead, the company cut wholesale prices and finally retooled its packaging, to put the pictures back in the context of a specific brand. At a time when other products, like the Aunt Jemima mixes, were readjusting the balance between pancakes and trademark personalities on their packaging in favor of melting butter pats and dripping syrup, General Mills moved in the opposite direction by superimposing a new logo (a large red spoon bearing the Betty Crocker signature) on the requisite photograph.[46] This design ploy tempered sheer appetite appeal, or the irrational need to buy a cake, with rational discrimination between one cake and another and ultimately established a sense of continuity, in the person of Betty Crocker, between convenience and real home cooking, between supermarket and kitchen. The author of the famous *Picture Cook Book*—herself about to undergo a facelift to keep pace with modern visual taste—was the same person whose name appeared in great, big letters on the boxes of cake mix.

Despite serious questions about the use of photography in food advertising, the aesthetic approach to marketing persisted throughout the decade. Color dominated the whole retail field. By 1957 nylons and panty girdles came in giddy pastels. Manufacturers of drygoods items sold in supermarkets, however, were among the first to capitulate to the craze. Kleenex added pink and yellow to its rainbow palette of toilet tissues and Dial Soap tested five shades, including a "new, improved gold," in several Midwestern cities. *Advertising Age* acknowledged that color and shape were often the only real points of difference between many similar products, a cynical method of giving the illusion of choice when there was none. But it was a fact of American life, nonetheless, this yen for things that looked rich, unusual, gay, decorative, or simply pretty. Prophets who dared to forecast the end of "recipe compulsiveness" (the disease that made 75 percent of all food ads look just alike, with their almost-too-good-to-eat pictures and instructions for making dishes that were minor works of art) had been proven wrong before. Would Campbell's soon be making purple soup? Would Heinz invent blue catsup? Would Wonder Bread someday come in big red loaves? "Hey, do you think the automobile industry started all this?" asked one food insider.[47] Maybe. But Americans were what they ate, and under the tutelage of *Betty Crocker's Picture Cook Book* they had learned to nibble their way through the 1950s on the basis of an enormous appetite for beauty. Life in the age of television was a feast for the eye.

Richard Nixon and Nikita Khrushchev survey
the American Exhibition in Moscow, 1959.

Seven

Nixon in Moscow: Appliances, Affluence, and Americanism

*T*he battle began in the morning, with a sharp exchange on the subject of automatic washers in the kitchen of a typical, six-room, $14,000 ranch house put up by a Long Island builder of subdivisions and furnished by Macy's. It resumed in the evening, in a $250,000 RCA Whirlpool "miracle" kitchen controlled by an electronic brain: at the push of a button, the dishwasher scurried to the dining table along an invisible track and a robot cleaner polished the floor. The combatants were two men lacking any prior association with household appliances, and the unlikely venue for their so-called Kitchen Debate was Sokolniki Park, in a leafy quarter of Moscow. But there, in July of 1959, at the height of the Cold War, the Soviet Premier and the Vice President of the United States locked horns over spin cycles, in-house intercom systems, and American domestic gadgetry in general. To Richard Nixon, the latest in kitchen consumerism stood for the basic tenets of the American way of life. Freedom. Freedom from drudgery for the housewife. And democracy, the opportunity to choose the very best model from the limitless assortment of colors, features, and prices the free market had to offer. To Nikita Khrushchev, the whole U.S. Exhibition was a display of wretched excess and bourgeois trivia. Where were the scientific displays, the American Sputniks? "What is this?" asked the newspaper *Izvestia.* "A national exhibit of a great country, or a branch department store?"[1]

The "Mechanical Maid" scrubbed the floor and then put itself away in the RCA Whirlpool Miracle Kitchen at Moscow.

Created under the provisions of a 1958 protocol agreement on the exchange of expositions of "science, technology and culture," the $5 million American show had suffered from congressional parsimony. As a result, many details, including the golden geodesic dome by the visionary architect Buckminster Fuller through which Russian visitors (with hard-to-come-by one-ruble tickets) entered the grounds, were borrowed from successful American outings at international trade fairs. The Whirlpool kitchen, for example, had already appeared at a 1958 product show in Milan, while other planned attractions, like a fashion show presented as a series of vignettes from American life, had been tried out at the Brussels World's Fair of the same year. Model homes and supermarkets dramatized the benefits of mass production for the average American family. As such, they were always important Cold War propaganda devices, offering compelling, tangible evidence of the superiority of the economic system that so casually spewed forth labor-saving marvels, frozen dinners (steak and french fries), and tasteful living rooms furnished by *House Beautiful.* Although official government policy held that displays of consumer goods would inspire businesses in underdeveloped countries to produce items suitable for the vast American market and open new markets for American firms in nations still recovering from the rav-

To Nixon, the appliance store represented American freedom of choice.

ages of World War II, these American showrooms also seem calculated to arouse envy and discontent at a basic level of appetite, haptic pleasure, and sensory overload. And the Moscow Exhibition was even more dazzling than most.[2]

Inside the Fuller dome, a new IBM computer programmed to answer questions about American life was overshadowed by a series of seven giant TV screens that showed in living color and material specificity what printed words on a punchcard could never capture. One twelve-minute show, by the designers Charles and Ray Eames, traced the American workday in 2,000 flashing images. A second, by Hollywood director Billy Wilder, celebrated weekend leisure. Like a Hollywood movie, the America conjured up in Moscow's multiscreen TV autobiography was pictorial—not logical or spiritual or poetic. It was a look, a dream, something tantalizing to touch kept just beyond

An earlier version of the Miracle Kitchen, bound for a Milan trade fair to represent the benefits of American-style democracy.

The U. S. kitchen in Milan: a showroom of Americanism.

the reach of yearning fingers. Behind the dome and the enticing pictures, a glass pavilion with a pleated, fan-shaped roof held a modular "jungle gym" or rack of metal with inset plastic panels in which more than 5,000 pots and pans, dishes, rolling pins, and small appliances were showcased like so many precious jewels: spectators could see the items from a special viewing balcony, but they remained just out of reach.[3]

Ironically, the Soviets themselves may have reinforced the impression that consumer products were forbidden fruit in the USSR by refusing to allow the distribution of free Coty lipsticks and, after long lines testified to public interest, by denying Russian women access to free makeovers at Helena Rubenstein's model beauty salon. When visitors did get close enough to touch, the result was pandemonium.

In the opening days, they mistook the contents of the model super-market for samples and nearly cleaned out the stock. They reached over the barriers and fingered the upholstery in the model home. Free glasses of Pepsi, dispensed from a kiosk between the glass pavilion and the model home, were consumed at a rate of 10,000 per hour for the forty-two-day duration of the show.[4]

There was a heart-lung machine in the dome, an art show in the pavilion, and a shed housing farm machinery adjacent to the

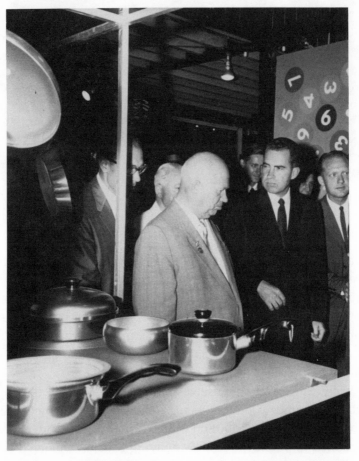

A modular rack in Moscow held alluring American consumer products, including kitchenware.

Model homes and models of American homes were weapons in the propaganda Cold War; when Khrushchev finally came to America, Ike proposed taking him to Levittown.

restrooms and the exit, but the overall tenor of the U.S. Exhibition in Moscow was as effervescent as a Pepsi-Cola. The ultimate consumer frivolity, Pepsi had taken aim squarely at the housewife in the late 1940s and 50s. Pepsi was the take-home drink in the elegant new "swirl" bottle. Less sugary, less substantial than the competition, it was the light drink, the one that guarded milady's slender, youthful image.[5] And image—specifically, an image of stylish domesticity, of exuberance and fizz—was the basis of the Moscow show.

The American home and the new iconographic center of that house, the kitchen, made up the core of the display, reinforced by the offerings of almost 800 manufacturers of sewing machines (a very popular demonstration), hi-fi sets, convenience foods, and lounge chairs. There were twenty-two cars, representing the latest 1959 models from all Detroit's leading automakers. There was a circular movie theater developed by Walt Disney. Under a cluster of plastic parasols planted in the park outside the buildings, the rituals of American family life, from the wedding and the honeymoon to the backyard barbecue and the country club dance, were enacted four times daily by fashion models in typical American outfits; in another outdoor enclosure were photographs and miniatures of typical American buildings, including churches, schools, and shopping centers. The Moscow Exhibition was "an American Showcase," concluded one business journal.[6] It was also a shopping center on a grand, international scale. And what was for sale was nothing less than "the American way of life."

The items on display in Moscow—the houses, the groceries, the fancy cars, the pretty clothes—came from the everyday experience of individual Americans. They weren't abstractions or constructs. They were somebody's, everybody's, definition of the good life in the affluent 1950s. As such, they were the decade's most powerful icons, the things everybody thought about first when that lifestyle came under attack. A bizarre example of such "contested" symbolism comes from a famous *Life* picture-essay on a Miami couple who spent their two-week honeymoon in a bomb shelter in August of 1959, less than a month after the Kitchen Debate in Moscow. Lured underground by a publicity-hungry builder, Mr. and Mrs. Minison did not go unprepared: their "wedding gifts" included an impressive array of canned goods, brand-name cereals, cigarettes, and assorted doodads spread out on the lawn around them for the benefit of *Life*'s photographer.[7]

In her recent book on American families in the Cold War era, the historian Elaine Tyler May takes the honeymoon story as a parable of the nuclear family "isolated, sexually charged, cushioned by abundance, and protected against impending doom by the wonders of modern technology."[8] But the story also highlights many of the specific material signs of an American way of life routinely invoked in moments of crisis. There was no car and fashion was hardly an issue twelve feet below the surface. The fallout shelter was still the private, single-family home organized around its kitchen functions, however. Nor was the photographic type an unfamiliar one in the 1950s. Corporations, propaganda agencies, and news magazines alike delighted in pictures showing American families surrounded by all the groceries they would consume in an average year. Like the endless shots taken in well-stocked supermarkets, such photos celebrated abundance, insisted on its reality, and served to ward off whatever threatened America's kitchens of tomorrow, crammed with instant mashed po-

The groceries consumed in a year by a typical middle-class family in Cleveland, Ohio, in 1952. The head of the household worked for DuPont.

tatoes and ready-to-heat-'n-eat, homestyle, frozen Salisbury steaks. *Life*'s underground kitchen was America's symbolic first line of defense against the bombs concealed in Russian satellites.

The America from which Richard Nixon departed on his mission to Moscow in 1959 was a jumpy sort of place, ripe for stories about nuclear honeymoons. Sputnik I, launched by the Soviets in October 1957, had been a blow to national self-confidence. Despite a splashy "You Auto Buy" campaign, the recession of 1958 lingered on. One of Ike's top aides was charged with taking expensive gifts in return for favors. Charles Van Doren, Columbia instructor and intellectual pin-up of the day, was indicted for cheating on a TV quiz show and then lying about it. Said Van Doren in his own defense: "But you know these are the Eisenhower years; there's money lying around every-where." The 1957 musical *Silk Stockings* showed Russians "swooning before capitalist luxuries." The Khrushchev who appeared in a tele-vised CBS interview in 1957 was a formidable character, however. Several years earlier, the sociologist David Riesman had jokingly suggested a "nylon war" instead of the Cold War: by bombarding the USSR with Toni wave kits, lipsticks, stoves, and refrigerators, he wrote, the United States would force Moscow to forget weaponry and concentrate on "consumers' goods, or face mass discontent on an increasing scale." But the tough-minded Soviet leader Americans saw on their own TV sets in 1957 did not seem likely to be toppled by a color-coordinated Bendix washer.[9]

With their space technology and their truculent resistance to fash-ion, the Russians were a constant reproach to bloated American con-sumerism. "It hardly seems worthwhile going to work, when you can stay home and play bingo for thousands of dollars, . . . or have a go at a dot game for a refrigerator," *Advertising Age* complained at the height of the quiz show mania. The novelist John Steinbeck, returning to the United States after a long absence in 1959, recorded his impres-sions for his friend Adlai Stevenson. Steinbeck smelled the "creeping, all-pervading nerve gas of immorality" and moral flabbiness. "If I wanted to destroy a nation," he concluded, "I would give it too much and I would have it on its knees, miserable, greedy and sick." An editorial in a special *Life* issue on "The Good Life" published in December of 1959 wondered aloud if high living in the form of credit cards, overdecorated, gas-guzzling Cadillacs, and an incessant bar-rage of hedonistic advertising had begun to sap the national purpose. According to presidential candidate John Kennedy ("Mr. Nixon may be experienced in kitchen debates," Kennedy would shortly quip, "but so are a great many other married men I know!"), the long slide into decadence had begun: "We have gone soft. . . . The slow corro-sion of luxury is already beginning to show." According to John Kenneth Galbraith's influential *The Affluent Society* (1958), America's legitimate material wants had been satisfied but the system depended on perpetual consumption of things that nobody needed. Corruption set in when advertising created lethal desires for chrome and color, on easy credit terms.[10]

Neo-Puritan asceticism made good copy in an age of affluence. But even in suburbia, where faith in the promise of a better life (and colored appliances) seldom faltered, all was not well in 1959, as Nixon left for Moscow. William Levitt, whose Long Island Levittown (begun in 1947) virtually invented the postwar suburb, built a new social construct there along with 17,400 Cape Cods, colonials, and ranch houses. Levitt made the owner-occupied, single-family home the American norm. He moved the kitchen to the front of the house, near the door, so mothers could keep an eye on their kids and, in the process, shifted the domestic focus from the parlors and sitting rooms of old to the work center of the new, servantless household. The modern technology that made affordable, assembly-line construction possible never asserted itself too blatantly in Levittown's exterior shutters and period roof lines, but in open-plan interiors arranged around the kitchen, the appliance acquired enormous visual promi-nence. In fact, Levitt used appliances as advertising come-ons for cash-poor home buyers: one easy monthly payment covered the house, an eight-inch TV set, and a brand-new Bendix washer. Such houses, the developer believed—a home of one's own—separated American capitalists from Russian communists. "No man who owns his own house and lot can be a Communist," Levitt joked. "He has too much to do."[11]

The rows of virtually identical $10,000 dream houses that marched across the once-rural landscape in the 1950s made suburbia an easy target for nay-sayers quick to equate stylistic sameness with middle-class conventionality and intellectual conformity. William H. Whyte, Jr., who studied the suburbs for *Fortune,* quoted with wry approval the description of a newcomer to the new community of Forest Park, Illinois: "a Russia with money." The apparently classless suburb ran-kled with some observers because it seemed to doom traditional hierarchies of wealth and class; if *anybody* could afford a house, and all houses were pretty much the same, what distinguished the occu-pants of one little box from their next-door neighbors? Surely not the contents of the living rooms and the adjacent, pass-through kitchens framed in every picture window, since moving to the suburbs meant acquiring a "standard package of consumer goods"—appliances were high on the list—that varied little from one address to another.[12]

Once upon a time, in movies and TV series, the upper crust moved to the country. With half the nation suddenly comparing notes on crabgrass, however, the old lines were harder to draw. Suburbia, USA, represented the breakdown of an established order, and as such it was a worrisome proposition for the guardians of American values. In 1959 it was also a headache to many of those who lived there. That was the year of the "suburban jitters," when paradise on the commuter line became "Ulcerville" and the American Medical Association issued stern warnings about the stresses associated with upward mobility and keeping up with the Joneses in the acquisition of house-

The open kitchen was at the front of this 1955 house, which a Soviet building expert bought with all its appointments and shipped back to Moscow for study.

hold gadgets.[13] Frustration was a particular problem for housewives, the experts concluded. Whether there was too much repetitious work to do, or too little to fill the time created by labor-saving appliances, women were not thriving in their push-button, dream kitchens.

The American Dream was the topic of one of the *Saturday Evening Post*'s smugly archetypal covers in the summer of 1959. As a young couple dreams of their future life together, its operative symbols appear in the starry sky above them, like signs of the zodiac retooled by Madison Avenue.[14] A split-level house. His and hers automobiles—one sports car, one station wagon. A boy and a girl. Two dogs. A hi-fi, a TV, and a nifty little transistor radio. Power tools. But most of all, electrical appliances: a giant refrigerator-freezer, a washer-dryer combination, a toaster, a Hoover Constellation vacuum cleaner (in the shape of a space satellite), a portable mixer, a steam iron, a percolator, an immersible fry-pan, and a rotisserie with a see-through window. If the whirring, purring appurtenances of the suburban good life were driving women mad, they were nonetheless central to the definition of an *American* way of life.

In the 1950s the United States bought fully three-fourths of all the appliances produced in the world. Along with cars and Levittowns (which Ike wanted Khrushchev to see if a planned state visit ever materialized), they stood for something fundamental to the postwar understanding of national identity: a sense of freedom, of effortless ease, of technological mastery, modernity, and access to conveniences formerly reserved for the very rich. A panel of thinkers assembled by the *New Republic* to ruminate on Steinbeck's disgust with American materialism suspected that the jitters of 1959 actually stemmed from fears of Soviet advances on the consumerist front, that "what we are really worried about is that the whole kit and caboodle of our American way of life—missiles and . . . pop-up toasters, our freedoms, fun, . . . and foolishness—is about to go down the drain." And if home appliances were really a litmus test for the American lifestyle, then why were there so many big, clunky, Communist-made refrigerators and washing machines in the Soviet Exhibition which debuted at the New York Coliseum in June of 1959?[15]

Khrushchev's ebullient deputy, Frol Kozlov, was dispatched from

The American Dream of limitless appliances and power tools, 1959. Illustration by Alajálov.

Moscow to open the show and to promulgate a new coda to the doctrine of "peaceful coexistence." Kozlov was one of the first Soviets to be seen at close quarters by the American media, and his reactions to normal features of American life were carefully studied. Reporters noted his astonishment that a shipyard hand could own a home and trailed the skeptical sightseer to a suburban Washington supermarket,

Shopping for major appliances, circa 1957–58.

which he insisted must be a phony, set up to impress foreigners. Not so, replied his tour guide, Richard Nixon. Besides, hadn't the Russians picked their prettiest girls to model at the New York exposition? Indeed, like the personable Kozlov himself, that display was meant to put an attractive, human face on Communism. So, when Dwight

Eisenhower and his vice president toured the Coliseum with Kozlov, they saw Sputniks and space capsules, heavy machinery, a model of a nuclear ice-breaker ("That's what we use atomic power for!"), and lots of Social Realist art glorifying the regime, but they also saw fashions, furs, dishes, and glasswear, a worker's apartment furnished in an ultra-modern style, console model TVs, Moskvich cars with more chrome than the average '59 Buick, and row upon row of washers and fridges.[16]

In official statements explaining the choice of exhibits, the Russians seemed almost apologetic for bringing so many displays of the Sputnik-and-steel-mill sort to New York in the first place, since the focus was on the future, in which an agrarian country proposed to transform itself into a consumer heaven. "By 1965," an embassy press release predicted, "88 billion rubles will have been spent on the production of household goods and appliances that take the drudgery out of housework." Nineteen sixty-five was the target date of a seven-year plan unveiled in Moscow by Nikita Khrushchev on June 29, 1959, in a long speech to the Communist Party's Central Committee. "We

Soviet-made refrigerators on display in New York, 1959.

U.S. propaganda agencies delighted in pictures of Russian women wearing fashions that looked dated and dowdy in comparison to American finery.

have launched a rocket into space," he shouted. How hard could it be to make washing machines? To match or better the United States in industrial output? Several days later, as Kozlov arrived in New York aboard a TU-114 turbo-prop plane said to be the biggest passenger airliner in the world, Khrushchev announced substantial price cuts aimed at getting existing supplies of consumer goods—nylons, hi-fi sets, watches—into the hands of citizens as quickly as possible.[17]

Veteran Soviet-watchers weren't swayed by talk of nylons, trade, and peaceful competition. They dismissed the show at the Coliseum as a propaganda ploy calculated to soften up the average America's prudent suspicion of the USSR. According to Max Frankel, the *New York Times*'s man in Moscow: "Many a Russian would agree with the one who expressed a desire to come to the New York exhibit to find out how he lives. . . . [It] strives for an image of abundance with an apartment that few Russians enjoy, with clothes and furs that are rarely seen." The *New Yorker*, on the other hand, found the Russian display captivating and, appalled by the dismissive attitude of the experts, offered a parody of the standard, sour-grapes commentary on what had turned out to be a very popular local attraction in the summer of 1959: "All these exhibits may strike poor, innocent you as absolutely wonderful, but they don't fool *us* for a moment. No matter how grand and shiny they are, we have something grander and shinier . . . [and] in any event, it makes no difference how wonderful they are, because the ordinary Russian doesn't have them." The current exchange program was tolerable, *Time* allowed, only because in Sokolniki Park, American know-how would finally have the chance to "make Russians more restlessly aware of the gulf between U.S. and Soviet standards of living."[18]

Under the terms of the agreement on reciprocal exhibitions, the Soviets were allowed to sell a percentage of the goods on display to Americans after the New York show was over. But there is no indication that buyers lined up to take home white, porcelain-finish appliances that looked like circa 1949 Sears Roebuck models, with bulbous, streamlined shapes and a crust of heavy chrome ornamentation in the form of aggressive handles and brand-name plates. They were hopelessly out of date. Appliances were squared-off nowadays.

The curvaceous, New Look styling popular in American durable goods of the late 1940s and early 50s connects appliance design to that of cars, similarly dependent on the use of large, unbroken areas of sheet metal. Since metal was tightly rationed during World War II, cars, stoves, and refrigerators were all in short supply. But that did not prevent manufacturers from advertising peacetime models of tomorrow and making extravagant promises for their performance. In 1945, for instance, Westinghouse anticipated the day when "you can put your whole dinner in the range, turn on the oven, toss away your apron, . . . and take the afternoon off." By the time the war ended, civilians expected a flow of consumer products with almost miraculous properties to transform the business of daily living. A steel strike slowed production in the 1949 model year, but Westinghouse and its competitors stockpiled materials and pressed forward with plans to hike their output by 15 percent per annum. Demand stood at an all-time high.[19]

The hankering for ranges and home freezers (subject of a major Truman administration scandal of 1951) struck some observers as symbolic of a whole new spectrum of possibilities open to the average American in a world of peace and plenty. "Here is a partial list of America's new frontiers," wrote *Look* with perfect seriousness in 1945: "The modern house . . . the automatic washer . . . express highways . . . television . . . quick freezing." Because the expectations were so high, because the desire was so strong, appliance design tended to be blatant, sculptural, and iconic. A *big* appliance, with an overall shape dependent on complex curves across the surface, dominated a room, intruded upon it, and showed that the customer had bought something significant. By covering the working parts of the mechanism in a smooth, polished carapace of glistening porcelain, designers also enhanced the magic and mystery of appliances, deemphasizing the human agency required to make them fulfill their advertised destiny. The "gorp" or chrome ornamentation that sprouted on many appliances in the early to mid-50s further identified a deluxe product on which no expense had been spared, much as a tail fin or a plated bumper connoted a car worth a long second look.[20]

In fact, the formal differences between a Chevrolet sedan and a Frigidaire refrigerator were often all but undetectable. General Motors sent its cars and its home appliances on a joint forty-four-city tour in 1950 and continued the practice throughout a decade in which the market for automobiles and kitchen equipment seemed fated to reach the saturation point simultaneously. In both cases, once the basic demand for the product was satisfied, surface appearance was proving more important to continuing sales than improvements in performance. Other bankable intangibles included iconography, social symbolism, and the way a given form made the consumer feel—or the sorts of problems that drove industrial designers to despair. "Once something becomes easier to make than it is to sell, its style assumes a paramount importance," wrote the design critic Eric Larrabee, in a fit of disgust with the commercial aesthetic in America. Yet there was a case to be made for style and for the attention-grabbing, Jell-O-like forms of appliances (and automobiles) in the early 1950s. Their exuberance matched the mood of the new suburbanite. Besides, stripped-down tract houses lacked architectural distinction; it was the furnishings that lent the standardized Cape Cod its character, and appliances functioned like large, expensive pieces of furniture for the kitchen in both placement and ornamental quality. As more and more market analysts began to predict a flat sales curve by 1954, however, advertisers and manufacturers turned to radical design changes, new-product development, and heavy doses of psychology to keep the wheels of commerce turning.[21]

Motivational researchers told clients that "in the minds of the consumer most . . . appliances have a definite masculine connotation." By that logic, housewives saw appliances as substitutes for men who did heavy work, or the man who paid for them, and felt vaguely guilty and lazy around certain not-strictly-necessary items, like clothes driers and dishwashers. Freezers, on the other hand, represented "the assurance that there is always food in the house; [and] food in the house represents security, warmth and safety." While psychologists could explain the reasons underlying consumer preferences, it took designers to change their minds about them. Resistance to all the second-tier appliances—freezers, dishwashers, dryers, and air conditioners, or what the industry began to make when it became apparent that everyone already owned a range, a fridge, and a washer—melted away only when the integrated, ensemble kitchen began to dominate women's magazines at mid-decade.[22]

Integrated kitchens spelled the end of gorp-covered, look-at-me refrigerators; all the component parts, from cabinetry to plumbing, from appliances to dinette sets, were carefully matched in color and form to create a total environment with a strong suggestion of an expensive, custom-built room. The new kitchen had a unified look,

Appliances were furniture for the kitchen. Front-loading washers
appealed on the basis of the TV-screen window.

with an unbroken flow of countertops and counter fronts over modular appliances that conformed to standard measurements and identified their electrical and mechanical components only by discreet
rows of pushbuttons. The age of the square appliance had dawned.[23]

The appliance-as-box was a byproduct of the integrated kitchen.
Since one box looked pretty much like another, with the same, unob-
trusive flat front and control panel, it was easier to sell more of them;
freezer, dryer, and dishwasher sales rose when they no longer stuck
out like sore thumbs, accusing the housewife of sloth by their bulky
presence. Color-coating also gained ground in ensemble kitchens.
While stoves, refrigerators, and steel cabinet units had been available
in a variety of hues since the late 40s, color tended to be just one more
extra. Unless all the major appliances were purchased at once, and

from the same manufacturer, a match was hard to achieve, too. And, until 1955 or so, curtains, canister sets, shelf paper, and other decorative accessories for kitchens generally came in white with contrasting touches of bright primaries, especially red, blue, and green. This fact suggests that most Americans played it safe by buying white appliances and adding color in the details. But the integrated kitchen depended on a single, monochromatic finish—one color intrinsic to all its basic functional components. Everything was pink, from the terrycloth towels and the plastic wastebasket to the new dishwasher and the counter-top range.[24]

More than any vaguely functional selling point of home appliances—more than new control panels or easy-to-use features, for instance—square corners and pink exteriors sparked debate about planned obsolescence. At a 1955 Museum of Modern Art symposium

Early dishwashers were a harder sell. They made housewives feel lazy.

New, box-like appliances on sale alongside older curvilinear models, 1956.

on American taste, the famed industrial designer Walter Dorwin Teague argued that an appliance with a predicted life of ten years should satisfy the homemaker for every last one of them and send her back to the same manufacturer for a replacement. The designer's job was merely to provide an efficient, convenient cover-up for the working parts. As motivational research had already suggested, however, appliances were more than tools to cook a meal or do the family wash. They were complex statements about a household's character and aspirations. As such, they were subject to psychological obsolescence long before the coils burned out and the motors failed, especially if the designer could be persuaded to join the manufacturer and the advertiser in a campaign to discredit existing kitchenware by making the latest models look as different as possible. Within the limits imposed by washer-ness and stove-hood, color, applied decoration (or the lack thereof), and angular vs. curvilinear shape became the weapons of the "merchants of discontent."[25]

Critics of obsolescence by design deplored the prodigal wastefulness and the cynicism of a system predicated on imagery, a system in which ads were more important than performance. "Color properly merchandized to the public," admitted one executive at the height of the pink appliance boom, "will . . . enable us to reduce significantly the trade-in span from eleven years to perhaps seven, or even lower." Big, expensive household machinery was being sold like cheap, ready-to-wear clothing, good for the current season only. The new Fridigaire "Sheer Look" line was introduced to the public by fashion models holding their hands at stiff, right angles to match the lines of the merchandise, and dressed in the same snooty shades: Mayfair pink, Sherwood green, Stratford yellow, and a charcoal gray derived from men's flannel suits.[26]

If the pink refrigerator-freezer was a pathetic status symbol, a warning sign of cultural decadence, a mark of deadening suburban sameness—there sat the heirs of Jefferson, wrote a bitter Lewis Mumford, "witnessing the same television performances, eating the same tasteless pre-fabricated foods from the same freezers"—in other quarters it was also a token of personal achievement, of an adventurous willingness to try something new. Or, according to the predilections of the observer, a snare for greedy housewives, in whom too great a longing for advertised novelties was often followed by disappointment, boredom, and discontent. "The Pushbutton Way to Leisure" promulgated by *Better Homes and Gardens* in the mid-50s, sometimes led straight to the psychiatrist's couch.[27]

Pushbutton strategies for maximizing leisure were premised largely on third-tier appliances, or tabletop models. Toasters and electric percolators weren't new products: they had been heavily promoted in the 1920s. But as manufacturers faced the possibility of a market glut of big-ticket items in 1954 and 1955, and as the lucrative trade tempted smaller firms into the appliance derby, electric blankets, deep fryers, fry pans, blenders, detached ovens, warmers, and the like came into their own. Many tabletop appliances performed a single, specialized task done as well or better on a stovetop. The advantage was mobility.

Ads for toasters in the early 50s showed them in use in the living room, in front of the TV set: the lady of the house could prepare a family snack without running into the kitchen and missing the better part of *I Love Lucy*. Give-away recipe booklets suggested dining on fingerfoods and "dips" (made in a new blender) during one's favorite shows. Plug-in tools freed women from the kitchen, or held out that possibility even when it was plainly impractical to roast turkeys and bake cakes wherever fancy dictated. And more than other kinds of appliances, they were unabashed luxuries, at relatively low cost. Specialized machines to make chip dip and ice-cream drinks at the flip of a switch weren't necessities in any sense of the word, but they made life sweeter and provided cheap, dramatic fulfillment of the promise of fingertip ease made by every dream kitchen constructed since World War II.[28]

Osaka. Izmir. Poznan. Home appliances big and small so dominated lists of American products considered representative of postwar life that they also dominated trade show exhibits prepared for foreign consumption. Europeans inspecting the comprehensive collection of housewares in the American pavilion at the Brussels World's Fair of 1958, for example, might have been forgiven for concluding that the United States had undergone some fundamental shift in values. "Now people no longer have any opinions; they have refrigerators," wrote a German critic of creeping American consumerism. "The only way to catch the spirit of the times is to write a handbook on home appliances." Given the ubiquity of U.S. cars and home appliances in such international venues, American critics realized how easy it was to confuse their country with its mechanical pets. Eric Larrabee remembered D. H. Lawrence's call for dishwashers to take care of life's dirty work. Yet now that American industry had obliged, he felt sure "Lawrence . . . would be the first to damn it as an example of our soul-less, gadget-ridden materialism."[29]

"Gadget" was the epithet of choice for appliances among most intellectuals, expressing their sense that freezers and blenders really amounted to so much trivia, on a par with Rube Goldberg's comic devices for doing simple jobs in the most complicated ways imaginable. In an essay on American art published in 1953, Louis Kronenberger found the "gadget aspect" rampant throughout a culture obsessed with anything useless *and* ferociously up to the minute. But

Russell Lynes, in his appraisal of 1950s suburbia, reckoned that look-alike, shoebox Cape Cods became homes mainly by virtue of "the gadgets that go into such houses": the freezers and the washer-driers were what had created the good life, American style.[30]

Gadget-haters thought them self-indulgent, soul-destroying, and fatal to American gastronomy. They were compensatory devices—the housewife's sorry reward for staying at home with the kids. In *Point of No Return* (1949), the novelist John Marquand shrewdly described a suburban wife at the breakfast table, cautioning her husband not to trip over the extension cords: "Instead of a typewriter she was ma-nipulating a toaster and an electric percolator." But they were, in the end, what separated us from the Russians. "Do Communists ever eat ice cream?" asked a cookbook writer, celebrating the sheer joy of wolfing down ice-cream desserts made by somebody else straight from the home freezer. Where but in the USA were the mysteries of atomic energy about to be unlocked in the average, suburban kitchen, so that busy cooks could serve up three-year-old gamma-radiated chicken dishes in less than four minutes, straight from a new micro-wave oven?[31] Indeed, the wonders of the American kitchen were profoundly interconnected with the military hardware of the Atomic Age. The same technological might that kept the armed forces poised to do battle against Godless atheism also kept the kitchens of America squared off and squared away. If there was any reason for worry, it was only that we seemed equally committed to appliances and rock-etry whereas the Soviets, a jittery market researcher mused, could "organize *all* their efforts in such a way as to make a moon shot possible."[32]

But to the staff of *House Beautiful* there was a distinct possibility that the rectilinear refrigerator was part of a Communist plot to strike at the very roots of the American way of life. In the spring of 1953 editor Elizabeth Gordon bought space in other journals to announce a special issue revealing the "*current* threat to the next America." "Something is rotten in the state of design," Gordon's April article boldly declared, and that something was "so-called modern things." As other design professionals were quick to point out, the page lay-out of Gordon's rambling diatribe boxed the names of well-known

International Style architects together with the word "Communist," creating the impression that modernism and Communism were synonymous. Gordon never actually accused Mies van der Rohe or Le Corbusier of party affiliation. But she did link their "stripped-down emptiness . . . and lack of possessions"—their spare, square, visual austerity—to social regimentation and un-American tendencies. Everything looked just the same in a modernist house, she argued, and that lean look was antithetical to the ethos of the cozy, comfort-filled American home. Furthermore, a person who bought a square appliance was in mortal danger of undermining the moral fiber of the nation, "for if the mind of man can be manipulated in one great phase of life to be made willing to accept less, it would be possible to go on and get him to accept less in all phases of life." Fewer gadgets, less chrome, less democracy.[33]

Elizabeth Gordon's distaste for modernism was common enough in the early 1950s when developers tacked superfluous shutters to houses specifically to make them seem unmodern and automakers added chrome sculpture to cars to give the customer some visible sign of having gotten a good deal. But an ideological justification for hating plain square shapes was uncommon. It came from a 1952 book by Lyman Bryson, *The Next America: Prophecy and Faith*, which advanced two central theories: first, that aesthetic issues have consequences in the world of politics and ideas; and second, that "the act of choice, the experience of seeing several ways of expressing a need and considering them, and taking one that appeals to some trait of . . . character" is the linchpin of democracy, even when choice is exercised in seemingly trivial matters, like picking an angular pink refrigerator over another model. By exerting an iron control over the forms that reach the marketplace, Bryson observed, the Russians were stifling the very possibility of intellectual and political freedom.[34]

In *House Beautiful*, side by side with Gordon's architectural Red-baiting, Bryson too waved the flag and smote the Communist enemy. At best, the modernists were misguided: "They may be expressing ideas that fit the spirit of some Europeans who are weary of trying for freedom and are seduced by totalitarian simplicities." Real *American* culture demanded diversity, comfort, a lush cornucopia of material goods responsive to human needs and desires. "We must expose the mechanistic forms, reject the authoritarian dogmas of the cult of stark, sterile modernism," Bryson thundered. "Liberty means choosing. . . . Men cannot choose what they have never heard of; ignorance is the greatest obstacle to freedom. In politics, we call the danger totalitarianism. . . . In the arts, we call it rigidity of taste. . . . We do not suspect political or ideological invasion of our homes by way of design or decoration. Yet it is indeed possible."[35]

While appliance design had never figured in the equation before, the charge that modern art was a weapon of the international Communist conspiracy was a cliché of Cold War politics. Congressman George A. Dondero of Michigan, the McCarthy of aesthetics, regularly published lists of artists suspected of ties to subversive organizations and pilloried federal agencies, like the USIA, for sending suspect works abroad on official government tours. Modern art. he theorized (apparently including all nonrepresentational and abstract styles from Van Gogh on up), was painted solely to "addle the brains of decent, innocent Americans." Dondero retired before the paintings for the Moscow exhibition were selected by a jury of distinguished artists and curators, but his crusade against modernism was taken up by Chairman Francis Walter of the House Committee on Un-American Activities. Of the sixty-seven artists represented in the display of American art mounted for Sokolniki Park, no fewer than thirty-four of them had past or present Communist affiliations, Walter declared. The poison in many of the pictures was subtle stuff. In at least one case, however—Jack Levine's *Welcome Home*—the anti-American sentiments were as plain as the noses on the crepe-faced generals gorging themselves at a patriotic banquet.[36] As for Levine himself, he was a member of "at least 21 Communist fronts and causes."[37]

The controversy over the paintings for the USSR came to a head at President Eisenhower's White House press conference on July 1, 1959. What did Ike think about the unflattering depiction of an American general, asked May Craig of the *Portland Press Herald?* "Well," replied the former general and spare-time amateur painter, choosing his words carefully, it "looks like a lampoon more than art, as far as I am concerned. But I am not going . . . to be the censor." What the President liked was *real* art—Andrew Wyeth's Moscow-bound, hyperrealist portrait of the pediatrician Dr. Margaret Handy (*Woman Doctor*, 1949), for example. In future, he opined, juries to select overseas exhibitions ought to include fewer experts and more ordinary Americans, folks who "are not too certain exactly what art is but we know what we like, and what America likes."[38]

In the end, the exhibition was not censored. But it was decontaminated by the addition of twenty-six older, more traditional pictures, including a still life of a dead duck hanging against a green wall lent by Ike from his personal collection. The art critic Frank Getlein, who was opposed to censorship but sick to death of the splatter-and-drip school of American modernism prevalent in touring shows for export, went to Moscow expecting not to like the U.S. paintings much. He came away impressed, despite himself, because the pictures had thoroughly alarmed the Soviet audience. "A lot of them," he noticed, "failed as completely as Eisenhower to understand why a painter should poke fun at generals." They were disconcerted by the Pollocks, and shocked by the lack of idealism or prettifying in the canvases with recognizable themes. After all the fuss and feathers, the art section turned out to be the best illustration in the park of the American virtues of diversity, self-criticism, and individual liberty.[39]

Nixon treated the show like a time bomb, of course. As the official party approached the exhibition space, he veered abruptly and turned his entourage downstairs, back into the displays of shoes and lingerie and appliances, avoiding a discussion with Khrushchev of satirized American generals. He was on surer ground among the washers and dryers that embodied diversity in less alarming ways. But the same disordered, unsorted, uncensored profusion of style defined both the art exhibition and the display of consumer goods, and it made little sense to Soviets used to hearty helpings of ideology on such occasions. What could this welter of stuff possibly *mean*? "I see no plan in all this," cried a sophisticated Russian guest. "The whole exhibition appeals only to bourgeois interests. . . . Your whole emphasis is on color, shape, comfort. We are more interested in the spirit behind things."[40]

Nixon's meeting with Khrushchev in Sokolniki Park should have been a bland ceremonial affair; the Vice President had come to Moscow to do the same honors Comrade Kozlov had performed so amiably at the New York Coliseum. And Ike pointedly reminded his second-in-command that he had no authority to negotiate with the Russians. What turned the encounter from a formality into an attention-grabbing debate was the Captive Nations Resolution. Passed by a Republican Congress every session since 1953, the legislation required the President to proclaim a week of prayer for people living under Communist tyranny. The document for 1959 was issued by the White House just as Nixon boarded his flight, and the coincidence enraged Khrushchev. With millions of Americans praying for the overthrow of his government, along came the U.S. Vice President, trying to stir up discontent with his TV sets and automatic washers! From their first meeting at the Kremlin, in which the Soviet leader used language that shocked the translators, it was clear that this was going to be no ordinary morning at the fair.[41]

Things began innocently enough in the Glass Pavilion, just before noon. The art show sparked no fireworks; Nixon adroitly guided the Premier past the greedy generals and downstairs, into the display of consumer products. For days the Soviet press had sniped at this particular portion of the exhibition, calling it unrepresentative of the life of the average American, and a "traditional Moscow fair" had suddenly opened to sell comparable items, rarely seen in Russian stores. As the party passed RCA's mock television studio, an engineer called out an invitation. Would Khrushchev and Nixon like to see themselves on the new color monitors and try out a system for recording and replaying programs? With the tape rolling, a truculent Khrushchev resumed discussion of the Captive Nations issue, throwing his arms around a nearby worker and asking whether the man looked like a slave. Nixon tried to divert his attention to the TV sets. Khrushchev dismissed them with a flick of the wrist: "In another seven years we will be on the same level as America. When we catch you up, in passing you by, we will wave to you," he blustered, wiggling his fingers at the camera once more. How about color television? Nixon replied. The Soviets were ahead in rockets, but wasn't the United States in the lead in *this* technology? "Nyet!" his adversary shot back, conceding nothing.[42]

Khrushchev had already appeared on American TV before Nixon went to Moscow. The Kitchen Debate over household items made him seem somewhat less menacing.

The next stop was the Pepsi-Cola booth, where the emerging theme of competition was taken up again. Originally the State Department had suggested a nose-to-nose clash between Coca-Cola and Pepsi at the Moscow Exhibition to illustrate the free enterprise system at work, but Coke had declined to participate. Instead, Pepsi presented two versions of its product, one imported from the United States and the other made with Moscow water and, through Ambassador Llewellyn Thompson, begged the Vice President to nudge Khrushchev toward the kiosk. The company's new advertising slogan was "Be Sociable,

Have a Pepsi!" What better ad than a picture of America's foremost adversary (and the scourge of Coca-Cola, which the Party in Europe equated with capitalist decadence) acting sociable over a Pepsi made in the USSR? "Don't worry," Nixon is said to have told Pepsi's CEO. "I'll bring him by." It wasn't hard to arrange, as things turned out: the contest suited Khrushchev's bellicose mood to a tee. He expressed a predictable disdain for American Pepsi, but the Russian version, he growled, was "very refreshing." And he drank seven bottles for the company photographers before the clutch of journalists and officials tromped off toward the exit, just beyond the model home.[43]

Richard Nixon would later insist that the Kitchen Debate was all an accident, that the domestic setting, sure to rivet the attention of his American audience, had not been chosen for political effect. But

Nixon and Khrushchev in a mock TV studio. The debate probably began only because the cameras were rolling.

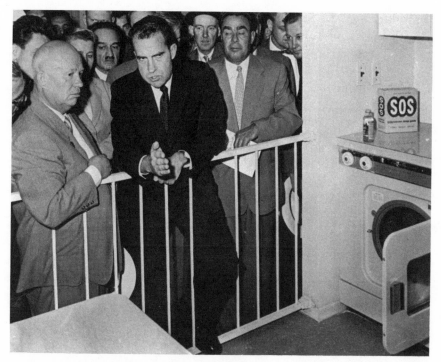

The famous Kitchen Debate, over an automatic washer.

it is worth noting that William Safire, a future Nixon speechwriter, was doing public relations for Macy's and the model house in Moscow and that photographer Elliot Erwitt was ready to shoot the exchange, moment by moment.[44] Erwitt recalls that Khrushchev was in high dudgeon by the time the entourage reached the viewing aisle that ran down the center of the bifurcated "Splitnik," as the Russians dubbed the three-bedroom house. He was spewing earthy profanities in all directions and Nixon, sensing an opportunity, was grandstanding for the press, citing facts and figures about home building. Suddenly, the Vice President pulled up short at the kitchen area and leaned over the railing in front of an automatic washer. "I want to show you this kitchen," he said. "It is like those of our houses in California." "We have such things," Khrushchev shot back. But anyone can afford a $14,000 house in the United States, Nixon continued—any steelworker, for instance: "This house costs about $100 a month to buy on a contract running twenty-five to thirty years." The house won't be standing then, the Premier scoffed. In America, builders want to sell everybody new houses every few years: "We build firmly. We build for our children and grandchildren."

"You Americans think that the Russian people will be astonished to see these things," he cried, in sheer frustration, gesturing toward the washer. "We hope to show our diversity and our right to choose," Nixon retorted, on a note of triumph. "We do not want our decisions made at the top by one government official that all houses should be the same. . . . [And] is it not far better to be talking about washing machines than machines of war, like rockets? Isn't this the kind of competition you want? . . . Let the people choose the kind of house, . . . the kind of ideas they want. We have many different manufacturers and many different kinds of washing machines, so that the housewives may have a choice." "Let's thank the housewife for letting us use her kitchen for our argument," Khrushchev countered, bowing to the American guide, and shot out the door, ending the second phase of the confrontation.[45]

That evening, at the formal opening of the American Exhibition, Nixon took Khrushchev on another tour of the premises, and led him straight into a second kitchen, a futuristic display of household robots in the Glass Pavilion. "In America, these are designed to make things easier for our women," he noted sanctimoniously. "Ha! These are mere gadgets!" huffed Khrushchev: "Don't you have a machine that puts food into the mouth and pushes it down?" A product demonstrator pushed a button, sending a dishwasher careening toward him like some creature out of science fiction. "This is not a rational approach. These are gadgets we will never adopt!" Khrushchev bellowed. Oblivious to his scorn, the uniformed guide in her pastel shirtwaist turned on a closed-circuit TV system designed to monitor activities in every corner of the house. Khrushchev's mood brightened visibly. "This is probably always out of order," he told Nixon, laughing. "Da," chortled the Vice President. And the Kitchen Debate ended on a note of bogus good humor with both sides in apparent agreement over the silliness of household gadgets.[46]

The robotic kitchen, operated by a TV-like computer at left.

In *The Culture of the Cold War*, the historian Stephen Whitfield takes the press corps on the scene to task for failing to understand the causal relationship between the arms race and American prosperity— and for discounting Khrushchev's righteous "anger at competition in both defense hardware and domestic software." Richard Nixon's opening address at the Exhibition, as well as his unprecedented televised speech to the Soviet people, lauded the American standard of living, depicted the Russian space program in strictly militaristic terms, and called for peaceful competition to raise the global standard of living, all without more than a passing mention of U.S. bases and weaponry.[47] As political theater his carefully staged skirmishes with Khrushchev, intensified by Nixon's one-sided rhetoric, were masterpieces of the genre. But there was more going on in Sokolniki Park than a political *pas de deux* performed by a calculating American and his long-suffering Soviet host, goaded beyond the limits of good manners. There was the matter of the multiple kitchens sent to Moscow to stand for the United States.

In any other setting, a day-long wrangle between representatives of the superpowers over fundamental issues of war and peace would have been just an argument: the kitchen raised the temperature of the debate by reminding those who saw the photos that what was at stake in an era of atomic bombs was existence—home, hearth, all the most basic human functions. Moreover, the kitchen was especially problematic for the Soviet government. In a collective state, the private home was, at best, a matter of housing; Nixon brought up the functional, hard-edged worker's apartment he had seen at the Coliseum by way of contrast with the single-family model house in Moscow, full of labor-saving devices and consumer comforts. The Russian Exhibition in New York showed rows of refrigerators as products of state industries. At the American Exhibition in Moscow, appliances were contextualized, as part of somebody's make-believe house. By concentrating on the private life of the family—their kitchen, their home, their new washer—the American Exhibition virtually denied the public claims of the state. It was this aspect of the show that led the Soviet press to wonder if Nixon had come to open "a national exhibit of a great country" or a department store and led the Soviet intelligentsia to deride the glut of housewares betraying a single-minded "emphasis . . . on color, shape, comfort." The washers and home freezers were effective propaganda devices, as the throng of enchanted visitors proved, but in ideological terms, the American show seemed casual, soft, personal, and flaccid.

Khrushchev was utterly baffled by Nixon's enthusiasm for product redundancy, too. When confronted with the automatic washer and the Vice President's smarmy assurance that this was only one of many styles from which the American housewife could make her selection, he argued for a single model, providing it worked. But Nixon wasn't interested in function, or rather, like the housewife he invoked, he trusted the machine to wash clothes (most of the time, at any rate). Instead, he was interested in style as a manifestation or a symbol of difference and in difference, multiplicity—the possibility of choice—

as the principle connecting idle consumer fetishism to ideology. The historian David Potter, in his influential 1954 study of the relationship between abundance and the national character, posited that American goods were the real force for change in the postwar world: "It was not our ideal of democracy but our export of goods and gadgets, of cheap . . . magic-working machines, which opened new vistas to the human mind and thus made us 'the terrible instigators of social change and revolution.'" Or, as Richard Nixon attempted to demonstrate in Moscow, the housewife's choice of a new appliance—pink, square, nonsensical, irrational: whatever—was a choice nonetheless and the habit of making them was a good working definition of the American way of life. The public virtues of democracy were woven into the fabric of private life, into the brand new, 1959-model textures and colors and shapes of the suburban kitchen. Pink porcelain, ersatz copper, or "the Platinum Look—the cool billion-dollar look" of brushed aluminum and everyday elegance: style meant leisure, pleasure, convenience, and the USA.[48]

On the left, elitism often takes the form of disdain for popular culture and mass enjoyment combined with a purist preference for production over consumption. That, in essence, was Khrushchev's response to the American kitchen. It was also a fashionable attitude among what Galbraith called "the more censorious social levels" in America itself, where gadget had become a pejorative term for durable goods. "In such circles," Galbraith noted shortly before the Kitchen Debate, "shiny rumpus rooms, imaginative barbecue pits, expensive television screens, and magnificent automobiles no longer win acclaim." To this list of suburban basics, he might have added home appliances. "But American suburbia, in global terms, may be the functional equivalent of what most peoples of the world seem, nowadays, to want," wrote a dissenting scholar in 1958. "For suburbia" with its color TVs and matching washer-dryer sets, "may be the highest reach of civilized life . . . within the grasp of common humanity."[49]

Common humanity as defined by the small, incremental details of daily life was the theme of *The Family of Man* exhibition also included in the American compound in Sokolniki Park. According to curator

Edward Steichen, the collection of photographs (originally assembled in 1955 for the Museum of Modern Art) was "a mirror of the universal elements and emotions in the everydayness of life—. . . a mirror of the essential oneness of mankind throughout the world." By presenting images of home life drawn from many cultures, the show underscored one subtext of the model kitchens: at the level of the family unit, political differences were meaningless, even dangerous abstractions. A record-breaking success in New York and the five other cities on its American circuit, the show had already toured Europe and Asia under USIA auspices before its stop in Moscow. Dwight Macdonald dismissed *The Family of Man* as so much "high-falutin'" twaddle and other critics found it repetitious, obvious, or politically naive, but the collection struck a responsive chord in audiences everywhere. Except for the Soviet journalist Victor Gorokhov, who wanted fewer sad pictures and more textual explication, the Russians loved it, too.[50]

In fact, the style of the show was particularly well suited to the direct, personal confrontation between Nixon and Khrushchev. Despite the genuine animosities evident in their serial conversation, it was in the face-to-face mode of *The Family of Man* that détente between Moscow and Washington seemed most likely to occur. And if the pair could agree on nothing of diplomatic substance, they were both willing to admire a bathing beauty, pay deference to a housewife, and drink a toast to "the ladies" in the course of their discussion. In swimsuits, ballgowns, or aprons, women were the common denominator, the human universal of the Kitchen Debate. When the day was over, when the posturing and fuming were all but done, Nixon and Khrushchev stood before the microphones on the darkened grounds of the Exhibition, glasses of California wine in hand.

> K: "We stand for peace [but] if you are not willing to eliminate bases then I won't drink this toast."
>
> N: "He doesn't like American wine!"
>
> K: "I like American wine, not its policy."
>
> N: "We'll talk about that later. Let's drink to talking, not fighting."

K: "Let's drink to the ladies!"

N: "We can all drink to the ladies."[51]

There were lots of American women attached to the Moscow Exhibition in an official capacity: seven pretty girls at the Pepsi counter, several bilingual home economists in the RCA kitchen, forty-odd fashion models, and twenty-eight guides. The models were a special case. After adverse reaction to racially integrated scenes in a New York runthrough and objections to some expensive garments "as being not representative of the American way of life," an amended fashion show in which clothes were shown in action at teen rock 'n' roll parties and patio barbecues proved very popular (although the young women in the Bermudas and playdresses were regarded as entirely "too skinny"). But the women who were actually doing the work of the Exposition were also expected to model "the type of clothes worn by everyday Americans." For the home economists, this meant pastel shirtwaists that could be washed and ironed in their model kitchens. For the guides, it meant a choice of five on-duty costumes (with coordinated hats and gloves) also based on the shirtwaist line, the uniform of the suburban housewife. In effect, then, whatever her profession, whatever her job at the Exhibition, the American woman became an attribute of the kitchen. The model kitchen was also a model of appropriate gender roles.[52]

But just as the accomplished, Russian-speaking guides dressed like housewives reflected a kind of double vision of women, so the kitchen itself signaled changes in their social status. By the end of 1959 fully 34 percent of the American workforce was made up of women, and economists believed it was the addition of a second breadwinner that gave families the discretionary income to remodel their kitchens and replace their appliances. The very structure and contents of the room also hinted at a shift in the homemaker's routine. A kitchen laid out by a woman architect on the basis of suggestions voiced by housewives at a 1956 forum sponsored by the Federal Housing Administration, for example, dissolved the existing open plan into a control center or island of major appliances entirely integrated with the rest of the ground floor. No longer a gendered space in any sense of the word, the kitchen became just another part of the family living room, the dining area, and the playroom.

By reducing the room to a few essential parts scattered across the floorplan, Margaret King Hunter's radial kitchen gave architectural expression to women's diversity of roles and to the concept of physical freedom inherent in the smaller, portable appliances of the later 1950s. Although framed with a different purpose in mind, the open-to-view model kitchens in Moscow, from which whole walls had been removed to permit direct access to the appliances, represented this new ideal of multiplicity, dispersal, and personal freedom. When Anastas Mikoyan, the Soviet Union's First Deputy Premier, visited the United States in 1958, he professed great admiration for the pushbutton appliances he was shown. "We have to free our housewives like you Americans!" he said. At Moscow in 1959, the shattered boundaries of the kitchen portended a freedom that went far beyond the

The open-plan kitchen gradually merged into the total floorplan.

dollops of increased leisure promised by ads for household appliances.[53]

As early as 1954, designers examining trends in kitchens saw an environment rife with contradictions: built-in appliances vs. the new generation of portables; mammoth, showy models vs. the more modest miniatures; quickie meals from packages vs. creeping gourmandism. But analysts at *Interior Design* also found a single, unifying factor in the open kitchen layout "which takes efficiency—and appliances— pretty much for granted and concentrates on social values. It is openly disintegrating into the rest of the house because it is an all-purpose room, an elegant headquarters for all the things the housewife chooses to get involved with. So what does she do," the study continued, "but pick up and leave."[54] The color of next year's refrigerator was a fashion imponderable. The serious, discussable issue for the future was the clash of housewife vs. appliance, or an emerging demand for home machinery that matched the consumer's new sense of self in both practical and symbolic terms. If she was bent on leaving the kitchen, then a dishwasher that followed her into the dining room and a floor polisher that did its job after she had gone made perfect sense. So did the kitchenless kitchen, the cluster of burnished and tinted electronic gadgets, the room without walls where Nixon met Khrushchev in 1959. The American kitchens in Moscow—today's kitchen and tomorrow's—provided a working demonstration of a culture that defined freedom as the capacity to change and to choose and dramatized its choices in the pink-with-pushbuttons aesthetic of everyday living.

The elegantly framed and gowned performer on the TV screen and her audience are mirror images of one another. So who's watching whom?

Afterword

The American exhibit at the Brussels World's Fair had featured Elvis pink and Mamie pink appliances. The kitchenware on display at the Moscow Trade Fair came in pink, turquoise, silver—a riotous choice of hue and tone. Mugging for the TV cameras in their drab business suits, Nixon and Khrushchev may have been the two least colorful items on display there. But color meant more than pink or turquoise blue. Black-and-white TV was profoundly coloristic, in terms of the vividness of life it brought into the American home. In that sense, color is a function of motion, of intensity—and if color TV had not been waiting in the wings of consumerism for most of the 1950s, then somebody would have had to invent it.

The Moscow kitchen was split in two, turned inside out for easy access by cameras and visitors. So, like a *real* kitchen in some suburb back home, it approached the condition of a mock-up used to represent a kitchen in a weekly TV series. It was a private space made public. The open-plan kitchen of the 1950s both dispersed and dramatized the act of cooking. When toasting and blending were not being done offhandedly on the coffee table during station breaks, home cooking became a true soap opera. If chip dip and the other new menu items of the suburban buffet blurred the distinction between social distance and intimacy, between company manners and family life, it was because such patterns of social discourse reflected television's ability to make the most private emotions public and the most public and rhetorical ones—like the Moscow Kitchen Debate—part of the decoration of the average living room.

The model kitchen in Moscow was sliced open, laid bare to the gaze of television. That, too, was the condition of the real-life home. The eye of the TV set opened private life on the sofa to the blandishments of advertisers, to the visual allure of the beautiful and the strange, to the political symbolism embedded in the charm bracelet or the washing machine. Dior's postwar dresses were called the "New Look." But TV made *everything* look new. Or rather, TV looked—and that was new.

Disneyland was the first made-for-TV place, in which the fictive content of the programming dictated the honest-to-gosh activity of Americans in physical space. It is probably no accident that Richard Nixon and his family were frequently called upon to inaugurate new attractions there: in his dark suit, Nixon looked both official and beguilingly normal as he emerged from a thrill ride down an ersatz Swiss mountain with his tie still welded in place. Unmoved alike by movement and violent shifts of scenery, he took the curse off strange new things. Shown on a Disney program waving and smiling from the bobsled run in Anaheim, Nixon made the scarier features of contemporary life—speed, danger, novelty—seem as normal as Grandma's (or Betty Crocker's) made-from-a-mix apple pie.

That was Grandma Moses's function, too. Disneyland was a critique of the suburban experience couched in terms derived from it; Main Street USA added a dose of pedestrian commerce and centeredness to the pastel uniformity of the empty suburban street. The work of Anna Moses helped to affirm the practice of moving to Levittown by pointing out that new patterns of country living in the postwar era might bear some resemblance to the sweet remembered joys of her rural girlhood in the 1800s. Walt Disney produced television shows recreating that golden age and Mrs. Moses painted it. Grandmaland and Disneyland were the pictorial ideals to which every housing tract aspired.

And Grandma was an amateur, somebody who painted in private life, at her kitchen table, and then, by accident it seems, became a public figure. The intense interest of the 50s in amateur art (and hobbycraft) again suggests the primacy of a television aesthetic that brought private things to public notice, living room by individual living room. Seeing, looking, appraising, exercising one's own taste: before the TV set, art and artfulness became public property. Who needed the sorts of artists designated as such by faceless cultural authorities, when you could do it yourself? When choosing a car, putting together an outfit, or baking a birthday cake summoned up all the aesthetic resources of the viewer-driver-shopper-baker and demanded their vigorous employment?

Old hierarchies tumbled. The aesthetic ground shifted and moved, as wildly as Elvis did, as inexorably as did the robotic floor scrubber that skittered out from under the cabinet in the Whirlpool kitchen in Moscow. As seen on TV, everything suddenly looked new to the 1950s.

Notes

Prologue

1. Quoted in Malcolm Forbes with Jeff Bloch, *They Went That-a-Way* (New York: Ballantine, 1988), 73.
2. Eugene Archer, "George Stevens and the American Dream," *Film Culture* 3 (1957), 27.
3. Edna Ferber, *Giant* (New York: Grosset and Dunlap, 1952), 434. Julie Goldsmith Gilbert, *Ferber: A Biography* (Garden City, N.Y.: Doubleday, 1978), 155, comments on her displeasure with the final lamb-and-calf scene in the script.
4. *Kirkus* quoted in Martice M. James and Dorothy Brown, eds., *Book Review Annual Digest*, vol. 48 (New York: H. W. Wilson, 1953), 301.
5. Peter Biskind, *Seeing Is Believing: How Hollywood Taught Us to Stop Worrying and Love the Fifties* (New York: Pantheon, 1983), 289. See also Nina C. Leibman, "Leave Mother Out: The Fifties Family in American Film and Television," *Wide Angle* 10 (1988), 29.
6. Stephen Harvey, *Directed by Vincente Minnelli* (New York: Harper and Row, 1989), 166–167.
7. "Desilu Formula for Top TV: Brains, Beauty, Now a Baby," *Newsweek*, Jan. 19, 1953, 58. Ad, *McCall's*, Nov. 1953, 13.
8. "Premier Khrushchev Angered When L.A. Police Bar Visit to Disneyland Because of Security," *New York Times*, Sept. 20, 1959. Phil Patton, *Open Road: A Celebration of the American Highway* (New York: Simon and Schuster, 1986), 88.
9. "Let's Go . . . to Monsanto's House of the Future," *Coed*, April 1958, 26–27; H. Ward Jandl, *Yesterday's Houses of Tomorrow: Innovative American Homes 1850 to 1950* (Washington, D.C.: Preservation Press, 1991), 206.

1. Mamie Eisenhower's New Look

1. Dior quoted in "Dictator by Demand," *Time*, March 4, 1957, 34. Jane Dorner, *Fashion in the Forties and Fifties* (New Rochelle, N.Y.: Arlington House, 1975), 28.

2. Quoted in Mary Ellen Roach and Joanne Bubolz Eicher, eds., *Dress, Adornment, and the Social Order* (New York: John Wiley, 1965), 328.

3. *Vogue*, April 1947, quoted in Phyllis Tortora and Keith Eubank, *A Survey of Historic Costume* (New York: Fairchild Publications, 1989), 321. Ellen Melinkoff, *What We Wore: An Offbeat Social History of Women's Clothing, 1950–1980* (New York: Quill, 1984), 20.

4. Quoted in Elizabeth Wilson, *Adorned in Dreams: Fashion and Modernity* (Berkeley: University of California Press, 1987), 94.

5. Christian Dior, *Dior by Dior* (London: Weidenfeld and Nicholson, 1957), 159–160. Bernard Roscho, *The Rag Race: How New York and Paris Run the Breakneck Business of Dressing American Women* (New York: Funk and Wagnalls, 1963), 176.

6. Wilson, *Adorned in Dreams*, 44, 225–226.

7. Sandra Ley, *Fashion for Everyone: The Story of Ready-to-Wear, 1870s-1970s* (New York: Scribner, 1975), 107. Cecil Beaton, *The Glass of Fashion* (Garden City, N.Y.: Doubleday, 1954), 296.

8. Lesley Jackson, *The New Look: Design in the Fifties* (London: Thames and Hudson, 1991), 8.

9. Thomas Hine, *Populuxe* (New York: Alfred A. Knopf, 1986), 3–14. For the Visi-door see ad in *American Home*, March 1954, 85.

10. E.g., Laura Mulvey, "Visual Pleasures and Narrative Cinema," *Screen* 16 (1975), 6–18.

11. Rachel Bowlby, in "Soft Sell: Marketing Rhetoric in Feminist Criticism," *Women: A Cultural Review* 1 (April 1990), 16–18, analyzes the failings of studies of women's victimization by patriarchal forces. Often, these have the paradoxical effect of ignoring the agency and will of women and making them seem wholly passive—or truly fitting pawns for manipulation by greedy capitalist and irate academic alike.

12. Umberto Eco, *Faith in Fakes* (London: Secker and Warburg, 1986), 193–194. Faust quoted in Wilson, *Adorned in Dreams*, 99–100.

13. E.g., Wini Breines, *Young, White, and Miserable: Growing Up Female in the Fifties* (Boston: Beacon Press, 1992), 105; Brett Harvey, *The Fifties: A Women's Oral History* (New York: HarperCollins, 1993), 110–124. Packard's influential text was *The Hidden Persuaders*.

14. Frederic Jameson, "Postmodernism and Consumer Society," in E. Ann Kaplan, ed., *Postmodernism and Its Discontents* (New York: Verso, 1988), 28; see also Stuart Ewen, *All Consuming Images: The Politics of Style in Contemporary Culture* (New York: Basic Books, 1988), 245–246. Stephen Bayley, *Taste:*

The Secret Meaning of Things (New York: Pantheon, 1991), 143. Margaret Halsey, *This Demi-Paradise: A Westchester Diary* (New York: Simon and Schuster, 1960), 55.

15. The ad campaign is described in *Advertising Age,* March 20, 1961, 3; see also "Maidenform Dreams Big," *Sales Management,* April 5, 1963, 35–39. The Surrealist painter Salvador Dali illustrated a feature article for *Vogue* in 1944 ("Dream vs. Reality") which may have been the inspiration for the series; see Richard Martin, *Fashion and Surrealism* (New York: Rizzoli, 1987), 214–215. The model is quoted in Carl Sferrazza Anthony, *First Ladies: The Saga of the Presidents' Wives and Their Power, 1789–1961* (New York: Quill, 1990), 552–553.

16. J. B. West with Mary Lynn Kotz, *Upstairs at the White House: My Life with the First Ladies* (New York: Coward, McCann, and Geoghegan, 1973), 146; Anthony, *First Ladies,* 557, 562.

17. Clipping, *Brownsville Herald,* April 8, 1948, in Dwight D. Eisenhower Library (DDEL), White House Social Office Files, Box 34 (Personal—Mamie Doud Eisenhower [4]), Folder: Photographs, Newsclippings. Maureen Turim, "Designing Women: The Emergence of the New Sweetheart Line," in Jane Gaines and Charlotte Herzog, eds., *Fabrications: Costume and the Female Body* (New York: Routledge, 1990), 215–220.

18. Vance Packard, *The Status Seekers* (New York: David McKay, 1959), 133. Mamie quoted in Lester David and Irene David, *Ike and Mamie: The Story of the General and His Lady* (New York: G. P. Putnam, 1981), 176–177; the same story appears in "The General's Lady," *Time,* June 2, 1952, 21.

19. Parnis quoted in Martha Weinman, "First Ladies—in Fashion, Too?" *New York Times Magazine,* Sept. 11, 1960, 132. "Mamie Emerges as a Poised Campaigner," *Life,* July 21, 1952, 22.

20. Helen Worden Erskine, "'Call Me Mamie,'" *Collier's,* Oct. 4, 1952, 46. Robert Wallace, "They Like Mamie, Too," *Life,* Oct. 13, 1952, 158; "The General's Lady," *Newsweek,* Oct. 13, 1952, 29.

21. Mrs. Eisenhower to Parnis, July 29, Oct. 4, Nov. 24, Dec. 17, and Dec. 20, 1952: all in DDEL, White House Social Office Files, Box 32, Folder: Parnis (Livingstone), Mollie.

22. Ley, *Fashion for Everyone,* 108; for a description of a typical "Mamie outfit," see "Mamie Leaves Politics to Ike," *U.S. News and World Report,* Oct. 15, 1954, 67. Anne Stegemeyer, *Who's Who in Fashion,* 2nd ed. (New York: Fairchild Publications, 1988), 154; see also "She Has Designs on Three First Ladies," *Life,* June 17, 1966, 43.

23. Parnis quoted in a wall label, Eisenhower Museum, DDEL; and in David and David, *Ike and Mamie,* 211–212.

24. See Donald Katz, *Home Fires* (New York: HarperCollins, 1992), 82; and draft of reply, MDE to Helen Thomas, Sept. 2, 1953, DDEL, WHSF, Box 35, Folder 2.

25. John Denson, "The Eisenhowers at Home Abroad," *Collier's,* July 28, 1951,

15; "The General's Lady," *Time*, 21. Anthony, *First Ladies*, 558. "Mamie Emerges as a Poised Campaigner," *Life*, 23; Chloris A. Maynard to MDE, Nov. 10, 1953, DDEL, WHSF, Box 35, Folder 2.

26. See *People Today*, Feb. 13, 1954, 63.

27. "The 'Mamie' Haircut Goes Over with a Bang," *New York Times*, Jan. 15, 1953.

28. Dorothy Brandon, *Mamie Doud Eisenhower: A Portrait of a First Lady* (New York: Scribner's, 1954), 300. Mort Weisinger, "An Industry of Charms," *Coronet*, April 1956, 146–148.

29. David McCullough, *Truman* (New York: Simon and Schuster, 1992) 863. Nixon quoted in J. Ronald Oakley, *God's Country: America in the Fifties* (New York: Dembner, 1990), 136. "Mamie Is Happy: She's to Run 54-Room Home," *U.S. News and World Report*, Dec. 12, 1952, 20; Anthony, *First Ladies*, 549.

30. Quoted in Weinman, "First Ladies," 130.

31. Sally Victor, "Reflecting the Heart," *New York Times Magazine*, March 25, 1951, 19. Second quotation from "Sally Victor," *Time*, March 30, 1959, 82.

32. Victor quoted in Inez Robb, "Sally's Sensational Hats," *Saturday Evening Post*, Feb. 17, 1962, 28. MDE quoted in "Mamie Emerges as a Poised Campaigner," *Life*, 23. MDE to Sally Victor, April 4, 1953, DDEL, WHSF, Box 43, Folder: "Vi."

33. Robb, "Sally's Sensational Hats," 29; Anthony, *First Ladies*, 584.

34. Jody Shields, *Hats* (New York: Clarkson Potter, 1991), 115; George Dugan, "Sally Victor, 83, a Hat Designer with Many 'Firsts' in Fashions," *New York Times*, May 16, 1977; "Ike Inspires Fashion," *Quick*, March 24, 1952, 40. There is a Victor hat similar to the inaugural model, white felt adorned with semicircular cuttings, in the collection of the Eisenhower Museum, DDEL; Victor's hats tended to run in design series.

35. "First Lady," *U.S. News and World Report*, March 20, 1953, 4. MDE to Sally Victor, Jan. 26, 1953, DDEL, WHSF, Box 43, Folder: "Vi."

36. See, e.g., *We Like Ike: The Eisenhower Presidency and 1950s America* (Wichita, Kan.: Wichita Art Museum, 1990), 100.

37. Press release, Jan. 13, 1953, DDEL, WHSF, Box 22, Folder: "Inauguration 1953 (1)."

38. "First Lady's Finery," *Life*, Jan. 26, 1953, 77. "The President's Lady," *Time*, Jan. 19, 1953, 17; "Mrs. Eisenhower on List of Best-Dressed Women," *New York Times*, Dec. 17, 1952.

39. White House Photo Album, April 8, 1954, DDEL; "Eisenhower Termed Well-Shod President," *New York Times*, Jan. 18, 1954; "First Lady Hops Ride in Family Plane for a Flying Round of Dress Shops Here," *New York Times*, Nov. 16, 1954.

40. "It Can Happen Even to the President's Wife," *New York Times*, April 1, 1955. "Taste in Garb Shown by Next First Lady," *New York Times*, Nov. 22, 1952.

41. See press releases, DDEL, WHSF, Box 35 [Press (1952–3)], Folder 1.

42. Bart Andrews, *The "I Love Lucy" Book*, rev. ed. (New York: Doubleday, 1985), 127, 130.

43. E.g., "First Lady Pink," *New York Times*, Feb. 17, 1953. Marie McNair, "Top Hat Time Again at the White House," *Washington Post*, Nov. 11, 1953 (clipping in DDEL, Mary Jane McCaffree Papers, Box 1, Folder 1); "The Eisenhowers: After 38 Years, a 'Dream House'," *Newsweek*, June 28, 1954, 29; Martha Weinman, "Mr. Eisenhower Builds His Dream House," *Collier's*, Sept. 17, 1954, 26; Helen Worden Erskine, "A Tour of 'Mamie's Cabin'," *Collier's*, Jan. 22, 1954, 26; "A Rare Picture Visit: The First Lady at Home," *Life*, Oct. 20, 1958, 64–65.

44. Jo B. Paoletti and Carol L. Kregloh, "The Children's Department," in Claudia Brush Kidwell and Valerie Steele, eds., *Men and Women: Dressing the Part* (Washington, D.C.: Smithsonian Institution Press, 1989), 22. Stanley Marcus, *Minding the Store: A Memoir* (Boston: Little, Brown, 1974), 302, 305.

45. See, e.g., "Steel Kitchen Cabinets," *Electrical Merchandising*, Jan. 1953, 116; G.E. ad, *Look*, Nov. 13, 1956, 94–95; Trix ad, *Look*, Jan. 22, 1957, 60. Martha Saxon, *Jayne Mansfield and the American Fifties* (Boston: Houghton Mifflin, 1975), 91. Dave Marsh, *Elvis* (New York: Thunder's Mouth Press, 1992), 10, 23, 27, 58; Chester Morrison, "The Great Elvis Presley Industry," *Look*, Nov. 13, 1956, 98.

46. *This Fabulous Century*, vol. 6 (New York: Time-Life Books, 1970), 78–79. Russell Lynes, *A Surfeit of Honey* (New York: Harper, 1957), 69. Lynn Schnurnberger, *Let There Be Clothes* (New York: Workman, 1991), 375.

47. "Good Buys," *Vogue*, Oct. 1, 1957, 174. Balenciaga's defenders claim he cut the first chemise in 1954, but Dior would produce 1952 sketches proving that he had primacy in the "liberation of the waist." See Charlette Calasibetta, *Fairchild's Dictionary of Fashion* (New York: Fairchild Publications, 1975), 154; Dorner, *Fashion in the Forties and Fifties*, 28–29; Stegemeyer, *Who's Who in Fashion*, 12; Dior, *Dior by Dior*, 163, 165; "Dior: Fashion's Ten-Year Wonder Leaves Couture Leadership a Question," *New York Times*, Oct. 25, 1957.

48. Nan Robertson, "Variations on the Chemise Theme of Fall Fashion," *New York Times*, July 15, 1958. "Letters," *Newsweek*, May 26, 1958, 13.

49. "Acheson Says Chemise Is Fashion 'In Horrors'," *New York Times*, March 9, 1958. Stevenson quoted in Roscho, *The Rag Race*, 174; see also editorial on the Acheson/Stevenson charges, *New York Times*, May 28, 1958. Hope quoted in "The Road to Moscow," *Time*, March 31, 1958, 40. "Getting the Sack," *Time*, June 30, 1958, 20.

50. "Elizabeth Admires American Chemise," *New York Times*, May 14, 1958; "People," *Time*, May 5, 1958, 34. Lollobrigida quoted in "But There's No Sag in the 'Sack'," *Newsweek*, March 24, 1958, 94. Barbara A. Schreier, *Mystique and Identity: Women's Fashions of the 1950s* (Norfolk, Va.: Chrysler Museum, 1984), 15.

51. "The Battle of the Chemise," *American Fabrics*, Winter 1957, 126. E.g., "Semantics," *International Textile Apparel Analysis*, Feb. 22, 1958, 8; "Strictly Sentimental," *Co-ed*, Feb. 1958, 11. Nan Robertson, "Chemise a Success, U.S. Stores Report," *New York Times*, March 11, 1958.

52. For the worst of the name-calling, see "The U.S. Gives the Bag the Eye," *Life*,

Sept. 16, 1957, 113; Paul Sann, *Fads, Follies and Delusions of the American People* (New York: Crown, 1967), 263. Agnes Ash, "Chemise Forces Sly Fox to Make a Comeback Try," *New York Times*, April 5, 1958.

53. "Eisenhower Gown," *New York Times*, April 4, 1958; Mary Prime, "Summer Chemises to Drape All Ages," *Atlanta Constitution*, March 10, 1958. "President's Wife Hints He Gave Sack the Sack," *New York Times*, Sept. 12, 1958.

54. "More Than Modern," *Time*, March 31, 1958, 56–64; Edward D. Stone, *The Evolution of an Architect* (New York: Horizon Press, 1962), 143–146, 188–193.

55. Christopher Rand, "Letter from Brussels," *New Yorker*, March 29, 1958, 43, 46. *Contributors to the United States Exhibition Program at the Brussels Universal and International Exhibitions, 1958,* unpaginated, in National Archives, Record Group 43, Box 18. "Brussels '58, Progress Report: The United States Speaks to the World," *Interiors*, Sept. 1957, 135–136, in which the planners promised to go beyond these obvious facts to show a society in ferment.

56. Thomas B. Hess, "Innocents to Brussels," *Art News* 57 (March 1958), 23. Philip Siekevitz, "The Decadent Pavilion," *Nation*, Oct. 11, 1958, 213; "America's Image," *Commonweal*, May 2, 1958, 116.

57. Madeleine May, "Overheard at the Fair," *Atlantic*, Aug. 1958, 70; Walter C. Emerson, Jr., "American Tragedy at Brussels," *American Mercury*, Oct. 1958, 6; Marjorie J. Harlepp, "American Styles Impress Visitors at Brussels Fair," *New York Times*, April 19, 1958. Siekevitz, "The Decadent Pavilion," 212.

58. Quoted in Harlepp, "American Styles Impress Visitors," 12.

59. Gloria Emerson, "Brussels to See American Styles Costing $4 to $25," *New York Times*, May 16, 1958.

2. Hyphenated Culture

1. "The Leisured Masses," *Business Week*, Sept. 12, 1953, 142, 145.

2. Daniel Seligman, "The Four-Day Week: How Soon?" *Fortune*, July 1954, 81–83. Dero A. Saunders and Sanford S. Parker, "$30 Billion for Fun," *Fortune*, June 1954, 115. The Twentieth Century Fund's massive study on employment and wages, edited by W. S. Woytinsky of Harvard, also predicted a five-hour cut in the work week by 1960, assuming that one-third of the predicted annual gain in productivity was used for increased leisure.

3. Lawrence S. Wittner, *Cold War America: From Hiroshima to Watergate* (New York: Praeger, 1974), 128. Mike Featherstone, "Consumer Culture: An Introduction," *Theory, Culture, and Society* 1 (1983), 5. David M. Potter, *People of Plenty: Economic Abundance and the American Character* (Chicago: University of Chicago Press, 1954), 70.

4. Saunders and Parker, "$30 Billion for Fun," 117–118. Como quoted in Lucy Goldthwaite, untitled column, *McCall's*, May 1954, 4. Ben Gedalecia, "The Communicators," in Edmund Woodling, ed., *Advertising and the Subconscious* (Ann Arbor: Bureau of Business Research, University of Michigan, 1959), 4.

"A $40 Billion Bill Just for Fun," *Life*, Dec. 28, 1959, 74. "The Leisured Masses," 142.

5. Arthur G. Scott, "Hobby Show at Boeing," *Recreation*, April 1952, 33. *Merchandising Hobbies* (New York[?]: Hobby Industry Association of America, 1959), 7.

6. W. T. Baxter, "Hobby Crafts for the U.S. Navy," *Industrial and Vocational Education*, Jan. 1949, 15–16. A New York lawyer who won a top prize in the amateur art contest mounted by *Art News* in 1951 was among the many who began to paint in the Pacific "to escape the boredom and the insects"; see "Amateur Big League," *Life*, April 16, 1951, 73.

7. Grace Mary Stutsman, "Finger Painting: Everybody's Art," *Profitable Hobby*, June 1951, 69. H. D. Edgren, "What Does a Hobby Get You . . .?" *Recreation*, Jan. 1951, 445. Menninger quoted in William P. Uhler, Jr., "Get More Out of Life with a Hobby," *Recreation*, April 1953, 25.

8. "What's *Your* Hobby?" *American Home*, Nov. 1954, 127.

9. "Cultivate a Hobby," *Saturday Review*, July 22, 1950, 20. Arthur Schlesinger, Jr., "The Crisis of American Masculinity," *Esquire*, Nov. 1958, 64–66.

10. Dorothy De Zouche, "Hobbies Are Our Undoing," *Parents*, Oct. 1947, 28; Penny and David Hellyer, "Keep Those Home Fires Burning . . . with Hobbies," *American Home*, Dec. 1948, 51–52; Frances Marshall, "Are These Your Teen-Agers?" *Better Homes and Gardens*, April 1950, 269–271; Reed Millard, "Hobbies That Hold Your Family Together," *Coronet*, Jan. 1952, 136–138; Dorothy Barclay, "Hobbies for Youngsters," *New York Times Magazine*, July 27, 1952, 24.

11. Margaret E. Mulac, *Hobbies: The Creative Use of Leisure* (New York: Harper, 1959), 1. Roland Marchand, "Visions of Classlessness, Quests for Dominion: American Popular Culture, 1945–1960," in Robert H. Bremner and Gary W. Reichard, eds., *Reshaping America: Society and Institutions, 1945–1960* (Columbus: Ohio State University Press, 1982), 168. "The Fabulous Market for Food," *Fortune*, Oct. 1953, 271. J. Paul Taylor, "4 Do-It-Yourself Trends," *Printer's Ink*, Oct. 2, 1953, 27.

12. Richard Nunn, "Hollywood Handymen," *Better Homes and Gardens*, Nov. 1957, 44. Ernest A. Kehr, "Tie In Your Advertising with Hobbies and You Have a Ready-Made Appeal," *Printer's Ink*, Oct. 23, 1953, 44. Ernest Dichter, *Handbook of Consumer Motivations: The Psychology of the World of Objects* (New York: McGraw-Hill, 1964), 146. First used by *McCall's* in a May 1954 ad, the term "togetherness" came into general circulation when Macy's appropriated it during that Christmas season. In practice it meant that husband and wife shared many household tasks, although critics argued that togetherness would emasculate American men.

13. Russell Lynes, *A Surfeit of Honey* (New York: Harper, 1957), 56.

14. Margaret L. Jones, "Hobbies Develop the Executive," *Recreation*, March 1955, 112. The forum for professional hobbyists in the 1950s was *Profitable Hobby*; see, e.g., Walter L. Harter, "A New Life for Old Records," *Profitable Hobby*,

Oct. 1951, 34; Lucile Flitton, "Salvage with a Paint Brush," Dec. 1951, 16–19; Charles De Mangin, "A Fabric Painter Grows in Brooklyn," March 1952, 28–30.

15. Richard C. Levy and Ronald O. Weingartner, *Inside Santa's Workshop* (New York: Henry Holt, 1990), 61. "Hobbies: Realism Is What Sells," *Business Week,* Feb. 27, 1954, 60. "From Toys to Hobbies: The Way to Men's Hearts," *Business Week,* Jan. 28, 1956, 56–57.

16. "Hobby Show," *New Yorker,* Aug. 18, 1956, 16.

17. See, e.g., "Tile Painting Kits," *American Artist,* Sept. 1953, 18; ad for Hassenfeld kits, *Life,* Nov. 26, 1956, advertising supplement. Douglas T. Miller and Marion Nowak, *The Fifties: The Way We Really Were* (Garden City, N.Y.: Doubleday, 1977), 9.

18. Peter L. Skolnik, *Fads: America's Crazes, Fevers & Fancies From the 1890's to the 1970's* (New York: Thomas Y. Crowell, 1978), 99. Paint-by-numbers box quoted in Michael O'Donoghue, "A Head for Numbers," *House and Garden,* Nov. 1992, 74. "These Fads Have Built a Billion-Dollar Business," *Business Week,* Nov. 28, 1953, 78.

19. See, e.g., "Filis Frederick, 71, Dies," *Los Angeles Times,* March 23, 1987; Gerald Fraser, "Richard C. Hess, 57; Artist Was Creator of Paint By Numbers," *New York Times,* Aug. 9, 1991. Jerome Ellison, "Anyone Can Paint a Picture," *Saturday Evening Post,* Dec. 19, 1953, 65.

20. Edward J. Beck, "Painting by Number, Current National Craze, Started in Detroit," *Detroit News Magazine,* March 29, 1953, 9. Unpaginated corporate history, courtesy Craft House Corporation, Toledo, Ohio; Picture Craft ad, *Good Housekeeping,* April 1952, 303. William H. Knowlton, "You, Too, Can Be an Artist!" *Sales Management,* Sept. 1, 1953, 126, 128.

21. Craig Wilson, "From Child's Play to Prized Possessions," *USA Today,* April 20, 1992.

22. Robbins and Baltimore woman quoted in Beck, "Painting by Number," 9. Corporate survey in "These Fads Have Built a Billion-Dollar Business," 86. Russell Lynes, "How Do You Rate in the New Leisure?" *Life,* Dec. 28, 1959, 87.

23. Store owner quoted in "These Fads Have Built a Billion-Dollar Business," 84. Ellison, "Anyone Can Paint a Picture," 65. Leonard Brooks, "You Too Can Paint," *Atlantic Monthly,* June 1955, 86. Alfred Werner, "The Painting Plague," *American Mercury,* Dec. 1952, 55–56.

24. "Those Ubiquitous Numbered Painting Sets," *American Artist,* Dec. 1953, 58–59.

25. O'Donoghue quoted in Wilson, "From Child's Play to Prized Possessions." "These Fads Have Built a Billion-Dollar Business," 78. Lois and Alan Gordon, *American Chronicle: Seven Decades of American Life, 1920–1989,* rev. ed. (New York: Crown, 1990), 296; see also "Paintings by Famous Amateurs," *Readers Digest,* Dec. 1951, 73.

26. Dorothy Brandon, *Mamie Doud Eisenhower: A Portrait of a First Lady* (New

York: Scribner's, 1954), 258–260; "People," *Time*, Aug. 23, 1954, 36. Andrew F. Tully, "Ike and Mamie at Home," *Collier's*, June 20, 1953, 17. J. B. West with Mary Lynn Kotz, *Upstairs at the White House: My Life with the First Ladies* (New York: Coward, McCann and Geoghegan, 1973), 171. Nelson ad, *McCall's*, Dec. 1953, 6.

27. Ad, *Good Housekeeping*, April 1952, 303. West, *Upstairs at the White House*, 159–160; John Denson, "The Eisenhowers at Home Abroad," *Collier's*, July 28, 1951, 14; Robert Wallace, "They Like Mamie, Too," *Life*, Oct. 13, 1952, 152. Miriam B. Reichl, *Hobbies for Everyone* (New York: Homemaker's Encyclopedia, 1952), 82.

28. "Bright Pinpricks in the Gloom," *Time*, July 5, 1954, 8. Churchill quotations from the following sources: Marie Benyon Ray, "You Can Be an Amateur Painter," *Coronet*, March 1954, 82; see also Mary Soames, *Winston Churchill: His Life as a Painter* (Boston: Houghton Mifflin, 1990), 17–20. Ellison, "Anyone Can Paint a Picture," 67; see also Winston Churchill, *Painting as a Pastime* (New York: Cornerstone Library, 1965). Emily Genauer, "The Ascending Id in Amateur Art," *House and Garden*, Feb. 1957, 21. Eric Newton, "Diagnosis of a New Disease: Amateur Paintisis," *New York Times Magazine*, Sept. 25, 1949, 17.

29. Erika Doss, *Benton, Pollock, and the Politics of Modernism: From Regionalism to Abstract Expressionism* (Chicago: University of Chicago Press, 1991), 345. Steven Naifeh and Gregory White Smith, *Jackson Pollock: An American Saga* (New York: Harper, 1989), 618–624.

30. "Escape," *Time*, Jan. 16, 1950, 36. Stephen Harvey, *Directed by Vincente Minnelli* (New York: Harper and Row, 1989), 221–224, 241–247.

31. Jacob Getlar Smith, "Everybody Wants to Get into the Act," *American Artist*, Summer 1957, 30, 90–92. "Escape to the Easel," *Newsweek*, Aug. 26, 1957, 94. Maurice Grosser, "Art," *Nation*, March 22, 1958, 263–264.

32. "Celebrated Artists," *New York Times Magazine*, Sept. 19, 1948, 39. Erika Doss, "Catering to Consumerism: Associated American Artists and the Marketing of Modern Art, 1934–1958," *Winterthur Portfolio* 26 (Summer/Autumn 1991), 143–167.

33. "Beat This, Television!" and "Kelly's Dancing Lens," in *The Chronicle of the Movies* (New York: Crescent, 1991), 164, 165. "Paintings by Famous Amateurs," 79. "Hollywood Hobbies," *McCall's*, Oct. 1955, 18. "Good Uses of Their Spare Time by Celebrated People," *Life*, Dec. 28, 1959, 81–82. Ray, "You Can Be an Amateur Painter," 102. John D. Morse, "It Was a Grand Festival!" *American Artist*, Sept. 1953, 57.

34. "A Nonpartisan Pastime," *Life*, June 21, 1954, 81–82. "Gallery in a Grocer's," *Life*, May 18, 1953, 151. "Art Conquers Attica," *Life*, Aug. 22, 1955, 81–86. "Amateur Painting: It's a 'Craze'," *Newsweek*, Jan. 11, 1954, 51. "Hobby Show," 16. E.g., Marion M. Mayer, "Of Course You Can Paint!" *American Home*, July 1953, 27–29. Ad, *Profitable Hobby*, Sept. 1956, 43.

35. Reuel Denney, "The Scientific Corps—A Sixth Estate?" *Confluence* 3 (1954),

220–229. E.g., Edward Kerr, "Recreation Through Art," *Recreation*, May 1952, 78.

36. "Amateur Painting: It's a 'Craze'," 50; Ray, "You Can Be an Amateur Painter," 102, illustrated with pages from the Famous Artists School text.

37. Karal Ann Marling, *Wall-to-Wall America: A Cultural History of Post-Office Murals in the Great Depression* (Minneapolis: University of Minnesota Press, 1982). Neil Harris, *Cultural Excursions: Marketing Appetites and Cultural Tastes in Modern America* (Chicago: University of Chicago Press, 1990), 372–374; Mitchell Douglas Kahan, *Art Inc.: American Paintings from Corporate Collections* (Montgomery, Ala.: Montgomery Museum of Fine Arts, 1979), 16–17. Karal Ann Marling and Helen A. Harrison, *Seven American Women: The Depression Decade* (New York: A.I.R. Gallery/Vassar College Art Gallery, 1976), 31–33.

38. Doris Lee and Arnold Blanch, *It's Fun to Paint* (New York: Tudor, 1947); quotation from p. 48. Copies were still being sold in art supply shops in the 1970s. For criticism of Lee's primitivism as merely cute, see "After Hours," *Harper's*, Sept. 1947, 286.

39. Jane Kallir, *Grandma Moses: The Artist Behind the Myth* (New York: Clarkson N. Potter, 1982), 18–19. Paul D. Casdorph, *Let the Good Times Roll: Life at Home During World War II* (New York: Paragon House, 1989), 78. Truman quoted in Wittner, *Cold War America*, 129.

40. Grandma Moses quoted in Ray, "You Can Be an Amateur Painter," 83. Kallir, *Grandma Moses*, 24–26. Jess Stern, "If Grandma Moses Can Do It . . . Everybody Is Painting Now, and We Don't Mean Houses," *New York News*, Oct. 27, 1949.

41. Macdonald quoted in Christopher Lasch, "The Cultural Cold War: A Short History of the Congress for Cultural Freedom," in Barton J. Bernstein, ed., *Towards a New Past: Dissenting Essays in American History* (New York: Pantheon, 1968), 331.

42. Truman quoted in Kallir, *Grandma Moses*, 23. Grandma Moses quoted in Saul Pett, "Grandma Moses, 90 This Week and Feeling Fine, Sniffs at Art Fame and Keeps Right On Painting," *Tulsa World*, Sept. 3, 1950.

43. Ellison, "Anyone Can Paint a Picture," 66. "What Is Happening to American Tastes?" *House Beautiful*, Oct. 1952, 173; for examples, see Richard Horn, *Fifties Style: Then and Now* (New York: Beech Tree, 1985), 98–102. "Everyday Pictures for Millions," *Time*, Dec. 17, 1951, 64.

44. Harry Castleman and Walter J. Podrazik, *Watching TV: Four Decades of American Television* (New York: McGraw-Hill, 1982), 94–96.

45. Ad, *Profitable Hobby*, June 1955, 40. For TV ads of the same type, see Cecelia Tichi, *Electronic Hearth: Creating an American Television Culture* (New York: Oxford, 1991), 133.

46. Jeffrey Hart, *When the Going Was Good: America Life in the Fifties* (New York: Crown, 1982), 151. Alvin Toffler, *The Culture Consumers: Art and Affluence in America* (Baltimore: Penguin, 1964), 28, 35.

47. Miller and Nowak, *The Fifties*, 140.
48. Hobby quoted in "Amateur Painting: It's a 'Craze'," 50. William H. Whyte, Jr., *The Organization Man* (New York: Simon and Schuster, 1956), 3–7.
49. "Amateur Painting: It's a 'Craze'," 51–52.
50. Dichter, *Handbook of Consumer Motivations*, 449.

3. Disneyland, 1955

1. Bob Thomas, *Walt Disney, An American Original* (New York: Simon and Schuster, 1976), 270; Randy Bright, *Disneyland: Inside Story* (New York: Abrams, 1987), 93. Bob Chandler, "Disneyland as 2-Headed Child of TV and H'wood Shoots for $18 Million B.O.," *Variety*, July 20, 1955; "'Davy Crockett' in Bowl July 14–15," *Los Angeles Examiner*, July 1, 1955.
2. Thomas M. Pryor, "Network Makes Big Plans for Opening of 'Disneyland' Park—Addenda," *New York Times*, July 3, 1955; Jack Lair, Jr., "On TV Today: Disneyland Opening, Channel 7, at 4:30," *Los Angeles Examiner*, July 17, 1955. *Disneyland: The First Thirty-Five Years* (Walt Disney Company, 1989), 30–33.
3. Jean Bosquet, "$17,000,000 Disney Dream Comes True," *Los Angeles Examiner*, July 18, 1955; "Disney Reveals Locking Himself in Own Firehouse," *Los Angeles Examiner*, July 18, 1955.
4. "Disneyland Gates Open: Play Park on Coast Jammed—15,000 on Line Before 10 A.M.," *New York Times*, July 19, 1955; "Crowds Jam Disneyland; Public Opening Brings 24,000 by 3:30," *Los Angeles Examiner*, July 19, 1955.
5. Quotations from Bright, *Disneyland*, 107, 108–109. Surprisingly, some business writers also seemed to think Disney was not entitled to a profit: Mitchell Gordon, "Disney's Land: Walt's Profit Formula: Dream, Diversify—And Never Miss an Angle," *Wall Street Journal*, Feb. 4, 1958.
6. Julian Halevy, "Disneyland and Las Vegas," *Nation*, June 7, 1958, 511. Ciardi in a *Saturday Review* article, quoted in Michael R. Real, *Mass-Mediated Culture* (Englewood Cliffs, N.J.: Prentice-Hall, 1977), 80.
7. Ray Bradbury, "The Machine-Tooled Happyland," *Holiday*, Oct. 1965, 100.
8. Harper Goff designed the ride with the movie in mind; Bright, *Disneyland*, 69.
9. Disney interview with *Hollywood Citizen*, quoted in Leonard Mosley, *Disney's World* (New York: Stein and Day, 1985), 230. Louis Kronenberger, *Company Manners: A Cultural Inquiry into America* (New York: Bobbs-Merrill, 1954), 28.
10. Diane Miller Disney with Pete Martin, "My Dad, Walt Disney," *Saturday Evening Post*, Jan. 5, 1957, 133; Christopher Finch, *Walt Disney's America* (New York: Abbeville, 1978), 42. Disney quoted in *Disneyland: The First Thirty-Five Years*, 11; and in Richard Schickel, *The Disney Version: The Life, Times, Art and Commerce of Walt Disney*, rev. ed. (New York: Simon and Schuster, 1985), 310.
11. "Walt Disney—Teacher of Tomorrow," *Look*, April 17, 1945, 25.
12. See, e.g., Betty Friedan, *The Feminine Mystique* (New York: Dell, 1963), 41–42.

13. Ford ad quoted in Phil Patton, *Open Road: A Celebration of the American Highway* (New York: Simon and Schuster, 1986), 88. The definitive anti-suburban diatribe of the period is John Keats, *The Crack in the Picture Window* (Boston: Houghton Mifflin, 1956).

14. Reyner Banham, *Los Angeles: The Architecture of Four Ecologies* (London: Penguin, 1971), 127–128.

15. Jack Alexander, "The Amazing Story of Walt Disney," *Saturday Evening Post,* Oct. 31, 1953, 66; John Seelye, "The Mouse in the Machine," *New Republic,* Dec. 22, 1973, 22; Miller and Martin, "My Dad," *Saturday Evening Post,* Nov. 24, 1956, 70, 75, 80; and Dec. 8, 1956, 85. For Walt and railroading, see "An Interview with Ward Kimball," *Storyboard: The Journal of Animation Art* 2 (Oct./Nov. 1991), 16–19, 34; Johnston quoted in Christopher Finch, *Walt Disney: From Mickey Mouse to Magic Kingdom* (New York: Abrams, 1973), 386.

16. Yi-Fu Tuan, *Dominance and Affection: The Making of Pets* (New Haven: Yale University Press, 1984), 18–36. Robert De Roos, "The Magic World of Walt Disney," *National Geographic,* Aug. 1963, 166; Mrs. Walt [Lillian Bounds] Disney, "I Live with a Genius," *McCall's,* Feb. 1953, 40.

17. Johnston quoted in Finch, *Walt Disney,* 387. See Michael Sorkin, ed., *Variations on a Theme Park* (New York: Hill and Wang, 1992), 206; in a factually inaccurate essay on Disneyland, Sorkin dismisses out of hand any search for the origins of the park. Kimball quoted in Mosley, *Disney's World,* 217.

18. "Twenty-three Railroads Cooperate in Twelve Feature Exhibits," *Railway Age,* July 24, 1948, 83. *Railway Age* quoted in "Glamour on Wheels," *Newsweek,* Aug. 2, 1948, 56.

19. Ward Walker, "Rails Attract Myriad Fans—with Cameras," *Chicago Tribune,* July 20, 1948.

20. "Villages Form an Interesting Part of Lake Front Show," *Chicago Tribune,* July 20, 1948.

21. "The 'Deadwood Central' Runs on Time," *New York Times,* Aug. 22, 1948.

22. Robert A. Messena, "Mr. Hungerford's Iron Horse Opera," *Trains,* Sept. 1977, 36–41; James E. Kranefeld, "Railroads on Parade at the World of Tomorrow," *National Railway Bulletin* 54 (1989), 4–29; "Scenes from Wheels-a-Rolling," *Railway Age,* Aug. 7, 1948, 32. "An Interview with Ward Kimball," 19.

23. Robert G. Athearn, *The Mythic West in Twentieth-Century America* (Lawrence: University Press of Kansas, 1986), 135–137. Kimball quoted in Mosley, *Disney's World,* 218.

24. John M. Findlay, *Magic Lands: Western Cityscapes and American Culture after 1940* (Berkeley: University of California Press, 1992), 105, takes exception to this line of reasoning.

25. Quoted in Thomas, *Walt Disney,* 218.

26. Huxley's *After Many a Summer Dies the Swan* (1939) quoted in Dennis Hale and Jonathan Eisen, eds., *The California Dream* (New York: Collier, 1968), 239.

27. Quoted in David Gebhard and Harriette von Breton, *L.A. in the Thirties: 1931–1941* (Layton, Utah: Peregrine Smith, 1975), 109.

28. Richard Hollis and Brian Sibley, *The Disney Studio Story* (New York: Crown, 1988), 66.

29. In-house memo quoted in Thomas, *Walt Disney*, 218–219. City council quoted in Bright, *Disneyland*, 41.

30. Quoted in Thomas, *Walt Disney*, 224.

31. David Riesman in collaboration with Reuel Denney and Nathan Glazer, *The Lonely Crowd: A Study of the Changing American Character* (New Haven: Yale University Press, 1950), v, 354.

32. Quoted in Real, *Mass-Mediated Culture*, 54.

33. Quoted in William L. O'Neill, ed., *American Society Since 1945* (Chicago: Quadrangle, 1969), 41.

34. William Irwin Thompson, *At the Edge of History* (New York: Harper and Row, 1971), 9. Moore quoted in Paul Goldberger, "Mickey Mouse Teaches the Architects," *New York Times Magazine*, Oct. 22, 1972, 95.

35. Kaufman quoted in Finch, *Walt Disney*, 447. Planner quoted in Bright, *Disneyland*, 237.

36. Richard V. Francaviglia, "Main Street U.S.A.: A Comparison/Contrast of Streetscapes in Disneyland and Walt Disney World," *Landscape* 21 (Spring/Summer 1977), 156. Brochure quoted in Leo E. Litwak, "A Fantasy That Paid Off," *New York Times Magazine*, June 27, 1965, 27.

37. See, e.g., Tom Tumbusch, *Tomart's Illustrated Disneyana Catalogue and Price Guide*, vol. 2 (Dayton, Ohio: Tomart Publications, 1985) 19–22.

38. Banham, *Los Angeles*, 127. Hollis and Sibley, *The Disney Studio Story*, 60.

39. "Disney Comes to TV," *Newsweek*, April 12, 1954, 85. Mosley, *Disney's World*, 244.

40. Thomas M. Pryor, "Disney to Enter TV Field in Fall," *New York Times*, March 30, 1954; *New York Times*, May 2, 1954.

41. Quoted in Schickel, *The Disney Version*, 313. See also "Disney on the Dial," *Newsweek*, Nov. 8, 1954, 62; "Growing Impact of Disney Art," *Newsweek*, April 18, 1955, 60, 62.

42. "Disney Does It Again," *Newsweek*, Dec. 27, 1954, 60; "The Mouse That Turned to Gold," *Business Week*, July 9, 1955, 72–73. The actor Kirk Douglas, who starred in the film, would later bring suit against Disney for invasion of privacy. He contended that home-movie footage of himself and his sons riding on Walt's backyard train had been improperly used on *Disneyland* to promote the movie. See Kirk Douglas, *The Ragman's Son* (New York: Simon and Schuster, 1988), 253–254.

43. Chandler, "Disneyland as 2-Headed Child of TV and H'wood," *Variety*, July 20, 1955.

44. Between 1955 and 1963, eight of the top ten shows were Westerns: see Ella Taylor, *Prime Time Families: Television Culture in Postwar America* (Berkeley: University of California Press, 1989), 32.

45. George Lipsitz, in a paper delivered at the annual meeting of the American Studies Association (Nov. 4, 1989), suggested the connection, quoting Lynn

Spigel, "Installing the Television Set: Popular Discourse on Television and Domestic Space, 1948–1955," *Camera Obscura* 16 (1988), 14–20.

46. Thompson, *At the Edge of History*, 13–14.

4. Autoeroticism

1. Gerald Jones, *Honey I'm Home. Sitcoms: Selling the American Dream* (New York: Grove Weidenfeld, 1992), 55, 92, 97, 100; Mary Beth Haralovich, "Sitcoms and Suburbs: Positioning the 1950s Homemaker," *Quarterly Review of Film and Video* 11 (May 1989) 62–63; Bob Eddy, "The Private Life of a Perfect Papa," *Saturday Evening Post*, April 27, 1957, 176.

2. Roland Marchand, "Visions of Classlessness, Quests for Dominion: American Popular Culture, 1945–1960," in Robert H. Bremner and Gary W. Reichard, eds., *Reshaping America: Society and Institutions, 1945–1960* (Columbus: Ohio State University Press, 1982), 167. "The California Way of Life: Climate and the Automobile Create a New Pattern of Indoor-Outdoor Living," *Life*, Oct. 22, 1945, 105.

3. See "Americana," *Time*, June 20, 1960, 14. Karal Ann Marling and John Wetenhall, *Iwo Jima: Monuments, Memories, and the American Hero* (Cambridge: Harvard University Press, 1991), 62–74.

4. Mumford quoted in John Keats, *The Insolent Chariots* (New York: J. B. Lippincott, 1958), 212–213. Bart Andrews, *The "I Love Lucy" Book*, rev. ed. (New York: Doubleday, 1985) 315–330, 370–380. Chevy ad quoted in Peter Lewis, *The Fifties* (New York: J. B. Lippincott, 1978), 21. J. Ronald Oakley, *God's Country: America in the Fifties* (New York: Dembner, 1990), 230. Martin Mayer, *Madison Avenue, U.S.A.* (New York: Harper, 1958), 26.

5. Kenneth L. Jackson, *Crabgrass Frontier: The Suburbanization of the United States* (New York: Oxford, 1985), 249. Reyner Banham, "Detroit Tin Re-Visited," in Thomas Faulkner, ed., *Studies in Design and Popular Culture of the 20th Century* (Newcastle-Upon-Tyne: Newcastle-Upon-Tyne Polytechnic, 1976), 120. Banham quoted in Bevis Hillier, *The Style of the Century, 1900–1980* (New York: E. P. Dutton, 1983), 147.

6. Slogan quoted in Paul Carter, *Another Part of the Fifties* (New York: Columbia University Press, 1983), 36. Keats, *Insolent Chariots*, 83. Christopher Finch, *Highways to Heaven: The AUTObiography of America* (New York: HarperCollins, 1992), 205. Thomas Hine, *Populuxe* (New York: Knopf, 1986), 87.

7. ©1955 Arc Music Corp. (BMI), quoted by permission. See also Warren Belasco, "Motivatin' with Chuck Berry and Frederick Jackson Turner," in David L. Lewis and Laurence Goldstein, eds., *The Automobile and American Culture* (Ann Arbor: University of Michigan Press, 1983), 262–279. For Jackie Brenston and the Kings of Rhythm, see E. L. Widmer, "The Automobile, Rock and Roll, and Democracy," in Jan Jennings, ed., *Roadside America: The Automobile in Design and Culture* (Ames: Iowa State University Press, 1990), 85–86.

8. Catchphrase quoted in Finch, *Highways to Heaven*, 215. For interplanetary

Buicks, see Robert Atwan, Donald McQuade, and John W. Wright, *Edsels, Luckies, and Frigidaires: Advertising the American Way* (New York: Dell, 1979), 180. Keats, *The Insolent Chariots*, 58.

9. Arthur J. Pulos, *American Design Ethic* (Cambridge, Mass.: MIT Press, 1983), 422–423. Arthur M. Johnson, "American Business in the Postwar Era," in Bremner and Reichard, eds., *Reshaping America*, 106.

10. Stephen King, *Christine* (New York: Viking, 1983). Kevin Allman, *TV Turkeys* (New York: Perigree, 1987), 68–75.

11. See Jeffrey L. Meikle, *Twentieth Century Limited* (Philadelphia: Temple University Press, 1979), 12–13, 106; Roland Marchand, *Advertising the American Dream* (Berkeley: University of California Press, 1985), 156–157. Sloan quoted in Julian Pettifer and Nigel Turner, *Automania* (Boston: Little, Brown, 1984), 131. Stephen Bayley, *Harley Earl and the Dream Machine* (New York: Knopf, 1983), 103–108. Ford design chief quoted in Jeffrey Hart, *When the Going Was Good! American Life in the Fifties* (New York: Crown, 1982), 34.

12. Martineau quoted in Vance Packard, *The Hidden Persuaders* (New York: David McKay, 1957), 52. Jane and Michael Stern, *Auto Ads* (New York: Random House, 1978), 84. Eric Larrabee, *The Self-Conscious Society* (Garden City, N.Y.: Doubleday, 1960), 39–40.

13. Marchand, *Advertising the American Dream*, 159; see also *The Automobile in American Life* (Dearborn, Mich.: Henry Ford Museum and Greenfield Village, 1987), 22–23. White quoted in Paul Rambali, *Car Culture* (New York: Delilah Books, 1984), 40. For the celebrated Jordan ad of 1926, see Julian Lewis Watkins, *The 100 Greatest Advertisements* (New York: Dover, 1959), 50–51; Paul A. Carter, *Another Part of the Twenties* (New York: Columbia University Press, 1977), 134.

14. Faulkner quoted in Cynthia Golomb Dettelbach, *In the Driver's Seat: The Automobile in American Literature and Popular Culture* (Westport, Conn.: Greenwood Press, 1976), 97. Ernest Dichter, *The Strategy of Desire* (Garden City, N.Y.: Doubleday, 1960), 34–36. James Gilbert, *Another Chance: Postwar America, 1945–1985*, 2nd ed. (Chicago: Dorsey Press, 1986), 119. Rambali, *Car Culture*, 40.

15. See Ian Logan and Henry Nield, *Classy Chassis* (New York: A&W Visual Library, 1977). William M. Freeman, *The Big Name* (New York: Printer's Ink Books, 1957), 58.

16. See, e.g., Donald J. Bush, *The Steamlined Decade* (New York: George Braziller, 1975). Phil Patton, *Made in the USA: The Secret Histories of the Things That Made America* (New York: Grove Weidenfeld, 1992), 184–185; Alan Hess, *Googie: Fifties Coffee Shop Architecture* (San Francisco: Chronicle Books, 1985), 57–58. Harley Earl with Arthur W. Baum, "I Dream Automobiles," *Saturday Evening Post*, Aug. 7, 1954, 82.

17. George Koether, "New Cars: 1958, The Battle of the Stylists," *Look*, Nov. 26, 1957, 125.

18. Bill Morris's *Motor City* (New York: Knopf, 1992) is a novel set in Detriot

during the 1954 model year, when competition over gaudy decor was at its height. One of the characters lampoons a Big Three stylist, "the Michelangelo of Motor City, [who] wants every car that comes off the line to have four-foot fins and enough chrome to anchor a fucking destroyer" (232–233). Chrysler ad copy quoted in Pettifer and Turner, *Automania*, 137.

19. Vladimir Nabokov, *The Annotated Lolita*, ed. Alfred Appel, Jr. (New York: Vintage, 1991), 227–228.

20. Eric Larrabee, "What's Happening to Hobbies?" *New York Times Magazine*, Dec. 27, 1953, 271. James J. Flink, *The Car Culture* (Cambridge: MIT Press, 1975), 194. The Big Three automakers also made appliances, so the design similarities are understandable. For a particularly carlike refrigerator with gold trim and a colored interior, see ad, *Life*, Nov. 26, 1951, 88–89.

21. Earl, "I Dream Automobiles," 82. John De Waard, quoted in Pettifer and Turner, *Automania*, 133.

22. Quoted in Hine, *Populuxe*, 101.

23. *Time* coined Walker's title; see Hart, *When the Going Was Good*, 34. "A New Kind of Car Market," *Fortune*, Sept. 1953, 102. Gilbert Burck and Sanford Parker, "The Changing American Market," *Fortune*, Aug. 1953, 193.

24. Hayakawa quoted in Flink, *Car Culture*, 194. David Riesman, *Abundance for What? And Other Essays* (Garden City, N.Y.: Doubleday, 1964), 273.

25. Alfred P. Sloan, *My Years with General Motors* (Garden City, N.Y.: Doubleday, 1963), ch. 15; Gerald Silk et al., *Automobile and Culture* (New York: Abrams, 1984), 237–239. *Detroit Style: Automotive Form 1925–1950* (Detroit: Detroit Institute of Arts, 1985), 101.

26. A Motorama-like unveiling of a new model is the centerpiece of the 1988 film *Tucker: A Man and His Dream*, directed by Francis Ford Coppola.

27. Car commercials of the period appear in several video collections, including *Cars of the Fabulous Fifties* (Union, N.J.: Video Treasures, 1987). Hillier, *The Style of the Century*, 118.

28. "Julia Meade: Small Parts Pay Off," *Look*, Sept. 8, 1953, 94, 97. Meade later appeared briefly with Sullivan in a Las Vegas lounge act; see "Ed Sullivan's Act," *Variety*, March 26, 1958.

29. A Foldes commercial is included in *Cars of the Fabulous Fifties*.

30. Raymond Loewy, "Jukebox on Wheels," *Atlantic Monthly*, April 1955, 36, 38, 37. His argument was summarized and discussed widely; see "Lunge by Loewy, or, Watch That Dagmar," *Industrial Design*, April 1955, 82–83.

31. Jane Fiske Mitarachi, "Harley Earl and His Product: The Styling Section," *Industrial Design*, Oct. 1955, 51. Joseph J. Seldin, *The Golden Fleece: Selling the Good Life to Americans* (New York: Macmillan, 1963), 101. For Dreyfuss, see Meikle, *Twentieth Century Limited*, 59, 104. Larrabee, "Autos in America," in Riesman, *Abundance for What?*, 271. "Cars '55," *Industrial Design*, Feb. 1955, 82.

32. Eric Larrabee, "The Great Love Affair: Autos and Americans," *Industrial*

Design, Oct. 1955, 97. John B. Rae, *The American Automobile: A Brief History* (Chicago: University of Chicago Press, 1965), 206.

33. Vance Packard, "The Hidden 'Whip' of Our Behavior," in Edmund Wooding, ed., *Advertising and the Subconscious* (Ann Arbor: Bureau of Business Research, University of Michigan, 1959), 44. "Fads of the Fifties," *Look*, Feb. 2, 1960, 86; "The Girl in the Gray Flannel Suit," *Look*, April 3, 1956, 61. Thomas Weyr, *Reaching for Paradise: The Playboy Vision of America* (New York: Times Books, 1978), 65.

34. Ashley Montagu, *The American Way of Life* (New York: Putnam's, 1966), 330–331. For jokes about women drivers see, e.g., a Steven Dohanos cover for the *Saturday Evening Post*, Aug. 4, 1956, showing two housewives backing into each other's cars in the middle of a deserted suburban street. Dodge used women in high heels and dresses in ads for the first pushbutton models, introduced in 1955 for the 1956 model year. Keats, *The Insolent Chariots*, 12–13.

35. Thomas Doherty, *Teenagers and Teenpix: The Juvenilization of American Movies in the 1950s* (Boston: Unwin Hyman, 1988), 53. "Pat Boone: All American Boy," *Look*, Aug. 5, 1958, 81; on Detroit sponsorship of 1950s TV shows, see Kenneth Hey, "Cars and Films in American Culture," in Lewis and Goldstein, eds., *The Automobile and American Culture*, 202.

36. Patton, *Made in USA*, 203. See, e.g., Tom Wolfe, *The Kandy-Kolored Tangerine-Flake Streamline Baby* (New York: Farrar, Straus and Giroux, 1965). Finch, *Highway to Heaven*, 22; David Dalton, intro., *James Dean Revealed!* (New York: Delta, 1991), 30.

37. Sundberg and Romney quoted in Paul C. Wilson, *Chrome Dreams: Automobile Styling Since 1893* (Radnor, Pa.: Chilton, 1976), 238. For gas guzzling, see Marty Jezer, *The Dark Ages: Life in the United States, 1945–1960* (Boston: South End Press, 1982), 144–145. Eric Larrabee, "The Edsel and How It Got That Way," *Harper's*, Sept. 1957, 71. Oakley, *God's Country*, 243.

38. Wallace quoted in Larrabee, "The Edsel and How It Got That Way," 73. Slogan quoted in Mayer, *Madison Avenue, U.S.A.*, 114.

39. Elvis quoted in Gary McRae, "Notes of a Fan-atic," in Jac L. Tharpe, ed., *Elvis: Images and Fancies* (Jackson: University Press of Mississippi, 1979), 177. "Elvis—a Different Kind of Idol," *Life*, Aug. 27, 1956, 106; Carlton Brown, "A Craze Called Elvis," *Coronet*, Sept. 1956, 157.

40. See, e.g., Thomas C. Ryan, "Rock 'n' Roll Battle: Boone vs. Presley," *Collier's*, Oct. 26, 1956, 109. "Presley Rolls in the Clear," *New York Times*, Oct. 20, 1956. Wendy Sauers, ed., *Elvis Presley: A Complete Reference* (Jefferson, N.C.: McFarland, 1984), 15.

41. Belasco, "Motivatin' with Chuck Berry," 274. The song was written by the black bluesman Arthur Gunter and reflects a minority fascination with the Cadillac. See entry for "Pink Cadillac" in Fred L. Worth and Steve D. Tamerius, *Elvis: His Life from A to Z* (Chicago: Contemporary Books, 1988), 154.

5. When Elvis Cut His Hair

1. E.g., "Elvis Starts His Army Life Early," *Chicago Daily News*, March 28, 1958; "Elvis Entering Service Today at $78 a Month," *Atlanta Constitution*, March 24, 1958. For a $500,000 offer for hairs clipped by the barber, see "Impresarios: The Man Who Sold Parsley," *Time*, May 16, 1960, 62.

2. James and Annette Baxter, "The Man in the Blue Suede Shoes," *Harper's*, Jan. 1958, 46. Lester Bangs, "Where Were You When Elvis Died?" in Kevin Quain, ed., *The Elvis Reader* (New York: Saint Martin's Press, 1992), 85. "Private Presley's Debut," *Life*, April 7, 1958, 118.

3. John P. Shanley, "Presley Performs on the Sinatra Show," *New York Times*, May 11, 1960. "Idols Team Up on TV," *Life*, May 16, 1960, 103.

4. "Topping Time in Idaho," *Life*, March 23, 1953, 123–124.

5. Frank Cameron, "The Kids Have Gone Nuts on Haircuts," *Saturday Evening Post*, April 23, 1955, 104.

6. For the connection between Riesman and Elvis, see Al Hurwitz, "Elvis Presley and Art," *School Arts*, Sept. 1957, 19. "Ain't Nothin' But a Hairdo," *Life*, March 25, 1957, 55–56. Harrison E. Salisbury, "Presley Records a Craze in Soviet," *New York Times*, Feb. 3, 1957.

7. Robert Mitgang, "About—Men's Haircuts," *New York Times Magazine*, June 2, 1957, 26.

8. E.g., "Elvis—a Different Kind of Idol," *Life*, Aug. 27, 1956, 101. "Elvis Presley: He Can't Be . . . But He Is," *Look*, Aug. 7, 1956, 82–85; on the motion or speed of Pollock's painting, see W. T. Lhamon, Jr., *Deliberate Speed: The Origins of a Cultural Style in the American 1950s* (Washington, D.C.: Smithsonian Institution Press, 1990), 184–186.

9. Jack Gould, "TV: New Phenomenon," *New York Times*, June 6, 1956. Dave Marsh, *Elvis* (New York: Thunder's Mouth Press, 1992), 55. For the poster, see *The Whole Pop Catalog* (New York: Avon, 1991), 234.

10. Carlton Brown, "A Craze Called Elvis," *Coronet*, Sept. 1956, 156. "Hillbilly on a Pedestal," *Time*, May 14, 1956, 82. Linda Ray Pratt, "Elvis, or the Ironies of Southern Identity," in Jac L. Tharpe, ed., *Elvis: Images and Fancies* (Jackson: University Press of Mississippi, 1979), 45.

11. "It was like a giant wedding ceremony," said the secretary who discovered Elvis; quoted in Greil Marcus, *Mystery Train: Images of America in Rock 'n' Roll Music* (New York: Dutton, 1976), 170. "Elvis Mops Up 308G in 9 Days," *Variety*, April 10, 1957; Fred L. Worth and Steve D. Tamerius, *Elvis: His Life from A to Z* (Chicago: Contemporary Books, 1988), 76.

12. Jac L. Tharpe, "Will the Real Elvis Presley . . .?" in Tharpe, ed., *Elvis: Images and Fancies*, 4. Marcus, *Mystery Train*, 182. Stella Verbit, a teen fan, called Elvis "The King" in a letter to the editor, *Life*, Sept. 17, 1956, 19.

13. For a brief history of Elvis and the pinks of the 1950s, see Colleen Sheehy, "The Flamingo in the Garden: Artifice, Aesthetics, and Popular Taste in American Yard Art" (Ph.D. diss., University of Minnesota, 1991), 108–109. "The Lush New Suburban Market," *Fortune*, Nov. 1953, 128.

14. Timothy E. Scheuer, "Elvis Presley and the Myth of America," in Timothy E. Scheuer, ed., *The Age of Rock* (Bowling Green, Ohio: Bowling Green State University Popular Press, 1989), 104–105. Marcus, *Mystery Train*, 204, notes Presley's "natural affection for big cars, flashy clothes, for the symbols of status that *give pleasure* [italics added] both as symbols and on their own terms. Elvis has long since become one of those status symbols himself."

15. Gerald Weales, "Movies: The Crazy, Mixed-Up Kids Take Over," *Reporter*, Dec. 13, 1956, 40. "Elvis Presley's Effect on Clothes Deplored," *New York Times*, Nov. 17, 1957. Louis M. Kohlmeier, "Heartbreak, Hound Dogs Put Sales Zip into Presley Products," *Wall Street Journal*, Dec. 31, 1956; Chester Morrison, "The Great Elvis Presley Industry," *Look*, Nov. 13, 1956, 98.

16. Ernest Dichter, quoted in Walter Goodman, *The Clowns of Commerce* (New York: Sagamore Press, 1957), 111. John Kenneth Galbraith, *The Affluent Society* (Boston: Houghton Mifflin, 1958), 123.

17. "Principals Toss a Rock at Presley-Mimic Role," *New York Times*, Feb. 25, 1957.

18. Bill Diehl, quoted in "Elvis Presley-digitation Churns Up Teen Tantrums, Scribe Raps, So-So B.O.," *Variety*, May 30, 1956. Gould, "TV: New Phenomenon." Ben Gross, quoted in "The Music Goes On and On," *Variety*, June 13, 1956. "Elvis Presley: He Can't Be . . . But He Is," 84; see also "Presley on Pan but Cash Keeps Rolling," *Billboard*, June 16, 1956, 18.

19. "Spellman in Plea to Save U.S. Youth," *New York Times*, Oct. 1, 1956; "Baptist Minister's Sermon vs. Elvis: He'll Hit the Skids," *Variety*, Oct. 17, 1956; "The Elvis Presley Story: He's Making Monkeys out of Singers," *Variety*, May 9, 1956; "Presley Termed a Passing Fad," *New York Times*, Dec. 17, 1956.

20. "The Eye and Ear Dept.," *Advertising Age*, Jan. 2, 1950, 34.

21. Weales, "Movies," 41; Nick Tosches, *Dino: Living High in the Dirty Business of Dreams* (New York: Doubleday, 1992), 204.

22. Gleason quoted in Henry Pleasants, *The Great American Popular Singers* (New York: Simon and Schuster, 1974), 273. See also W. J. Weatherby, *Jackie Gleason: An Intimate Portrait of the Great One* (New York: Pharos, 1992), 108. Steve Vineberg, in *Method Actors: Three Generations of an American Acting Style* (New York: Schirmer, 1991), 91, also makes the connection between teen culture and the work of the Actors Studio.

23. Several video versions of the Presley TV appearances are available; see *Elvis: The Great Performances*, vols. 1 and 2 (Burbank, Calif.: Buena Vista Home Video, 1990). "Lonely & Shook Up," *Time*, May 27, 1957, 101. Elvis quoted in "Elvis Presley: He Can't Be . . . But He Is," 84.

24. "Elvis Presley-digitation," *Variety*. John Sharnik, "The War of the Generations," *House and Garden*, Oct. 1956, 41.

25. John Lardner, "Devitalizing Elvis," *Newsweek*, July 16, 1956, 59. "Presley Signed by Ed Sullivan," *New York Times*, July 14, 1956.

26. Jack Gould, "Elvis Presley: Lack of Responsibility Is Shown by TV in Exploiting Teen-Agers," *New York Times*, Sept. 16, 1956. Sullivan quoted in Worth and Tamerius, eds, *Elvis: His Life from A to Z*, 326. See also Arnold Shaw, *The Rockin' 50s* (New York: Dutton, 1974), 151.

27. "Shows of the Week," *Newsweek*, Sept. 24, 1956, 68. H. Wiley Hitchcock and Stanley Sadie, *The New Grove Dictionary of Music and Musicians* (New York: Grove Press, 1986), 218.

28. Brown, "A Craze Called Elvis," 153. Pleasants, *The Great American Popular Singers*, 265, quoting Charles Gillett. E.g., "A Howling Hillbilly Success," *Life*, April 30, 1956, 64. Lyric transliterated in "Elvis—A Different Kind of Idol," 102.

29. Baxter and Baxter, "The Man in the Blue Suede Shoes," 46. Richard Middleton, "'All Shook Up': Innovation and Continuity in Elvis Presley's Vocal Style," in Tharpe, ed., *Elvis: Images and Fancies*, 153–154. Scheuer, *The Age of Rock*, 108.

30. Alan Levy, "Elvis Comes Marching Home," *TV Guide*, May 7–13, 1960, 11. Richard S. Tedlow, "The TV Quiz Show Scandals of the 1950s," in Leonard Dinnerstein and Kenneth L. Jackson, eds., *American Vistas, 1877 to the Present*, 4th ed. (New York: Oxford, 1983), 314–320. Kent Anderson, *Television Fraud: The History and Implications of the Quiz Show Scandals* (Westport, Conn.: Greenwood Press, 1978), 54–67, 70.

31. See Helen Beal Woodward, "The Smitten Female," *Mademoiselle*, July 1957, 104. "Junk Wins TV Quiz Shows," *Life*, Sept. 23, 1957, 137–138.

32. One of the best known "misery" shows, which offered prizes to contestants willing to tell tales of woe to the camera, was called *Strike It Rich!* For the quiz show in general, see William Boddy, *Fifties Television: The Industry and Its Critics* (Urbana: University of Illinois Press, 1990), 81–84.

33. Cadillac convertibles were doled out on *The $64,000 Question*. According to Eric Barnouw, *Tube of Plenty: The Evolution of American Television*, rev. ed. (New York: Oxford, 1982), 198, the 1956–57 season, when Elvis and the quiz shows were the sensations of the airwaves, was the TV boom year of the 50s: 85 percent of all homes watched five hours a day and ads brought in $1 billion.

34. Murrow quoted in Anderson, *Television Fraud*, 160. Gilbert Seldes, *The Public Arts* (New York: Simon and Schuster, 1956), 15.

35. "What TV Is Doing to America," *U.S. News and World Report*, Sept. 2, 1955, 36–38.

36. Merle Curti, "The Changing Concept of 'Human Nature' in the Literature of American Advertising," *Business History Review* 41 (Winter 1967), 357. Martin Mayer, *Madison Avenue, U.S.A.* (New York: Harper, 1958), 244. Richard L. Cutler, "Current Research in Subliminal Perception," in Edmund Wooding, ed., *Advertising and the Subconscious* (Ann Arbor: Bureau of Business Research, University of Michigan, 1959), 56.

37. "7th Annual *Look* TV Awards," *Look*, Jan. 8, 1957, 61. Vladimir Nabokov, *The Annotated Lolita*, ed. Alfred Appel, Jr. (New York: Vintage, 1991), 151–154; Jack Kerouac, *On the Road*, in Ann Charters, ed., *The Portable Beat Reader* (New York: Viking, 1992), 24; Warren Belasco, "Motivatin' with Chuck Berry and Frederick Jackson Turner," in David L. Lewis and Laurence Goldstein, eds., *The Automobile and American Culture* (Ann Arbor: University of Michigan Press, 1991), 262–279.

38. Goodman, *Clowns of Commerce*, 118–120.

39. E.g., Lynn Spigel, "Installing the Television Set: Popular Discourses on Television and Domestic Space, 1948–1955," in Lynn Spigel and Denise Mann, eds., *Private Screenings: Television and the Female Consumer* (Minneapolis: University of Minnesota Press, 1992), 25–27; Lynn Spigel, *Make Room for TV: Television and the Family Ideal in Postwar America* (Chicago: University of Chicago Press, 1992), 117–126; Cecelia Tichi, *Electronic Hearth: Creating an American Television Culture* (New York: Oxford, 1991), 18–23. TV tray ad, *Better Homes and Gardens*, Jan. 1953, 114.

40. Carl Sferrazza Anthony, *First Ladies: The Saga of the Presidents' Wives and Their Power 1789–1961* (New York: Quill, 1990), 559, describing the period ca. 1953; at a party held several years later at the Gettysburg farm in observance of their wedding anniversary, the White House staff gave the Eisenhowers wooden tray-tables for their new house. Niblets ad, *National Grocers Bulletin*, March 1953, 65. Ads, *House and Garden*, Feb. 1953, 99; *Good Housekeeping*, Feb. 1952, 236; "The Pushbutton Way to Leisure," *Better Homes and Gardens*, March 1954, 135.

41. *High Styles: Twentieth-Century American Design* (New York: Whitney Museum of American Art, 1986), 130–145.

42. Ads, *Saturday Evening Post*, Feb. 18, 1950, 121; and *Good Housekeeping*, April 1954, 167.

43. Elvis quoted in Gary McRae, "Notes of a Fan-atic," in Tharpe, ed., *Elvis: Images and Fancies*, 177. For a Cadillac giveaway, see announcement of a Swanson's contest, *Progressive Grocer*, July 1954, 27.

44. Thomas Doherty, *Teenagers and Teenpix: The Juvenilization of American Movies in the 1950s* (Boston: Unwin Hyman, 1988), 53. Thomas C. Ryan, "Rock 'n' Roll Battle: Boone vs. Presley," *Collier's*, Oct. 26, 1956, 109.

45. Simon Frith, *Sound Effects* (New York: Pantheon, 1981), 64.

46. *Time* quoted in Quain, ed., *The Elvis Reader*, 38–41. "Dance Expert Predicts Rock 'n' Roll, Presley Will Be Around for Years," *Variety*, Aug. 7, 1957.

47. "Army to Give Elvis a G.I. Haircut," *Billboard*, Oct. 27, 1956, 1. Mike Kaplan, "Mdse. Swells Record Take," *Variety*, Oct. 24, 1956; "Impresarios," 62.

48. "The Red Line Doesn't Wiggle," *Atlanta Constitution*, March 11, 1958. Steven and Boris Zmijewsky, *Elvis: The Films and Career of Elvis Presley* (Secaucus, N.J.: Citadel Press, 1976), 55. "Leipzig Presley Fans Jailed," *New York Times*, Nov. 3, 1959.

49. "Elvis: Bigger Than the Generals Who Watch over Him," *Variety*, Nov. 5, 1958.

50. Parker quoted in "Impresarios," 62. Gossip quoted in Earl Wilson, "It Happened Last Night," *New York Post*, Sept. 23, 1958.

51. Janet Winn, "A Star Is Borne," *New Republic*, Dec. 24, 1956, 22; for *Love Me Tender*, see also Steve Pond, *Elvis in Hollywood* (New York: Plume, 1990). "Halo, Everybody, Halo: Latest Presley Pitch," *Variety*, Sept. 26, 1956. Marcus, *Mystery Train*, 182.

52. "Presley Case Assailed," *New York Times*, Jan. 3, 1958. "Rock-a-Bye Role for Presley," *Time*, Oct. 10, 1960, 121. Elvis quoted in Murray Schumach, "Holly-

wood Civilian," *New York Times*, May 22, 1960. Producer quoted in Jon Whitcomb, "Elvis and Juliet," *Cosmopolitan*, Oct. 1960, 14.

53. Quoted in "Is This a 'New' Presley?" *Newsweek*, May 30, 1960, 91.

6. Betty Crocker's Picture Cook Book

1. Patrick L. Coyle, Jr., *Cooks' Books: An Affectionate Guide to the Literature of Food and Cooking* (New York: Facts on File Publications, 1952), 25; ad, *Minneapolis Tribune*, Aug. 27, 1950. Lois Gordon and Alan Gordon, *American Chronicle: Six Decades in American Life, 1920–1980* (New York: Atheneum, 1987), 294; see also Hubbard Cobb, *Your Dream Home: How To Build It for Less Than $3500* (New York: Wise, 1950). "Betty Crocker Honors Mother of the Year," *General Mills Horizons,* June 1951, 12; "Project of the Year," *General Mills Annual Report,* June 1, 1952–May 31, 1953, 12.

2. John Wickland, "Huge Sale Seen for Cook Book," *Minneapolis Morning Tribune,* Sept. 2, 1950.

3. "How Betty Crocker Wrote the *Picture Cook Book,*" promotional reprint from *Journal of Home Economics* (Dec. 1956), unpaginated, in General Mills Archive (GMA), Betty Crocker Food and Publications Center, Minneapolis; tearsheet for ad (ca. 1952), "Why it took 10 years to serve this dish," GMA; "Cook Book Offers 1,000 Photographs," *New York Times*, Sept. 7, 1950. Margaret A. Gram, "Seasoned with Glamour," *Saturday Review,* March 10, 1951, 48. Morrison Wood, "How to Cook the Way Mother Used To," *Chicago Sunday Tribune,* Sept. 10, 1950.

4. Harvey Levenstein, *Paradox of Plenty: A Social History of Eating in Modern America* (New York: Oxford, 1993), 33, points out that before the McMein portrait codified her image, the Betty of the 1920s was sometimes young and blonde and modern in cartoon-style ads. Nor was she the only radio homemaker of the period; see Evelyn Birkby, *Neighboring on the Air: Cooking with the KMA Radio Homemakers* (Iowa City: University of Iowa Press, 1991).

5. Jean Lipman Block, "The Secret Life of Betty Crocker," *Woman's Home Companion*, Dec. 1954, 28, 78, 80; "General Mills of Minneapolis," *Fortune,* April 1945, 18; "The Story of Betty Crocker," promotional leaflet (ca. 1986), GMA; Jane Simon, "Mix Trust, Blend Ease, Cook Till Sales Are High," *Compass Readings* [Northwest Airlines], Nov. 1990, 35–38.

6. See Al Sicherman, ". . . And the Ladies of the Club Sandwich," *Minneapolis Star Tribune*, July 10, 1991. For a wide variety of such spokeswomen, see a single issue of *Good Housekeeping*, April 1952, 29, 157, 207, 220, etc.

7. James Gray, *Business without Boundary: The Story of General Mills* (Minneapolis: University of Minnesota Press, 1954), 178.

8. Levenstein, *Paradox of Plenty*, 31. John Mariani, *America Eats Out* (New York: William Morrow, 1991), 161, says that the phrase "just like Mom used to make" carried little weight on American menus after World War II, when Grandma began to be invoked instead.

9. "General Mills of Minneapolis," 10. The Betty Crocker recipe ad series appeared in several magazines: see, e.g., *Better Homes and Gardens*, Sept. 1949–April 1950. For the 1950 Gift Box, see *General Mills Horizons*, Nov. 1950, 12.

10. Adelaide Cummings Hawley was a blonde Park Avenue fashion reporter, a sophisticate who did not resemble the McMein picture in the slightest. For a summary of the company's sponsorships, see *General Mills Horizons*, Nov. 1951, 4. Hawley went before the cameras for the first time on Nov. 3, 1951. *Betty Crocker . . . 1921–1954* (Minneapolis: General Mills, [1960]), 11–12.

11. Ernest Dichter, *The Strategy of Desire* (Garden City, N.Y.: Doubleday, 1960), 230. Vance Packard, *The Hidden Persuaders* (New York: David McKay, 1957), 78; Ernest Dichter, *Handbook of Consumer Motivations: The Psychology of the World of Objects* (New York: McGraw-Hill, 1964), 14, 21, 37. *Betty Crocker . . . 1921–1954*, 13.

12. "The Story of Betty Crocker," GMA. On the occasion of her next overhaul, in the 1960s, Betty lost fifteen pounds and ten years. She came to resemble an older Mrs. Kennedy or a younger Mrs. Johnson, with heavily sprayed hair, a suit, and an unkitcheny rope of pearls. *Betty Crocker . . . 1921–1954*, 14.

13. Virginia Roberts, *The Photo-Method for Cake* (Minneapolis: Home Baking Institute, 1944). Jane and Michael Stern, *American Gourmet* (New York: Harper-Collins, 1991), 98–99.

14. The standard Kraft commercial began in 1952–1953 and appeared for years on variety shows as well as dramas. New York's Museum of Broadcasting has a collection of ads from the *Kraft Television Theater*, 1953–1955.

15. Lynn Spigel, "Television in the Family Circle: The Popular Reception of a New Medium," in Patricia Mellencamp, ed., *Logics of Television: Essays in Cultural Criticism* (Bloomington: Indiana University Press, 1990), 76. *Betty Crocker's Picture Cook Book* (Minneapolis: General Mills, 1950), 2–3. The new test kitchens were installed in 1946. For ads offering similar products for sale, see, e.g., *Better Homes and Gardens*, Feb. 1950, 22, for St. Charles Kitchens in assorted colors, and *Better Homes and Gardens*, Oct. 1950, 247, for redesigned Chambers gas ranges, also in color.

16. According to Jane and Michael Stern, *Square Meals* (New York: Knopf, 1984), 264, the classic California dip was created in 1954, when Lipton published a recipe combining dry soup mix with a carton of sour cream. But the idea predates 1954. Californian Helen Evans Brown introduced dipping foods and many other easy-eating recipes to the rest of the nation in the 1940s; see M. F. K. Fisher, introduction, *Helen Brown's Holiday Cook Book* (Boston, Little, Brown, 1952), xi.

17. *Betty Crocker's Picture Cook Book*, 49, 80. *The Sunset Barbecue Book* (1947) was only one of many to suggest—as Helen Brown did—that outdoor dining, buffet-style, was the new norm between the Rockies and the Pacific. Mary Douglas, *Implicit Meanings: Essays in Anthropology* (London: Routledge and Kegan Paul, 1975), 257, suggests that barbecues and cocktail parties act as social bridges between intimacy and distance. They seem to erode the dis-

tinction in a particularly suburban way, making "Californian" the preferred dining style of the housing tract.

18. Richard Sexton, *American Style* (San Francisco: Chronicle Books, 1987), 38–40. Harry Botsford, "Outdoor Hospitality: The Gentleman Plays with Fire," in *"Esquire's" Handbook for Hosts* (New York: Grosset and Dunlap, 1953), 97–98. "The Fabulous Market for Food," *Fortune*, Oct. 1953, 135, 137. Levenstein, *Paradox of Plenty*, 109.

19. "Short Cuts," in *Betty Crocker's Picture Cook Book*, 427–428. For Brown 'n' Serve rolls, see "A Year of Customer Service," *General Mills Annual Report*, June 1, 1949–May 31, 1950, 3; Gray, *Business without Boundary*, 253–254; "New Whole Wheat 'Brown 'n' Serve' Ups Sales by 50 percent," *Vitality News*, Aug. 1950, 1. *Vitality News* was a General Mills newsletter for the commercial baking industry.

20. Sally Bedell Smith, *In All His Glory: The Life of William S. Paley* (New York: Simon and Schuster, 1990), 479.

21. *Betty Crocker's Picture Cook Book*, 118–119. *General Mills Horizons*, Nov. 1951, 2.

22. *Betty Crocker's Picture Cook Book*, 152–153.

23. M. F. K. Fisher, *The Art of Eating* (Cleveland: World, 1954), 643–644. Jennie S. Wilmot and Margaret Q. Batjer, *Food for the Family: An Elementary College Text*, 4th ed. (Philadelphia: J. B. Lippincott, 1955), 368–369. *Betty Crocker's Picture Cook Book*, 271, 274, 276.

24. Laura Shapiro, *Perfection Salad: Women and Cooking at the Turn of the Century* (New York: Farrar, Straus and Giroux, 1986), 84–91. Margaret Cussler and Mary L. DeGive, *'Twixt the Cup and the Lip: Psychological and Socio-Cultural Factors Affecting Food Habits* (New York: Twayne, 1952), 48.

25. Levenstein, *Paradox of Plenty*, 102. *Betty Crocker's Picture Cook Book*, 5. Poppy Cannon (of *Better Homes and Gardens* and NBC's *Home* show), quoted in John L. Hess and Karen Hess, *The Taste of America*, 3rd ed. (Columbia: University of South Carolina Press, 1989), 154.

26. "32 Food Concerns, a Governor Mobilized to Entertain Editors," *Food Field Reporter*, Oct. 19, 1953, 1; Susan Strasser, *Never Done: A History of American Housework* (New York: Pantheon, 1982), 276–277; the imagery of containment is obvious in the examples cited: modernity was kept under control when the convenience food was stuffed into a traditional one.

27. Ad, *American Home*, Jan. 1954, 65. For another view of convenience foods of the 1950s, see Harvey A. Levenstein, *Revolution at the Table: The Transformation of the American Diet* (New York: Oxford, 1988), 202–203. *Harper's* editor Bernard De Voto mockingly called the aesthetic cookery espoused by the women's pages "fancy compositions," unfit for men.

28. The cake is described as a symbol of "Home Life" in a famous Betty Crocker motto: see *Betty Crocker's Picture Cook Book*, 115. The song, written by Al Hoffman, Bob Merrill, and Clem Wats, was introduced in Chicago on the popular *Breakfast Club* radio show in 1950 and spent fifteen weeks on the charts; see Joseph Murrells, *Million Selling Records from the 1900s to the 1980s: An Illustrated Directory* (New York: Arco, 1984), 62.

29. See "Roses-in-Snow Cake Kit for '50," *Vitality News*, March 1950, 1; "It's a Sweetheart," ibid., Jan. 1950, 1; and ads, *Baker's Digest*, Feb. 1951, 46, and April 1951, 49. Dichter, *Handbook of Consumer Motivations*, 37. He also thought women made fancy desserts when they were bored.

30. Walter Goodman, *The Clowns of Commerce* (New York: Sagamore Press, 1957), 20–28, describes such a brainstorming session, with a framed picture of Betty Crocker hung on the wall for inspiration. On freezers, see "NARGUS Reports to Retailers," *National Grocers Bulletin*, Feb. 1953, 3. Dichter, *Handbook of Consumer Motivations*, 15, comments on avoiding public cake-eating.

31. Mary Fisher Langmuir, Ph.D., "Wife Trouble? Get Her a Job!" *American Magazine*, Jan. 1950, 36–37. For Minute Rice, see "Wonder-quick . . . and oh, so Wonderful!" *Ladies Home Journal*, Jan. 1950, 32. For Readi-Whip, see Sam Martin and Saul Beck, "Forty Years of Quick Frozen Foods," *Quick Frozen Foods*, Aug. 1978, 49. For "Dinner-in-a-Shell," see ad, *Better Homes and Gardens*, Sept. 1949, 73. For a collection of published recipes for TV snacks and tabletop meals, see *Recipes of Tomorrow by Betty Crocker* (Minneapolis: General Mills, 1954), 10–11.

32. Gray, *Business without Boundary*, 251–252. The popularity of cakes was not wasted on General Mills executives, who had already decided that bread would be less of a staple in the postwar period and concluded that, to make a profit, food-processing concerns had to develop new, convenience products. "Betty Crocker Chiffon Cake Makes History," *General Mills Annual Report*, June 1, 1947–May 31, 1948, 9. Recipe-ad, *Better Home and Gardens*, Oct. 1949, 23.

33. Dichter on fear of failure quoted in Martin Mayer, *Madison Avenue, U.S.A.* (New York: Harper, 1958), 123; BBD&O built the Betty Crocker "I Guarantee" campaign around this statement. Dichter, *Handbook of Consumer Motivations*, 28.

34. Dichter, *The Strategy of Desire*, 183–184. "Ready-mixes," he would write in *Advertising Age*, "are . . . correct psychological answers to the conflict between individuality and [the] mass mind"; see Goodman, *Clowns of Commerce*, 112.

35. "Eat Your Cake and Have It, Too," *Progress Thru Research* 4 (Fall 1949), 9–11. "NARGUS Reports," *National Grocers Bulletin*, Jan. 1953, 3. Competition increased and sales reached a plateau and finally began to decline as the 1950s wore on. "Old Favorite Food Items Lose Ground to Newer Products, Cleveland Survey Shows," *Advertising Age*, Jan. 4, 1954, 20, noted that Pillsbury had pulled ahead in the cake-mix wars with 26.6 percent of the market, whereas Betty Crocker (21.6 percent) and the new Duncan Hines brand (17.5 percent) trailed behind. In 1957 four in ten households used mixes regularly; see "Convenience Foods Have Scant Impact on Housewife, Ag Department Study Says," *Advertising Age*, Feb. 4, 1957, 46.

36. Packard, *The Hidden Persuaders*, 62–63. The potential for failure rose as the castles of gelatin did, of course. "Recipes: Too Elaborate?" *Food Field Reporter*, Aug. 24, 1953, 16.

37. The most famous study of the period linked women to red packaging and men to blue; Packard, *The Hidden Persuaders*, 109. See also Container Corporation of America ad, *Ice Cream Review*, Oct. 1951, 137. The red Marlboro package was a subtle exception to the rule of gender.

38. Joseph J. Seldin, *The Golden Fleece: Selling the Good Life to Americans* (New York: Macmillan, 1963), 90. The fugue state that supposedly overtook shoppers in the presence of pictorial cake-mix boxes is described in Packard, *The Hidden Persuaders*, 108.

39. "Biggest Show on Television Promotes Ice Cream," *Ice Cream Review*, Oct. 1951, 108, 110. "NARGUS Reports," *National Grocers Bulletin*, March 1953, 3; Loewy also redesigned the packaging for the Armour meat line in the 1950s. Untitled column, *Progressive Grocer*, Dec. 1954, 95; "The Coming of Color," *Food Field Reporter*, Jan. 25, 1954, 36.

40. Bill Culp, "Swanson's TV Dinner: Behind the Debut of a *New* Product," *Frosted Food Field*, Feb. 1954, 78. Ad, *Quick Frozen Foods*, March 1951, 166; untitled article, *Quick Frozen Foods*, April 1951, 118; "Frigidinner to Sell in Grocery Stores," *Food Field Reporter*, Aug. 10, 1953, 28.

41. Quotes from *Frosted Food Field*: "Quaker State Markets Complete Frozen Meals," Feb. 1953, 20; "Restaurant Chain Plans to Sell Frozen Dinners," March 1953, 1, 5; "Quaker State Pushed Frozen meals, Sees Big Market," Aug. 1953, 29. Martin and Beck, "Forty Years," 51, 58, believe that the first such product was an airline dinner in a circular dish (a "sky plate") sold briefly in a New Jersey department store under the name of Maxson's Strato-Meals.

42. "Swanson Claims Packaging 'First' for Its TV Dinner's Outer Wrap," *Food Field Reporter*, Jan. 11, 1954, 24.

43. See ad, *Quick Frozen Foods*, Feb. 1951, 258G. Commentator quoted in Culp, "Swanson's TV Dinner," 82. Armour ad, *Progressive Grocer*, Sept. 1954, 159; note on TV Dessert in "Frozen Desserts Coming," *Frozen Food Center*, Feb. 1954, 12; "Packaging Notes," *Food* [Great Britain], Dec. 1954, 463–464; untitled article, *Progressive Grocer*, Aug. 1954, 149, and ad, 220. Formerly a concession food, popcorn was growth industry in the 1950s thanks to home entertainment; see "NARGUS Reports," *National Grocers Bulletin*, May 1954, 3.

44. Sales of the chicken dinner surpassed those of the popular (and cheaper) frozen pot pie by 419 percent for a comparable introductory period; untitled article, *Food Field Reporter*, June 28, 1954, 8. For the printing process, see untitled article, *Frozen Food Field*, June 1953, 13. For the food scare, untitled article, ibid., Feb. 1955, 3, 8.

45. "Ullman Returned, Shuns Picture Use, Hails the Unusual," *Food Field Reporter*, Oct. 5, 1953, 41. "Cake Mix Gallery of Pictures Steals Story from Brand Names, Nash Tells Conclave," ibid., Oct. 5, 1953, 43. "U.S. Supermarket in Yugoslavia," *New York Times Magazine*, Sept. 22, 1957, 88.

46. "Betty Crocker Cuts Its Cake Mix Prices," *Food Field Reporter*, April 5, 1954, 38; "Red Spoon Is Selected as Betty Crocker Sign," ibid., May 17, 1954, 31. The spoon was designed by Lippincott and Margulies of New York.

47. Quotes from *Advertising Age:* untitled article, March 11, 1957, 21; "Armour Tests Dial Soap in 5 New Colors in 2 Midwest Cities," April 1, 1957, 1; E. B. Weiss, "Packaged Meals Pose New Problems for Advertisers, Merchandizers," Jan. 18, 1954, 66; editorial, "Who Started It, Anyway?" Sept. 2, 1957, 62.

7. Nixon in Moscow

1. Stephen J. Whitfield, *The Culture of the Cold War* (Baltimore: Johns Hopkins University Press, 1991), 73; "'Made in U.S.A.'—in Red Capital," *U.S. News and World Report,* Aug. 3, 1959, 38. Gereon Zimmerman and Bob Lerner, "What the Russians Will See," *Look,* July 21, 1959, 52–54. *Izvestia* quoted in "'Ivan' Takes a Look at American Life," *U.S. News and World Report,* Aug. 10, 1959, 42.
2. "U.S. and U.S.S.R. Agree to Exchange Exhibitions in 1959," *Department of State Bulletin,* Jan. 26, 1958, 132–134. "Architecture: Umbrella Man," *Newsweek,* July 13, 1959, 84. See, e.g., note on 1955 trade fairs in Paris and Milan, *Industrial Design,* Aug. 1955, 72–77. Arthur J. Pulos. *The American Design Adventure* (Cambridge, Mass.: MIT Press, 1990), 242–247.
3. "The Vice President in Russia: A Barnstorming Masterpiece," *Life,* Aug. 10, 1959, 34.
4. Milward W. Martin, *Twelve Full Ounces* (New York: Holt, Rinehart and Winston, 1962), 109.
5. Alvin Toffler, "Coca-Cola vs. Pepsi-Cola: The Competition That Refreshes," *Fortune,* May 1961, 127.
6. "'Made in U.S.A.'—in Red Capital," 39.
7. "Their Sheltered Honeymoon," *Life,* Aug. 10, 1959, 51.
8. Elaine Tyler May, *Homeward Bound: American Families in the Cold War Era* (New York: Basic Books, 1988), 3.
9. Van Doren quoted in Paul A. Carter, *Another Part of the Fifties* (New York: Columbia University Press, 1983), 188; Douglas T. Miller and Marion Nowak, *The Fifties: The Way We Really Were* (Garden City, N.Y.: Doubleday, 1977), 16–17. Whitfield, *The Culture of the Cold War,* 72. David Riesman, *Abundance for What? And Other Essays* (Garden City, N.Y.: Doubleday, 1964), 67.
10. *Advertising Age* quoted in Joseph J. Seldin, *The Golden Fleece: Selling the Good Life to Americans* (New York: Macmillan, 1963), 128. Steinbeck quoted in Thurston N. Davis, Arthur M. Schlesinger, Sr., et al., "Have We Gone Soft?" *New Republic,* Feb. 15, 1960, 11. "Leisure Could Mean a Better Civilization," *Life,* Dec. 28, 1959, 62. Kennedy quoted in J. Ronald Oakley, *God's Country: America in the Fifties* (New York: Dembner, 1990), 418. John Kenneth Galbraith, *The Affluent Society* (Boston: Houghton Mifflin, 1958), 139–140.
11. Kenneth T. Jackson, *Crabgrass Frontier: The Suburbanization of the United States* (New York: Oxford, 1985), 235–236; Jan Cohn, *The Palace or the Poorhouse: The American House as a Cultural Symbol* (East Lansing: Michigan State University

Press, 1979), 239. Levitt quoted in Jackson, *Crabgrass Frontier*, 231; Eric Larrabee, "The Six Thousand Houses That Levitt Built," *Harper's*, Sept. 1948, 82–84.

12. Wendell Bell, "Social Choice, Life Styles, and Suburban Residence," in William M. Dobriner, ed., *The Suburban Community* (New York: G. P. Putnam, 1958), 266. William H. Whyte, Jr., "The Future c/o Park Forest," *Fortune*, June 1953, 126, and "The Transients," ibid., May 1953, 113. Riesman, *Abundance For What?* 107.

13. "On the 5:19 to Ulcerville," *Newsweek*, Aug. 17, 1959, 32.

14. Cover, *Saturday Evening Post*, Aug. 15, 1959.

15. Gilbert Burk and Stanford Parker, "The Changing American Market," *Fortune*, Aug. 1953, 98. Davis, "Have We Gone Soft?" 12.

16. "'Peaceful Coexistence'," *Time*, July 13, 1959, 13; "On Tour with Russia's New No. 2 Man," *U.S. News and World Report*, July 13, 1959, 43. Vasili Zakharchenko, "In New York," *U.S.S.R.* 6 (1959), 1–9.

17. "Khrushchev: A 7-Year Plan, and Frills, Too," *U.S. News and World Report*, July 13, 1959, 8.

18. Frankel quoted in "'Peaceful Coeexistence'," 11. "The Talk of the Town," *New Yorker*, July 11, 1959, 17. "'Peaceful Cooexistence'," 9.

19. Paul D. Casdorph, *Let the Good Times Roll: Life at Home in America During World War II* (New York: Paragon House, 1989), 41. Westinghouse ad, *Life*, Oct. 22, 1945, 28. "Westinghouse to Hike Its Appliance Output 15 percent, Price Declares," *Advertising Age*, Jan. 2, 1950, 14.

20. *Look* quoted in James Gilbert, *Another Chance: Postwar America, 1945–1985*, 2nd ed. (Chicago: Dorsey Press, 1986), 3. Dr. Daniel E. Schneider, "The Creative Process in Industrial Design," *Industrial Design*, Jan. 1957, 71. Don Wallance, *Shaping America's Products* (New York: Reinhold, 1956), 71.

21. Eric Larrabee, "Autos and Americans: The Great Love Affair," *Industrial Design*, Aug. 1955, 97; untitled news item, *Printer's Ink*, Feb. 3, 1950, 70; "3 Dream Kitchens," *Industrial Design*, Feb. 1955, 67. Russell Lynes, *The Domesticated Americans* (New York: Harper and Row, 1963), 269.

22. Ernest Dichter, *Handbook of Consumer Motivations: The Psychology of the World of Objects* (New York: McGraw-Hill, 1964), 130. Quote about freezers in Vance Packard, *The Hidden Persuaders* (New York: David McKay, 1957), 73. Daniel Seligman and Sanford S. Parker, "Upheaval in Home Goods," *Fortune*, March 1954, 97–99.

23. Vance Packard, "The Hidden 'Whip' of Our Behavior," in Edmund Wooding, ed., *Advertising and the Subconscious* (Ann Arbor: Bureau of Business Research, University of Michigan, 1959), 44; "Westinghouse Ads Push Its 'Family' of Major Appliances," *Advertising Age*, Sept. 2, 1957, 3.

24. E.g., Madeline Holland, "Colors Make Your Kitchen Easy to Live In," *Chicago Sunday Tribune*, Sept. 17, 1950. Ruth Ellen Church, *Mary Meade's Kitchen Companion: The Indispensable Guide for the Modern Cook* (New York: Bobbs-Merrill, 1955), 14.

25. "What's Happening to America's Taste?" *Industrial Design,* June 1955, 16. Packard, *The Hidden Persuaders,* 22.

26. Seldin, *The Golden Fleece,* 90–91.

27. Mary Ellen Chase, "She Misses Some Goals," *Life,* Dec. 24, 1956, 25. "The Pushbutton Way to Leisure," *Better Homes and Gardens,* March 1954, 135.

28. E.g., *Recipes of Tomorrow by Betty Crocker* (Minneapolis: General Mills, 1954), 10. For the small appliances of choice in 1956, see "How to Be Happy and Stay out of Debt," *Newsweek,* Dec. 17, 1956, 83.

29. German critic quoted in Lawrence S. Wittner, *Cold War America: From Hiroshima to Watergate* (New York: Praeger, 1974), 120. Eric Larrabee, *The Self-Conscious Society* (Garden City, N.Y.: Doubleday, 1960), 15.

30. Louis Kronenberger, "America and Art," *American Scholar* 22 (Autumn 1953), 403–403. Lynes, *The Domesticated Americans,* 269.

31. Bernard Rudofsky, *Behind the Picture Window* (New York: Oxford, 1955), 7. John P. Marquand, *Point of No Return* (Boston: Little, Brown, 1949), 9. Church, *Mary Meade's Kitchen Companion,* 11, 162.

32. Godfrey Hodgson, *America in Our Time* (Garden City, N.Y.: Doubleday, 1976), 6. See also Allan M. Winkler, *Life under a Cloud: American Anxiety about the Atom* (New York: Oxford, 1993); Robert A. Divine, *The Sputnik Challenge: Eisenhower's Response to the Soviet Satellite* (New York: Oxford, 1993). Quotation from Ernest Dichter, *The Strategy of Desire* (Garden City, N.Y.: Doubleday, 1960), 227.

33. Ad, *Interiors,* April 1953, 44. Elizabeth Gordon, "The Threat to the Next America," *House Beautiful,* April 1953, 126–127. For responses see, e.g., Thomas H. Creighton, open letter to Gordon, *Progressive Architecture,* May 1953, 234; see also O.G., "Viewing with Alarm," *Interiors,* April 1953, 75; Alfred Auerbach, "Modern . . . From Where to Where," ibid., July 1953, 42a-42h; draft of undated letter, Russel Wright to Gordon, in Russel Wright Papers, Syracuse University Libraries, Box 1, Folder: Articles and Magazines.

34. Lyman Bryson, *The Next America: Prophecy and Faith* (New York: Harper, 1952), 124–126.

35. Lyman Bryson, "The Greatest Good—and Goods—for the Greatest Number," *House Beautiful,* April 1953, 114–115, 172.

36. Jane De Hart Mathews, "Art and Politics in Cold War America," *American Historical Review* 81 (Oct. 1976), 771–773. Dondero quoted in Frank Getlein, "Politicians as Art Critics: Thoughts on the U.S. Exhibition in Moscow," *New Republic,* July 27, 1959, 13. "Jury Appointed To Select Works for U.S. Exhibit at Moscow," *Department of State Bulletin,* March 16, 1959, 381. "Like It or Not," *Newsweek,* July 13, 1959, 20.

37. Quoted in "Now An Art Show Has U.S. Leaders in a Stew," *U.S. News and World Report,* July 13, 1959, 79. See also Richard M. Fried, *Nightmare in Red: The McCarthy Era in Perspective* (New York: Oxford, 1990), 33.

38. Transcript in Getlein, "Politicians as Art Critics," 12.

39. Added paintings illustrated in "'Made in U.S.A.'—in Red Capital," 39. Frank Getlein, "Pictures at an Exhibition: Russia's Reaction to the U.S. Show In Moscow," *New Republic*, Aug. 24, 1959, 13–14. For the use of Abstract Expressionism as anti-Communist propaganda in the later 1940s, see Serge Guilbaut, *How New York Stole the Idea of Modern Art: Abstract Expressionism, Freedom, and the Cold War* (Chicago: University of Chicago Press, 1983), 149–151.

40. Quoted in Getlein, "Pictures at an Exhibition," 15.

41. Stephen E. Ambrose, *Nixon: The Education of a Politician* (New York: Simon and Schuster, 1987), 520–521. Richard M. Nixon, *Six Crises* (Garden City, N.Y.: Doubleday, 1962), 252.

42. For transcripts of the debate, see "'Better to See Once'," *Time*, Aug. 3, 1959, 12–14; "Encounter," *Newsweek*, Aug. 3, 1959, 15–17; "The Two Worlds: A Day-Long Debate," *New York Times*, July 25, 1959.

43. Herbert S. Parmet, *Richard Nixon and His America* (Boston: Little, Brown, 1990), 398–399. Martin, *Twelve Full Ounces*, 109–110.

44. J. C. Louis and Harvey Z. Yazijian, *The Cola Wars* (New York: Everest House, 1980), 93.

45. There is no complete sound recording of this portion of the event, and wording varies from account to account. My reconstruction depends on a variety of published stories; see note 42 above.

46. "That Famous Debate in Close-Up Pictures," *Life*, Aug. 3, 1959, 28.

47. Whitfield, *Culture of the Cold War*, 75. "Vice President Nixon Opens American Exhibtion at Moscow," *Department of State Bulletin*, Aug. 17, 1959, 227–237.

48. David M. Potter, *People of Plenty: Economic Abundance and the American Character* (Chicago: University of Chicago Press, 1954), 135. "The Fabulous Fifties: America Enters an Age of Everyday Elegance," *Look*, Oct. 2, 1956, 71.

49. Mike Featherstone, "Consumer Culture: An Introduction," *Theory, Culture and Society* 1 (1983), 5. Galbraith, *The Affluent Society*, 193. Daniel Lerner, "Comfort and Fun: Morality in a Nice Society," *American Scholar* 27 (Spring 1958), 163.

50. Edward Steichen, Introduction, *The Family of Man* (New York: Simon and Schuster, 1955), n.p. Dwight Macdonald, *Against the American Grain* (New York: Random House, 1962), 44. Getlein, "Pictures at an Exhibition," 13.

51. Quoted in "Encounter," 17.

52. Eleanor Graves, "Propaganda Goof over U.S. Fashions," *Life*, July 27, 1959, 71–72, 75; Richard M. Nixon, "Russia As I Saw It," *National Geographic*, Dec. 1959, 718. "The Vice President in Russia," 32–33.

53. "Housewife's House," *Life*, Dec. 24, 1956, 134–137. Mikoyan quoted in Zimmerman and Lerner, "What the Russians Will See," 54.

54. Jane Fiske Mitarachi, "Is the Kitchen Disintegrating?" *Interior Design*, Aug. 1954, 66.

Illustration Credits

Prologue

Chapter 1

Chapter 2

Chapter 3

pages 86, 89, 100, 110, 111, 113: ©The Walt Disney Company, used by permission
pages 91, 109, 115, 118: Photo, Gregory Marling
pages 94, 95, 97, 99, 117, 125: National Archives
pages 102, 104, 107: Chicago Historical Society (page 102 photo, Dr. Frank E. Rice)
page 120: American Museum of the Moving Image; photo, David Allison

Chapter 4

pages 128, 145, 149, 150, 151, 152, 157: Video Treasures
pages 130, 143, 147: National Archives
page 131: Pennsylvania Academy of the Fine Arts; Temple Purchase Fund
page 135: Collection of the author
page 139: Courtesy *Design Quarterly*
page 161: ©Elvis Presley Enterprises, Inc., reproduced with permission; photo, Mike Rutherford

Chapter 5

page 164: ©Elvis Presley Enterprises, Inc., reproduced with permission
page 166: Wide World Photos
page 171: Courtesy RCA
page 172: Black Star; photo, Fred Ward
page 178: American Museum of the Moving Image, gift of Don Logan; photo, David Allison
pages 181, 199: National Archives
page 184: Library of Congress
page 196: Courtesy Binney & Smith
pages 200, 201: Wisconsin Center for Film and Theater Research

Chapter 6

pages 202, 205, 207, 215, 218: General Mills
page 204: Collection of the author
pages 210, 211, 229, 233, 238: National Archives
page 212: International News
pages 219, 234, 235: Courtesy College of Human Ecology, University of Minnesota
page 225: ©Del Monte Foods, used by permission
page 230: Kraft General Foods. Jell-O® is a registered trademark of Kraft General Foods, Inc.

Chapter 7

pages 242, 244, 246, 277: Whirlpool Corporation
pages 245, 247, 248, 249, 251, 254, 259, 263, 264, 273, 274, 282: National Archives
page 256: University of Minnesota Photo Archive
pages 257, 265: Library of Congress
page 275: Associated Press/Wide World

Acknowledgments

Early versions of several chapters were published in journals: Chapter 3 in *American Art* 5 (1991); Chapter 4 in *Design Quarterly* 146 (1989); and Chapter 6 in *Prospects, An Annual of American Cultural Studies* 17 (1992). The material appears here by the gracious permission of the National Museum of American Art, Smithsonian Institution; the Walker Art Center; and Jack Salzman, respectively.

In 1991 I was appointed Senior Fellow at the Society for the Humanities, Cornell University. Much of the research for this book was completed in Olin, Uris, and Mann Libraries and the Business Administration Library there. I am grateful to fellow Fellow Simon Frith for discussing Elvis with me almost daily in the Society's dignified quarters in A. D. White House and to Professor Michael Kammen and his students for challenging luncheon conversation.

The Graduate School of the University of Minnesota provided generous funding for my research assistants: Robert Haddow, Barbara Coleman, and Lisa Fischman. Bob Haddow, now a Fellow at the National Museum of American History, has been unfailingly generous and critical; our pilgrimage to Graceland was a high point in the genesis of this book.

The Dwight D. Eisenhower Library in Abilene, Kansas, was a key resource. Dennis Medina of the Eisenhower Museum kindly allowed me access to Mrs. Eisenhower's wardrobe and lent an encouraging ear to my first, tentative thoughts on the New Look.

Mildred Friedman, former editor of *Design Quarterly* and curator of design at the Walker Art Center, asked me to look into automotive styling back in 1988. Indirectly, it was she who set me on the route that led to this broader study of 1950s artifacts.

Steve Benson, my colleague at station KUOM, and Debby Dane, my producer at Minnesota Public Radio, have given me the chance to try out my ideas about the 1950s on the air. The listeners who called and wrote with their responses encouraged me to explore themes I would not otherwise have considered. I first met Jane and Michael Stern in my capacity as a part-time radio commentator; they have been most supportive over the years and contributed materially to my understanding of both cooking and painting by numbers.

Gabe and Yvonne Weisberg gave me a cozy room in Washington and dragged me to the movies for the good of my soul.

As always, Lindsay Waters, my old friend and my editor at Harvard University Press, has been an author's good guardian angel. I particularly valued his flying trip to Cornell to restore my confidence when the theorists had me (temporarily) cornered.

Finally, I am grateful to my brother, Gregory, for keeping me company on a long field trip to Los Angeles, and for supplying his fine photos on demand.

Index

Abstract Expressionism, 14, 67, 74, 79, 80, 83–84, 153

Acheson, Dean, 42

The Adventures of Ozzie and Harriet, 217. *See also* Nelson, Ozzie, and family

Advertising, 16, 17, 18, 57, 65, 69, 72, 84, 96, 121, 122, 128, 132, 133, 136, 148–149, 151–153, 155–156, 158, 187, 191, 193, 214–216, 221, 228–229, 231, 235, 251, 265; subliminal, 186–187; use of female symbols in, 207–208, 209–210, 211; agencies, 224

The Affluent Society, 252

The African Queen, 91, 92

Alice in Wonderland, 108, 119, 121

Allen, Steve, 177, 179–180

Americana, 79, 101

American Exhibition in Moscow. *See* Moscow, American Exhibition in

An American in Paris, 69–70

Anthony, Carl Sferrazza, 27

Anthony, John, 70

Appliances, 2, 6, 30, 47, 58, 123, 153, 157, 206, 216, 217, 243, 253–254, 256, 265; glass doors on, 4, 5, 6, 14; color of, 14, 220, 221, 243, 253, 263–266, 283; design similarities to automobiles, 142, 143, 261; for use with TV set, 191–192; sold on TV, 214–216; symbol of freedom of choice, 245, 247, 267, 270, 278–279, 282, 283; squared-off, 260–261, 263, 269; tabletop models, 266–267. *See also specific appliances*

Arden, Elizabeth, 27, 28, 35, 38, 48

Arnaz, Desi, 3–5; merchandizing, 4–5. *See also* Ball, Lucille; *I Love Lucy*

Art: instruction, 59, 70–75; amateur, 66, 69, 70, 287; calendar, 80; Soviet, 258; modern, opposition to, 269, 270, 271. *See also* Churchill, Winston; Famous Artists Schools; *individual artists*

Art shows, 68–69, 70–71; of U.S. art abroad, 79, 248, 270–271, 279–280; automobiles exhibited as art, 146–147, 148, 149, 152–153; food as art, 230. *See also The Family of Man*

Associated American Artists, 69, 74

Automobiles, 6, 83, 94–95, 96, 123–124, 126, 139, 142, 143, 158–162, 217, 249, 267, 287; convertibles, 4, 169; model cars, 58; and families, 95–97, 112, 129–132, 144–145, 155–157; depicted on TV sitcoms, 129; imagery of, 132–136, 140–141, 144, 146, 154, 187; and women, 136–138; and the American Dream, 255. *See also specific makes*

Baking, 212, 217; at home, 209; iconography of, 213

Ball, Lucille, 3–4, 5, 6, 38. *See also I Love Lucy*

Balmain, Pierre, 20, 22

Banham, Reyner, 98, 132

Bangs, Lester, 166

Barbecues, 41, 49, 96, 124, 173, 191, 218, 219, 249, 279

Baxter, James and Annette, 182

Bayley, Stephen, 17

Beaton, Cecil, 12

Beauvoir, Simone de, 12

Benny, Jack, 58

Bergler, Edmund, 11

Berle, Milton, 169, 178, 179

Berry, Chuck, 133–134, 142, 162

Better Homes and Gardens, 57, 217, 266